CO-ATX-368

Beyond Beijing

Economic liberalization and preferential treatment have led to widening income disparities between the wealthier coastal areas and the interior regions in post-Mao China. The widening regional disparities have in turn increased regional tensions and elicited demands for regional policy change.

Beyond Beijing offers a balanced assessment of the dynamics of economic liberalization and decentralization and their consequences for regional relations and regional policy. The book is organized into three parts. The first reviews the patterns of regional development from Mao to Deng; the second discusses the dynamics of competition and emulation among local governments and analyzes the trends in regional cleavages amid economic liberalization; while the third covers the politics of regional policy and examines government efforts to address regional disparities.

Dali L. Yang has produced an authoritative study of an issue that will remain highly visible on China's political agenda for the foreseeable future.

Dali L. Yang is Assistant Professor of Political Science at the University of Chicago and author of *Calamity and Reform in China*.

Routledge Studies in China in Transition
Series Editor: David S.G. Goodman

Beyond Beijing

Liberalization and the Regions in China

Dali L. Yang

London and New York

For Ling

First published 1997
by Routledge
11 New Fetter Lane, London EC4P 4EE

Simultaneously published in the USA and Canada
by Routledge
29 West 35th Street, New York, NY 10001

© 1997 Dali L. Yang

Typeset in Times by LaserScript Limited, Mitcham, Surrey
Printed and bound in Great Britain by
T. J. International Ltd.

All rights reserved. No part of this book may be reprinted or
reproduced or utilized in any form or by any electronic,
mechanical, or other means, now known or hereafter
invented, including photocopying and recording, or in any
information storage or retrieval system, without permission in
writing from the publishers.

British Library Cataloguing in Publication Data

A catalogue record for this book is available from the British Library.

Library of Congress Cataloguing in Publication Data

Yang, Dali L.
    Beyond Beijing: liberalization and the regions in China / Dali L. Yang.
        p. cm. – (China in transition)
    Includes bibliographical references and index.
    1. China – Economic conditions – 1976-   2. China – Economic
conditions – Regional disparities.   3. China – Economic policy – 1976-
I. Title.   II. Series.
HC427.92.Y3723 1997
338.951–dc21   96–40110
                                              CIP

ISBN 0–415–14501–5

Contents

Figures and tables

FIGURES

TABLES

Preface

In the late 1970s, as China's reform era opened, the Communist Party of China committed itself to first doubling and then redoubling the aggregate size of the economy of the People's Republic of China by the end of the millennium. At the time and into the early and mid-1980s it was a prospect greeted as a desirable aspiration by most academic observers of China, but as little more. Many economists in particular pointed out the difficulties in the project and the near-impossibility of its achievement. In the event, the target was attained with almost five years to spare, sometime in 1995.

The rapid growth of China's economy is a useful starting-point for this series, intellectually as well as chronologically. It is not only that China has developed so spectacularly so quickly, nor that in the process its experience has proved some economists to be too cautious. Rather, its importance is to demonstrate the need for explanatory theories of social and economic change to themselves adapt and change as they encompass the processes under way in China, and not to assume that previous assumptions about either China or social change in general are immutable.

China in Transition aims to participate in these intellectual developments through its focus on social, political, economic and culture change in the China of the 1990s and beyond. Its aim is to draw on new, often cross-disciplinary research from scholars in East Asia, Australasia, North America and Europe, as well as that based in the more traditional disciplines. In the process, the series will not only interpret the consequences of reform in China, but also monitor and reflect the changes of the future.

The regional dimensions of change in contemporary China present a prime example of the need to adjust perspectives, and in *Beyond Bejing* Dali Yang has risen admirably to the challenge. Unlike many of the more instantaneous reactions to growth in political profile for the regions and regional leaders – that subsequently stress China's potential to disintegrate – this is a carefully grounded study of the political economy of relations between the central regions, the inland provinces and central government. It argues cogently that to understand the dynamics of regional change it is necessary to consider the attitudes of inland provinces and central government separately and in relation to the coastal regions, rather than only through examining the development and behaviour of the coastal regions. Its conclusions suggest that, rather than disintegration, a more complex political future, based on economic federalism, is already emerging.

Beyond Bejing has two particular methodological devices that provide it with its cutting edge. The first is that it is concerned more with the economics of politics rather than the politics of economics, which is the more usual approach to the study of regionalism in China. The second is that (good to his analytical approach) Dali Yang looks not just at the early policy stage results of the coastal strategy but also in detail at the responses of the interior. In the process, he highlights what is clearly becoming the case – that inland provinces, despite national policy, have already taken the initiative to redress their perceived inequalities. This is a point that rarely surfaces in much of the literature on regional issues or political change more generally in China, stuck as they often are in consideration of a single national forum of political conflict.

David S. G. Goodman
Institute for International Studies, UTS
May 1997

Acknowledgments

For a country of China's size, spatial economic disparities are unavoidable. Because of economic decentralization, the restoration of economic incentives, and the Chinese government's unbalanced regional development strategy, rapid economic growth in China has been accompanied by widening income inequalities between the more prosperous coastal region and inland areas. As in other parts of the world, the widening regional disparities have been of much political concern, causing resentment among the population in areas that are lagging behind and prompting elites in these areas to demand remedial policies from the central government. In this small book, I seek to go beyond the headlines and offer a balanced assessment of the political economy of regional policy and regional change in post-Mao China. Moreover, this study contributes to answering two major questions about China's economic reforms: What accounts for the spatial extension of economic liberalization in China under communist rule? Has the Chinese economy become more fragmented or more integrated under the market-oriented reforms?

This book had its beginning in a seminar paper I initially wrote in 1988 (D. Yang 1990). Since that first paper I have pursued this research topic as a sideline to my research on the Great Leap Famine and reform and have benefitted from the generous assistance of many people. I would like to single out a few people who have especially made this volume possible, beginning with my immense debt to David Bachman. For reasons beyond my control, David's comments and assistance went unacknowledged when my first paper on this subject saw the light of day. I would like to make up for that omission now and express my deep gratitude for his encouragement and support for this project. I am also equally indebted to Lynn White III for his unfailing support and comments over the years.

I would like especially to thank Houkai Wei of the Institute of Industrial Economics of the Chinese Academy of Social Sciences for collaborating with me in writing the case study of rural enterprise policy that appears in chapter 6 and for extended discussions on the subject. Xiaomin Rong helped me formalize the game-theoretic model that appears in chapter 3. Others who have commented on one or more of the chapters include Henry Bienen, Michael Dawson, Robert Gilpin Jr, Avery Goldstein, David S.G. Goodman, Mel Gurtov, David Laitin,

Nicholas Lardy, Nan Lin, Barry Naughton, William L. Parish, Bruce Reynolds, Lloyd and Suzanne Rudolph, Gerald Segal, Susan Shirk, Bernard Silberman, Dorothy Solinger, Shaoguang Wang, and Edwin Winckler. I am especially indebted to colleagues and students at the University of Chicago for fostering a friendly but challenging atmosphere for social science research.

James Myers deserves a special thank you for eliciting an earlier version of the chapter on regional cleavages. Anonymous readers for Routledge and a number of scholarly journals offered comments that improved both the substance and the style of this volume. I am much indebted to several students at the University of Chicago for providing essential research support for this project at one time or another: they are, in chronological order, Ben Klemens, Leah Bartelt, Samuel Wilkin, and especially Yuan Bai and Fubing Su. Katherine Hannaford prepared the map on p. 6.

David S.G. Goodman was the ideal series editor in combining the force of suasion with humor, qualities that won me over to the "China in Transition" book series. At Routledge, Victoria Smith and Diane Stafford looked after the project with care and efficiency. Susan Cope did the copy-editing.

A number of institutions offered generous support for this project. At the University of Chicago, my research has been nurtured by grants from the Social Sciences Divisional Research Fund and the Committee on Chinese Studies. Houkai Wei's visit to the United States in 1995 was financed by a fellowship from the Chinese Fellowships for Scholarly Development Program of the Committee on Scholarly Communication with China and a grant from the Committee on International Studies of the University of Chicago. Wei and I are also indebted to the Spencer Foundation for funding a study on Decentralization and Regional Educational Disparities in China in 1995. The final manuscript was put together during my stay at the Institute of East Asian Political Economy at the National University of Singapore. I wish to thank the Institute's staff for providing me with a wonderful research environment to complete this project.

I am grateful to the following journals and book publishers for granting me permission to draw on previously published materials, all of which have been extensively revised and updated: "Patterns of China's Regional Development Strategy," *China Quarterly*, no. 122 (June 1990): 230–57; "Reforms, Resources, and Regional Cleavages: The Political Economy of Coast-Interior Cleavages in China," *Issues and Studies*, vol. 27, no. 9 (September 1991), pp. 43–69; "Reform and the Restructuring of Central–Local Relations," in David S.G. Goodman and Gerald Segal (eds), *China Deconstructs: Politics, Trade and Regionalism*, London and New York: Routledge, 1994, pp. 59–98; Dali L. Yang and Houkai Wei, "Rural Enterprise Development and Regional Policy in China," *Asian Perspective*, vol. 2, no. 1 (1996), pp. 71–94.

This book is dedicated to my wife, Ling. Thanks to the computer revolution, she has had little to do with the manuscript, but her support in everything else has been both indispensable and deeply appreciated.

Abbreviations

AWSJW	*Asian Wall Street Journal Weekly*
CCP	Chinese Communist Party
CD	*China Daily*
CDBW	*China Daily Business Weekly*
DJN	Dow Jones Newswire
FBIS-CHI/	
FBIS-China	Foreign Broadcast Information Service, daily report: China
FEER	*Far Eastern Economic Review*
FT	*Financial Times*
JJRB	*Jingji ribao* (Economic daily), Beijing
JJWTTS	*Jingji wenti tansuo* (Explorations in economic issues), Yunnan
JJYJ	*Jingji yanjiu* (Economic research), Beijing
JXSHKX	*Jiangxi shehui kexue* (Jiangxi social sciences)
NPC	National People's Congress
QB	*Qiao bao* (China press)
RMRB	*Renmin ribao* (People's daily)
RMRBO	*Renmin ribao* (People's daily), overseas edition
SCMP	*South China Morning Post*
SCMPIW	*South China Morning Post* International Weekly
SEZ	Special Economic Zone
SPC	State Planning Commission
STB	*Shenzhen tequ bao* (Shenzhen special economic zone tribune)
WSJ	*Wall Street Journal*
WWW	World Wide Web
Xinhua	Xinhua News Agency
ZGJJWT	*Zhongguo jingji wenti* (Chinese economic issues), Fujian
ZGSBZK	*Zhongguo shibao zhoukan* (The China Times Magazine), US edition
ZGTJNJ	*Zhongguo tongji nianjian* (Statistical yearbook of China)
ZGGYJJTJNJ	*Zhongguo gongye jingji tongji nianjian* (Statistical yearbook of China's industrial economy)
ZXS	Zhongguo Xinwen She (China News Service)

Part I

Introduction

1 Analytical perspectives

A major issue that confronts policy-makers in large economies is uneven development in different parts of the country. When economic disparities become entwined with ethnic differences, regional inequality acquires special political significance, as has been the case in Canada, Italy, Nigeria, Spain, the former Yugoslavia, and other countries. Until very recently, however, China has been noticeably absent from the list of countries in which regional disparities rank among the most prominent political issues. Indeed, Maoist China was held to be the paragon of balanced regional development.

When I first started research on the political economy of regional disparities in China (D. Yang 1990), research on the topic was dominated by economists and geographers. Making use of the steady stream of data then becoming available on China, their emphasis in research was on finding out what was going on in the patterns of regional, especially inter-provincial, disparities in China rather than on explicating the political dynamics of regional policy change.[1] This was to be expected because central politicians and planners dominated the allocation of scarce resources in China until not very long ago. While the spatial dimension has always been a major aspect of China's developmental experience, it has until recently not been considered central to the study of contemporary Chinese politics.

Yet China's regional development policy and practice have undergone a dramatic shift since the late 1970s. Moving away from the Maoist emphasis on investment in inland areas, China's regional policy during the reform period has been decidedly in favor of the more prosperous coastal region. Occurring during China's transition from a planned to a market-oriented economy, the shift in regional policy and widening regional disparities have raised serious questions about distributive justice and touched off a heated debate on the economic and political implications of uneven regional development. Indeed, as I put the finishing touches to this book, the issue of uneven development has become one of the most salient political issues facing China's leadership. Judging by the rhetoric of the debate, few areas of public policy in China are as complex, divisive, and potentially explosive politically. Some Chinese commentators have even made an analogy between present-day China and the United States of the mid-nineteenth century and suggested that acute regional disparities may cause socio-political instability and even lead China onto the path of civil war. Reports of acute disparities in China now appear regularly in the Western media and have been featured on the front pages of major publications such as the *New York Times* (Tyler 1995) and *The Economist* (1993a, 1996).

While this book participates in the raging debate over China's regional policy, it is also intended to contribute to the resurgence of interest in spatial issues among social scientists, especially economists (Krugman 1991a, 1995; Storper and Walker 1989). While economists seek to (re)model regional development, my goal is to explore the linkages between the worlds of regional development and Chinese politics during an era of economic liberalization. Specifically, this study seeks to provide:

(a) an empirical description and analysis of the changing patterns of regional disparities;
(b) a model and empirical test of the dynamics of competitive liberalization among local governments;
(c) an examination of the patterns of regional cleavages and cooperation during economic transformation and their implications for regional change;
(d) a description and analysis of the political economy of regional policy reorientation since the late 1980s.

All in all, this study will allow us better to understand the causal dynamics of regional development, market formation and integration, and regional dominance in contemporary China.

DEFINING THE REGION

Some readers have probably noted that I have already mentioned two different measures of regional disparities above: inter-provincial disparities and coast–interior disparities. This brings us to the issue of how to define a "region." Some scholars, such as Mumford (1938: 367) and Skinner (1977), have emphasized the resilience of natural regions in economic change. For most regional scientists, economists, and regional planners, however, the region is merely a taxonomic category, a subunit of national space that may be divided into a variety of abstract divisions depending on the criteria used (Friedmann and Weaver 1979: 31). Regional issues are thus by nature relative and constructed.

Yet the choice of a regional unit of analysis is consequential for the measurement of regional disparities. As Mathur (1983: 498) points out, the absolute magnitude of a measure of regional inequality is highly sensitive to the areal unit used for measurement. Inequality is sometimes more significant *within* rather than among regional units (such as provinces) (Fields and Schultz 1980: 447–67). Economists and regional scientists frequently adopt a number of regional definitions in order to achieve a balanced assessment of regional disparities. In the meantime, much debate on regional issues arises from practitioners talking past each other by adopting different definitions of regions.

Occupying around 7 percent of the earth's land area, China is an immensely varied subcontinent and has been subject to a variety of regionalization schemes. Most broadly, one may point to the contrasts between northern versus southern China (Fairbank 1992: 4–14; Xin Xiangyang and Ni Jianzhong 1993) or the disparities between coast versus hinterland or interior. At the intermediate level, there are the macro-regions emphasized by Skinner (1977) as well as the great administrative regions that were adopted in the early 1950s and continue to find much currency in Chinese analyses of regional development and in the organization of military forces.[2] There have also been serious efforts by different levels of government to organize cooperative development along the Yangtze River and Yellow River valleys and the Bohai Bay as well numerous economic cooperation zones across various administrative boundaries. Further down the scale are the standard units of political administration, the provinces; economists have usually emphasized economic disparities among provincial units in studies of contemporary China.[3] Finally, in light of the size of the average provincial unit (the average population per province is about 40 million), intra-provincial disparities, particularly among counties, offer insights that may be obscured by studies of regional change at the provincial and macro-regional levels.[4]

These different regionalization schemes should not be regarded as exclusive of each other. Instead, I believe they offer complementary perspectives on regional change in China. Nevertheless, this study will focus on the political economy of coast–interior disparities, and only occasionally on the results derived from other types of regionalization schemes, including inter- and intra-provincial disparities. This book is thus not a study of the political economy of Chinese spatial disparities in all their permutations.

I am fully aware that the focus on coast–interior disparities paints a relatively stark picture and obscures significant variations within regions and even smaller units (Wang Zhiyuan and Zeng Xinqun 1988; Skinner 1994: 9; Wu Zhe 1994; D. Yang 1995b; and Solinger 1996: 2). Yet, as a political scientist, my choice of research focus has been an easy one. As far as political saliency is concerned coast–interior disparities rank far ahead of any other regional disparities and, as I hope the reader will agree, the emphasis on coast versus interior does capture a very significant aspect of China's political economy. The appendix to this volume offers a preliminary examination of the patterns and determinants of intra-provincial disparities.

The map in Figure 1.1 shows China according to the coast–interior regionalization scheme.[5] The coastal region is a narrow strip along the sea coast. It includes 12 provincial units: Liaoning, Beijing, Tianjin, Hebei, Shandong, Jiangsu, Shanghai, Zhejiang, Fujian, Guangdong, Hainan (since 1988), and Guangxi. A large proportion of the nation's major industrial cities and all the special economic zones are located in the coastal region.[6] The interior, which is further divided into the central and western regions,

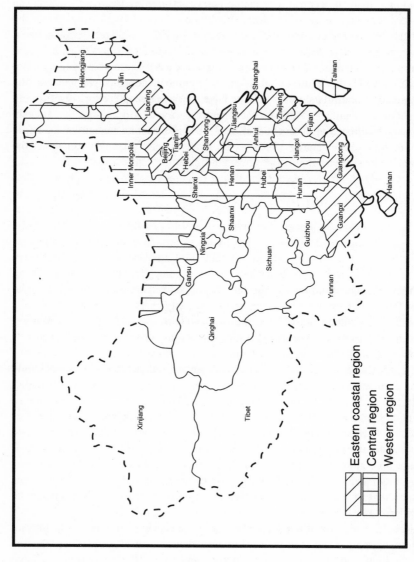

Figure 1.1 Map of China's regions

currently has 18 provincial-level units. Chongqing became the nineteenth in March 1997 when it was designated a centrally administered municipality.

Table 1.1 presents data comparing the population and geographic size of the provinces and regions. It is evident that the coastal region is much more developed than the central region; the central region is in turn superior to the western region in terms of economic development. From Table 1.1, we can see that the coastal region, with slightly less than 14 per cent of the total land area, supports more than 41 per cent of the nation's population. In 1983 the coastal region produced about 60 per cent of the national gross value of industrial output (GVIO) while the central and western regions together accounted for the remainder. Therefore, significant regional disparities exist between the coast and the interior regions in China. The vast majority of China's poor, currently officially estimated at 80 million, live in the interior and especially the western region (Shang Rongguang 1996), as do most of the 100 million or so of the population of ethnic minorities.

MARKETS AND REGIONAL DISPARITIES

Existing literature on regional development has emphasized the tendency toward uneven regional development in developing countries if market forces are left alone (Williamson 1965). Myrdal (1957) used the principle of circular and cumulative causation to explain the patterns of uneven regional development in underdeveloped countries. For the sake of market potential, firms tend to locate near large markets that are comprised of lots of other firms. Thus, production tends to be geographically concentrated owing to the influence of increasing returns, positive externalities, and strategic complementaries. This process is known as self-reinforcing agglomeration in regional development (Krugman 1995: 46; see also Arthur 1994). The localities and regions that started first would gain a competitive advantage and reap increasing returns, be it in banking or industry, and would tend to retain their dominance while other localities or regions would suffer from relative stagnation. In consequence, market forces tended to increase, rather than decrease, the inequalities between regions. Even in the United States, a huge, fertile, and economically developed country, most people live along parts of two coasts and the Great Lakes, and manufacturing was, until recently, concentrated in a relatively small part of the Northeast and the eastern part of the Midwest (Krugman 1991a; Pred 1966). As Albert Hirschman noted in one of the most widely cited texts on economic development, not only does economic growth tend to be spatially concentrated around some starting points, it also has the ability and tendency "to round itself out for a long time within some subgroup, region, or country while backwardness retains its hold elsewhere" (Hirschman 1958: 184). The geographic transmission of development is far from automatic and tends to become polarized.

For Myrdal, the tendency toward uneven development between center and periphery is the net effect of two causal processes that are at work

Table 1.1 Population and area by province and region

Province/Region	Area (km²)	% of total	1984 Population (10,000)	1984 % of total	1994 Population (10,000)	1994 % of total
COASTAL REGION						
Beijing	16,807	0.17	947	0.91	1,125	0.95
Tianjin	11,305	0.12	799	0.77	935	0.79
Hebei	187,700	1.95	5,478	5.27	6,388	5.38
Liaoning	145,900	1.52	3,655	3.52	4,067	3.43
Shanghai	6,341	0.07	1,205	1.16	1,356	1.14
Zhejiang	102,000	1.06	3,993	3.84	4,294	3.62
Fujian	120,000	1.25	2,677	2.58	3,183	2.68
Guangxi	236,600	2.46	3,806	3.66	4,493	3.79
Jiangsu	102,600	1.07	6,171	5.94	7,021	5.92
Guangdong	177,900	1.85	6,166	5.94	6,689	5.64
Hainan	34,000	0.35	n/a	n/a	711	0.60
Shandong	153,300	1.59	7,637	7.35	8,671	7.31
Coastal total	1,294,453	13.46	42,534	40.95	48,933	41.25
CENTRAL REGION						
Inner Mongolia	1,183,000	12.30	1,985	1.91	2,260	1.91
Shanxi	156,300	1.63	3,421	3.29	3,045	2.57
Heilongjiang	454,000	4.72	3,295	3.17	3,672	3.10
Jilin	187,400	1.95	2,284	2.20	2,574	2.17
Anhui	139,700	1.45	5,103	4.91	5,955	5.02
Jiangxi	166,900	1.74	3,421	3.29	4,015	3.38
Henan	167,000	1.74	7,646	7.36	9,027	7.61
Hubei	185,900	1.93	4,876	4.69	5,719	4.82
Hunan	211,800	2.20	5,561	5.35	6,355	5.36
Central total	2,852,000	29.66	37,592	36.19	42,622	35.93
WESTERN REGION						
Sichuan	570,000	5.93	10,112	9.74	11,214	9.45
Guizhou	176,100	1.83	2,932	2.82	3,458	2.91
Yunnan	394,000	4.10	3,362	3.24	3,939	3.32
Shaanxi	205,600	2.14	2,966	2.86	3,481	2.93
Gansu	454,300	4.73	2,016	1.94	2,378	2.00
Qinghai	721,200	7.50	402	0.39	474	0.40
Ningxia	66,400	0.69	406	0.39	504	0.42
Tibet	1,220,000	12.69	197	0.19	236	0.20
Xinjiang	1,660,400	17.27	1,344	1.29	1,632	1.38
Western total	5,468,000	56.87	23,737	22.85	27,080	22.83
National total	9,614,453	100.00	103,863	100.00	118,635	100.00

Sources: Zhongguo baike nianjian 1994: 32–35; Zhongguo renkou tongji nianjian 1990: 585; ZGTJNJ 1995: 60.

simultaneously. On the one hand, the rise of one region or locality tends to produce what he calls "backwash effects" (or polarization for Hirschman), with the movements of labor, capital, and trade helping the rising region to move further upwards. Meanwhile the lagging regions suffer from "current account" and human capital deficits and find it difficult to keep up in investments in infrastructure (including roads, public utilities, and education) and thus to stay competitive. On the other hand, through increased demand and other mechanisms, the faster-growing region will produce "spread effects" (or trickle-down effects for Hirschman) to somewhat counteract the backwash effects (Myrdal 1957: 23–32). Drawing on studies of regional disparities in Europe, Myrdal points out that the spread effects become stronger as an economy becomes more developed, a proposition Williamson (1965) later verified through cross-national studies. Yet such spread effects are weak in an underdeveloped country. Myrdal thus concludes that "as a rule the free play of the market forces in a poor country will work more powerfully to create regional inequalities and to widen those which already exist" (Myrdal 1957: 34). In short, "the tendency of capitalist systems is to reproduce patterns of inequality. The financial inducements offered by governments to private enterprise are usually much too weak to achieve a permanent restructuring of spatial organization" (Friedmann and Weaver 1979: 173).

If Hirschman and Myrdal's arguments are correct, then it is expected that, given China's low level of economic development, disparities between the coastal core and the periphery or hinterland (interior) in China will increase as China converts from central planning to a market economy. In fact, one of my earlier studies (D. Yang 1990) reported rising coast–interior disparities under the reforms, providing empirical support for the Hirschman–Myrdal thesis in the Chinese context.[7]

Yet the Chinese case is far from an unalloyed test of the Hirschman–Myrdal thesis. Even though it is undeniably true that market forces now play a far greater role in the Chinese economy than they did in the early 1980s, it is also true that the Chinese state, which remains heavily involved in the economy in spite of more than a decade and a half of reforms, has not given market forces a free rein. As will be detailed in chapter 2, the Chinese government has been a key participant in setting the terms of regional development by skewing the rules of the game in favor of the more prosperous coastal region. A true test of the Hirschman–Myrdal thesis would have to answer the counterfactual question of whether the coast–interior disparities would still have risen had the Chinese central government not explicitly favored the coast. More important, an answer to this counterfactual question would help us assess with greater accuracy whether the Chinese central government is in a position to reverse the trends in regional disparities if it chooses to do so.

STATE, REGIME TYPE, AND REGIONAL DISPARITIES

Myrdal certainly believed that the state could play a major role in determining changes in regional disparity. He pointed out that the European welfare states had used a complex array of state policies and institutions to counteract the backwash effects and support the spread effects of market forces, thereby promoting greater regional equality (Myrdal 1957: 25, 39). Recognizing the weaker spread effects and weaker governments in less developed countries, however, Myrdal was not optimistic that these countries could do equally well. Indeed, he conceded that "at that stage the inequalities were a necessary condition for progress, and perhaps also the lack of political democracy which made their continuation possible" (Myrdal 1957: 46). Nevertheless, Myrdal called for the recognition that national integration toward greater social mobility and regional economic equality was conducive to rapid and sustained economic growth in the country as a whole and argued that underdeveloped countries should use national economic development plans and policies to strengthen the spread effects and promote regional equality (Myrdal 1957: 79–81). Later John Friedmann put forward the agripolitan approach to development, which to some extent drew on China's developmental experience in the 1970s. Friedmann called for a strong central government to balance increased power at district and regional levels in order to manage territorial tensions and conflicts. For Friedmann, "the role of the state is at once protective, developmental, facilitative, regulatory, and redistributive" (Friedmann and Weaver 1979: 203).

While Chinese leaders were unaware of Myrdal's writings during the 1960s–70s, they nevertheless possessed vast powers in channelling resources into targeted industries and regions. As will be described in chapter 2, over this period, Chinese economic development under Mao was heavily oriented toward the interior and produced a reduction in coast–interior economic inequalities, albeit with dubious economic results. The turn to the coast under the reforms was in part a reaction to the draconian Maoist development policies.

The recent rise in coast–interior inequalities has led Chinese politicians and economists to reconsider the post-Mao emphasis on coastal development. As I shall discuss in Part III of the book, following an extensive debate, national politicians in China now espouse the position that the state should endeavor to bring about a more balanced economic development among the regions. The question is whether the Chinese state will be able effectively to promote balanced economic development in a market economy.

If one follows Myrdal's argument about the patterns of regional disparities, then the answer to the question on the future of China's regional development is a pessimistic one. With the conversion to a market economy and extensive decentralization of economic powers, the backwash effects will tend to overwhelm the spread effects. As a result, the central government in China will be hard put to counteract the backwash effects for a long time to come.

A drastic remedy would be to change China's political governing regime.

Myrdal believed that effective democratic institutions, by empowering the poor and downtrodden, would provide the political basis for more egalitarian regional policies (Myrdal 1957: 41, 83).[8] For now, however, such a political transformation in China looks unlikely in the next several years at the national level. Indeed, an underdeveloped country such as China is caught in a poverty trap: the weakness of the spread effects leads to greater regional economic inequalities which are in turn "inimical to the growth of an effective democracy" (Myrdal 1957: 41; Huntington 1991: 46–58). We are thus back to square one.

Hirschman (1958: 187) has characterized Myrdal's analysis as "excessively dismal." Instead, he argues that once regional polarization has proceeded for some time "strong forces making for a turning point" will emerge and "deliberate economic policy will come into play to correct the situation" (Hirschman 1958: 187–90). In other words, the famous advocate of disequilibrium and unbalanced growth nevertheless posits that regional imbalances will unleash forces that will tend toward some sort of spatial equilibrium (Friedmann 1988: 95).

Hirschman's hypothesis was premised on the realization of the following elite career choice mechanism. While the more prosperous region tends to produce elites who are content to stay in business, "the poorer sections of the country, where careers in industry and trade are not promising, often produce, for this very reason, a majority of the country's successful politicians and thereby acquire influential spokesmen in the councils of government" (Hirschman 1958: 193). Owing to the rising influence of politicians from poor areas, "the government will, to the best of its ability, attempt to counteract in part the polarization effects that result from the operation of market forces" by counterbalancing the emigration of capital and talent from the poor regions and offering special tax advantages and public investment in these areas (*Ibid.*: 194).

Hirschman made no attempt to offer a systematic and empirical test of his regional career choice mechanism. While the mechanism makes some intuitive sense, I believe it is by no means the whole story, at least in the case of China. Indeed, a counter-argument can be made that even though a greater proportion of the elite pool in poor areas may choose to go into politics, the elite pool in prosperous areas is larger because of greater access to higher education and other avenues of mobility. Even if a smaller proportion of the pool of elites chooses to go into politics in prosperous areas than in poor areas, the larger size of the pool in prosperous areas will probably cancel out the effect of the lack of drive for political careers in prosperous areas.

My alternative hypothesis emphasizes the fusion of politics and economics. It is likely that the prosperous areas will want to translate their economic muscle into political power, the better to preserve their economic achievements. If the system of political mobility is porous enough, then the rise in a region's economic fortune will also be likely to translate into improvement in that region's political influence in national politics. National politicians have powerful incentives to include politicians from rich areas in order to secure the economic foundations of their power and other forms of political support. Greater representation of rich areas at the pinnacle of political power will in turn reinforce the process of cumulative causation in regional development that Myrdal has identified.

A striking case of such regional domination is South Korea. Ever since the country embarked on its rapid development in the early 1960s, its political elite has hailed mainly from the eastern Taegu and Kyongsang regions, which have received more government investment and are now the most prosperous and industrialized. In contrast, areas such as the Northern Cholla province have been discriminated against (Choi 1993; Glain 1995), leading to the perpetuation of economic disparities between eastern and western Korea.

In the case of China, similar patterns of regional elite representation have also emerged. Whereas Mao and a significant number of his senior colleagues hailed from the interior regions, there is striking evidence that the economically strong provinces are also the most politically preeminent in China of the late 1980s and early 1990s. While most top leaders hail from the coastal region and leaders from several coastal provincial units, including Beijing, Shanghai, Guangdong, and Shandong, have enjoyed membership on the powerful Political Bureau in the last few years, at the present none of the interior provincial leaders sits on the Political Bureau even though there are 18 interior provinces versus 12 for the coastal region. The interior provinces may again have one representative on the Political Bureau, but the balance has clearly been in favor of the coastal interests.

THE BALANCING ACT IN REGIONAL POLICY

With the composition of the top elite stratum being stacked in favor of prosperous coastal provinces, it may be easy to postulate that central leaders will continue to favor the coastal region and reinforce the dominance of coastal interests in Chinese politics. On this view, even though the central government adopted preferential policies for the coastal region on the premise that it would eventually turn around and help the interior to develop, once the coastal region has reasserted its economic dominance, the pattern of regional policies becomes self-reinforcing as the coastal region parleys its economic dominance into political dominance. The positive feedbacks will thus become difficult to counteract.

Yet such an extrapolation rests on fairly strong assumptions that the Chinese leadership cares only about economic growth and economic interests, that central leaders are practically transmission belts for local economic interests and possess little autonomy *vis-à-vis* such local interests, and that local leaders in peripheral areas such as the interior have little political power and influence as long as they are economically weak. As Friedmann pointed out, however, while the centers of innovation in the core tend to penetrate and dominate the periphery through trade, production, and market relations, new desires and frustrations will grow in the peripheral areas, giving rise to political demands and prolonged conflict with the core (Friedmann 1972: 90–99). In setting China's regional development policies, central leaders will have to balance between economic interests and the political demands from the interior regions. When the center is preoccupied with the maximization of China's economic growth rate, as was the case in the 1980s, then China's regional development policies are likely to be in favor of the coastal region. In contrast, when the other demands from the interior can claim equal priority with rapid economic growth, then the central leadership will probably call for more balanced regional development. Thus a key determinant of China's regional development policy will be the effectiveness with which the interior interests can make the central leadership perceive their political significance in the Chinese regime's search for political stability and survival. As will be discussed in chapter 5, in the late 1980s and early 1990s a confluence of factors led the central leadership to perceive the interior regions as a potential source of instability and prompted it to pay more attention to seeking a more balanced regional development strategy. The story of China's regional policy evolution is thus a story about how Chinese leaders have tried to balance these various concerns.

Moreover, a formulated policy may not be implemented. Implementation of China's regional policies will be a function of how the economic system has been reshaped. While the central government's regional policy will almost certainly be implemented under a tightly controlled central planning system, relaxation of economic control will tend to weaken implementation of central policies. As the Chinese economy becomes more decentralized and market-oriented, implementation of the regional policies will crucially depend on the center's leverage over economic resources. The effectiveness of regional policy implementation will depend not only on the will of the center but also the interests of local governments and other economic actors. Any assessment of the effectiveness of regional policy must therefore pay attention to the interaction among these actors.

PREVIEW

This book is comprised of three parts. Part I (chapters 1 and 2) provides an overview of the swings in China's regional development policies and practices from Mao to Deng. Whereas under Mao Chinese regional development was oriented toward the interior, it has been decidedly biased in favor of the more developed coastal region under Deng. In consequence, after more than four decades of communist rule, the patterns of regional development have reverted to those that prevailed when the communist movement first came to power.

Part II (chapters 3 and 4) examines the dynamics of regional relations during the post-Mao reform era. In chapter 3, I introduce a simple game-theoretic model to illustrate the incentives and mechanisms for competitive liberalization among local governments and account for the spatial spread of liberal economic policies in China as epitomized by the proliferation of various types of development zones. The geographic diffusion of liberal practices has not only added impetus to the reforms but has also gradually eased a major source of resentment harbored by the interior toward the southeastern coastal provinces.

Another major source of coast–interior cleavages has concerned the pricing and allocation of energy and raw materials. Chapter 4 examines the dynamics of resource-based cleavages and their behavioral consequences for regional cooperation and competition and market formation in China. In the 1980s, this set of cleavages was manifested in the interior's push for building local processing industries. Unfortunately, while that push helped increase the interior's share of industrial output in the short run, the empirical evidence suggests that since the late 1980s the coastal region has reasserted its economic dominance. Nevertheless, this source of regional cleavages has also seen alleviation as prices have largely been freed up.

In many ways, the year of 1989 marked a major turning point for China's regional policy. In Part III, I examine the reorientation of China's regional development policies away from the single-minded emphasis on the coastal region. The ground for such a transition was laid prior to 1989 in the growing current of opinion against the pro-coast regional development strategy. Chapter 5 first provides a look back at this current and then examines the confluence of political and economic factors that made it possible for the argument against unbalanced development to be reflected in central government policy. The central leadership not only began to phase out preferential treatment for the coastal region but also promised more investment for interior regions.

Chapters 6–8 examine the substance and limits of the reorientation. I argue that both the structure of the fiscal and taxation reforms and the marketization of the Chinese economy will make it difficult for the center to sharply increase the share of investment in the interior. As a result, the central government has pushed for inter-regional cooperation in the hope of facilitating the spread of economic growth from the coast to the interior. Similarly, a regionally oriented rural enterprise policy to promote rural enterprise development in the interior has emphasized development demonstration rather than grants-in-aid. Further evidence of the center's efforts to please both coast and interior and the limits of the reorientation can be seen from the debate over and decision on the future of the special economic zones.

In the concluding chapter, I briefly go over the main findings of this study but focus on the interrelations between political and economic changes. I begin with an overview of the regional policy reorientation. This is followed by a discussion of the replication of regional development patterns and the vicious cycle of development that traps underdeveloped areas. In a sense, Chinese politics is dominated by an oligarchy from the coastal region. Nevertheless, I suggest that a more pluralistic China provides a number of opportunities for the interior to pursue its political and economic interests.

2 From Mao to Deng
Regional development policies and practices

As I mentioned in the last chapter, China's regional development policies, like practically everything else, have undergone dramatic swings since the communist takeover. Using statistical data on patterns of domestic and foreign direct investment, changes in the regional share of gross value of industrial output (GVIO), and other economic and policy indicators, this chapter delineates the shift in China's regional development strategy over time. Whereas the emphasis during the Maoist era was on eradicating regional industrial disparities through interior-oriented investments, China under Deng Xiaoping has unabashedly pursued a strategy of unbalanced regional growth. More concretely, the post-Mao Chinese leadership has not only relaxed the straitjacket on the coastal region but has come to rely on the coastal region to provide the "engine of growth" for China as it strives to catch up with its neighbors in economic development. Deng Xiaoping died on 19 February 1997. For technical reasons, this book has retained the present tense in references to Deng. President Jiang Zemin has avowed that China will continue with Deng's policies of reform and opening up.

For the sake of simplicity, I will call the development strategy of the 1953–78 period the "Maoist development strategy." Though it varied in degrees in different sub-periods, the Maoist strategy dominated China's industrialization efforts until it faded out in the late 1970s. It was anchored on the construction of a military industrial complex, relied on vigorous redistributive measures to equalize regional economic development, preferred heavy to light industrial investment, emphasized extensive rather than intensive modes of growth, and allowed no foreign direct investment.

In contrast, China under Deng Xiaoping has gradually, but decidedly, reversed the Maoist development strategy and come to adopt a new development strategy that has been associated with Deng's call for some people and some areas to become rich first before attaining the goal of common prosperity.[1] It emphasizes the harnessing of regional comparative advantage, accepts regional disparities as inevitable, and encourages foreign investment and international interaction in order to bring China out of economic backwardness and isolation and to catch up with the rest of the world. Deng's advocacy for unbalanced development reached a plateau during his celebrated tour of southern China in

1992. In his talks on the trip, Deng reiterated that those areas that had favorable conditions should strive to grow faster. While he mentioned that those areas that became prosperous first should pay more to help less developed areas, he nevertheless concluded that that time would not come until the end of the twentieth century (Deng 1993: 374–76).

Overall, central government policies have favored the coast more than the interior during the post-Mao era. To be sure, the interior regions have also experienced rapid economic growth, but in relative terms they have lagged behind the coastal region. As a result, alarms have been sounded about the widening coast–interior economic inequalities. In the rest of the chapter, I will first review the regional aspects of the Maoist development strategy. I will argue that, in regional terms, the Maoist development strategy was subverted internally by the Maoist dictum of self-reliance at various levels. I will then examine the post-Mao leadership's rationale for regional policy change and discuss the shift to an unbalanced regional development strategy that favors the coast and its actual impact on regional disparities.

REGIONAL ASPECTS OF THE MAOIST DEVELOPMENT STRATEGY

The economy taken over by the Chinese communist leadership in 1949 was not only rudimentary and war-devastated, but also extremely imbalanced regionally. Centuries of cumulative change beginning in at least the Song Dynasty (960– 1279) had shifted China's economic center to the coast. Even though much of China's national industry moved inland during the Sino-Japanese War (Sun Guoda 1991), by the end of the 1940s over 70 percent of the industrial assets and output (including handicraft output) were concentrated in the coastal areas, especially Shanghai, Jiangsu, and Liaoning, while the rest of the country shared the remainder (State Statistical Bureau 1984: 64–65). Within the coastal region, modern industrial production was again heavily concentrated in just a handful of urban centers. The gross value of output of eight cities (Beijing, Tianjin, Shanghai, Shenyang, Anshan, Benxi, Dalian, Fushun) accounted for 55 percent of the total for the coastal region (Roll and Yeh 1975: 82). Like a typical underdeveloped country, the Chinese economy was dualistic and the few industrial centers were surrounded by a vast agricultural hinterland.

As it embarked on the road to rapid industrialization in the early 1950s, the Chinese leadership, partly influenced by the Soviet theories of regional development, regarded the huge coast–interior imbalance in China as irrational for both economic and national security reasons.[2] First, areas of industrial production (the coast) were usually located too far away from energy and raw materials supply areas and the interior market. This not only entailed substantial long-distance transport costs but also put undue strain on China's undeveloped transport system. Second, the rich resources in inland areas could not be properly exploited (State Statistical Bureau 1984: 64). Third, since the coastal region was easily exposed to foreign military power, the heavy concentration of industry along the coast was regarded as a national security risk, as was the case during the Sino-Japanese War when Japanese troops took control of most of the coast (Roll and Yeh 1975: 84). These considerations led the Chinese leadership to emphasize the pursuit of regional balance, thereby giving priority to investment in inland areas, from which Mao and most of his revolutionary lieutenants had originated (Mao Zedong 1974). Moreover, from the late 1950s onward Mao and others called on local authorities to build up relatively independent industrial systems, thus encouraging self-reliance and economic fragmentation along administrative boundaries (Lyons 1987).

Unlike previous Chinese governments, the communist leadership was able to tap a powerful war-state to rectify China's regional imbalance. The establishment of a centrally planned economy in the 1950s furnished Chinese leaders with the levers of centrally directed investment and greatly facilitated the channelling of investment into targeted areas. The First Five-Year Plan stipulated that new industrial bases were to be built to rectify the irrational spatial distribution of Chinese industry (Fang Weizhong 1984). During the First Five-Year Plan period (1953–57), almost two-thirds of the major projects, including three-quarters of the projects built with Soviet aid, such as the Taiyuan Steel Works in Shanxi and First Autoworks in Jilin, were located in the interior (Roll and Yeh 1975: 84). None of the Soviet-aided projects was located in major coastal provinces such as Shanghai, Jiangsu, Zhejiang, Fujian, Shandong, Tianjin, and Guangdong. Despite allowance made to help rehabilitate war-devastated coastal industrial facilities (such as the Anshan Iron and Steel Works), nearly 56 percent of the state investment in fixed assets went to heavy industrial projects in the interior during this period (Table 2.1).

The interior-oriented regional investment policy took its toll in terms of economic efficiency as coastal industrial growth was sorely needed as a foundation for the development of the whole country. More concentrated efforts at rehabilitation and improvement of old enterprises in the coastal region could have produced more immediate economic pay-offs than scattering investments, sometimes in places such as Fulaerji of Heilongjiang that lacked infrastructural support. Nevertheless, in light of what was to come in the 1960s–70s, most factories constructed during the First Five-Year Plan were built near existing cities or mineral deposits in the interior and were reasonably coordinated. Many of these factories would remain China's backbone enterprises in the 1980s.

Partly as a result of the preference for the interior, coastal industrial growth lagged behind that of the interior by 3.4 percentage points over 1952–57. Nevertheless, the underlying economic strength of the coastal region was unmistakable. Aided by the arrival of peace and the strength of the non-state economic entities, and because it took time for the interior projects to be completed, the coastal region's share of national income grew steadily in the 1950s, rising from 46.3 percent in 1952 to 50.3 percent in 1958 (State Statistical Bureau 1990).

Yet there is no denying that preexisting coastal industrial centers were neglected and even skimmed during this period. Thus, Mao Zedong (1974: 65–67), in his

Table 2.1 Fixed-asset investment in state enterprises (Rmb 100 million)

Period	Coastal region		Interior regions	
	Amount	*% of total*	*Amount*	*% of total*
1953–57 (1st FYP)	217.26	44.1	275.57	55.9
1958–62 (2nd FYP)	462.62	40.6	675.61	59.4
1963–65	147.38	37.5	245.77	62.5
1966–70 (3nd FYP)	262.85	29.4	631.21	70.6
1971–75 (4th FYP)	625.36	39.5	959.34	60.5
1976–80 (5th FYP)	988.21	45.8	1,171.59	54.2
1953–80 total	2,703.68	40.6	3,959.09	59.4
1978	200.83	44.0	255.35	56.0
1979	221.09	45.7	262.95	54.3
1980	248.69	47.2	278.46	52.8
1981	212.20	50.3	209.53	49.7
1982	266.50	50.8	257.95	49.2
1983	277.96	49.6	282.80	50.4

Source: State Statistical Bureau 1984: 40.
Note: Non-region-specific investments in railway engines, ships, aircraft, and civil defence are excluded. Consequently, the sum of investments in the regions for a period = total state investment − non-region-specific investments.

celebrated speech of April 1956, "On the Ten Great Relationships," commented that in "the past few years we have not laid enough stress on industry in the coastal region" so that the productive power of coastal industry could be used for the full development of the whole country, especially the interior. In the same speech, however, Mao also revealed economic efficiency was not his top concern; he was in favor of building most of China's heavy industry, "90 percent or perhaps still more," in the interior.

The First Five-Year Plan was for a long time the only plan that was even partially implemented (Bachman 1990).[3] In 1958–62, China's economic development was caught in the notorious Great Leap Forward that relied on mass mobilization and institutional transformation to speed up agricultural growth and industrial development (MacFarquhar 1983). The Great Leap emphasized heavy industry in general, and the iron and steel industry in particular. In any case, the Great Leap came to be a leap into disaster and led to the worst famine in history (Bernstein 1984; D. Yang 1996a). During this period state investment in industrial assets in the interior continued to increase. It averaged 59.4 percent of the national total during 1958–62 and rose further to 62.5 percent in the post-Leap adjustment period (1963–65). Much of the money was poured into projects that came to nothing.

In the meantime, worsening Sino-Soviet relations and US involvement in Vietnam led Mao to perceive rising threat and insecurity in China's strategic environment and thus an urgent need to enhance China's national defense capabilities to prepare for a world war that was believed to be both inevitable and imminent (Deng Xiaoping 1993: 127). In consequence, despite the much felt need in the aftermath of the Great Leap to invigorate existing industrial production and restore consumption levels, Mao in fall 1964 made the momentous decision that China should concentrate its resources on the construction of defense-oriented industries in the interior so that the industrial infrastructure would survive a foreign invasion and provide for a protracted defensive war in an era of nuclear missiles and atomic bombs. The country was divided into three fronts, roughly corresponding to the three regions (coastal, central, and western). Most new industrial projects were located in the third-front areas and thus the military-industrial build-up in these areas has been known as the third-front program (Naughton 1988, 1991). The program experienced two waves. The first wave lasted from 1964 to 1966 and was concentrated in Sichuan, Hubei, and Gansu. After the Cultural Revolution was brought under control and with the intensification of the Sino-Soviet confrontation, a second push came into being in 1969; it lasted until 1972 and most projects built during this period were located in Sichuan, Hubei, Shaanxi, Henan, and Guizhou.

The third-front program was massive by any standard and in sharp contradiction to Mao's statement on regional balance in his speech on the ten great relationships. During the Third Five-Year Plan period (1966–70), third-front areas were allocated 52.7 percent of China's basic construction investment funds, compared with 20.6 percent over 1953–57 and 36.9 percent over 1958–62 (Lu Dadao *et al.* 1990: 26; see also Naughton 1991). Major projects included the Panzhihua iron and steel complex in Sichuan, the Chengdu–Kunming railways, the Second Autoworks in Hubei, and aircraft manufacturing in Shaanxi. By the late 1970s some 29,000 third-front entities, including almost 2,000 research institutes, had been built or were being built, leading to a very substantial increase in the industrial capacity of third-front areas (Li Yongzeng and Li Shuzhong 1985: 10; Zhang Huaiyu 1985: 10).

Though it centered on heavy industry, the entire third-front build-up was dictated by considerations of military strategy rather than economic efficiency. Many of the projects were decided on by a few leaders and with no feasibility study of any sort whatsoever. Following Defense Minister and Mao-heir-apparent Lin Biao's watchword of building "in mountains, in dispersion, and in caves (*shan, san, dong*)," most third-front projects were built in areas that lacked proper infrastructure. Because limited funds were spread over too many projects, the third-front projects generally took a long time to build and thus tied up great amounts of investment funds and yielded poor economic results. According to one official estimate, only half of the factories built performed to design specifications and the rest were either only partially completed (30 percent) or not completed at all (20 percent). Fully one-third of the total investment was wasted (Zhang Huaiyu 1985: 10–11). In the mid-1980s, the central government surveyed the existing third-front enterprises and found that 48 percent of them were doing reasonably well while 45 percent were performing badly owing to poor location and other reasons. The remaining 7 percent (121 projects) were simply hopeless and were relocated to urban centers or merged into other enterprises in the late 1980s or early 1990s at considerable expense (2 billion yuan over 1986–90 alone) (Lang Yihuan and Li Dai 1991: 33–34).

This centrally directed effort pushed the interior's share of total state investment in fixed assets to a little over 70 percent between 1966 and 1970. Despite the chaos of the Cultural Revolution (1966–69), third-front construction continued in the early 1970s for several reasons. First was the renewed war scare arising out of the 1969 Sino-Soviet border clashes. Second was the investment momentum itself; it was both politically and economically difficult for the leadership to leave projects half-finished. Third was the decentralization in economic decision-making, which made it difficult for leaders in Beijing to control investment scale as various localities used the funds under their control to build "little third-front" projects in each locality. In consequence, during the 1971–75 period the interior's share of state investment still averaged a high 60.5 percent and third-front areas took in 41.1 percent of the state basic construction funds. Nevertheless, as will be discussed later in this chapter, the opening of Sino-American relations in 1972 was beginning to usher in a limited reorientation of China's regional development.

REASSESSING THE MAOIST REGIONAL DEVELOPMENT STRATEGY

As can be seen in Table 2.1, from 1953 to 1980, 59.4 percent of the total state investment in fixed assets was allocated to the interior provinces, leaving 40.6 percent to the coast. This roughly corresponded to the regional population distribution (Table 1.1). Nevertheless, since most of the industrial projects were capital intensive, they were necessarily concentrated in selected areas (Taiyuan, Changchun, Baotou, Fulaerji, for example, during the First Five-Year Plan period; Chongqing, Panzhihua, Guiyang, Shiyan, Xi'an, among others, after 1964) rather than evenly spread throughout the interior.

At various stages, different development objectives prevailed. In the 1950s the objective was mainly to achieve "balance" in China's industrial distribution and hence in the distribution of regional economic power. After 1964 interior industrialization was dominated by military–strategic considerations. Most of the projects were built in areas that were not easily accessible and were lacking in infrastructure. Often the projects had few linkages to local economies because of the choice of isolated locales. In Yunnan, for example, heavy industry's share of capital construction investment over the 1952–78 period was 52 percent. As a result, heavy industry's share of gross industrial output increased from 36 percent in 1949 to 57 percent in 1978. Nevertheless, most people in the province benefitted little from these investments (He Zhiqiang 1991: 6).

Did the Chinese leadership succeed in redressing the coast–interior imbalance in industrial configuration? The answer is ambiguous at best. A look at Table 2.2 reveals why. In terms of the value of fixed assets, the interior was clearly the beneficiary. Its share of the total rose sharply from 28 percent in 1952 to nearly 57 percent by 1983, with a corresponding reduction in the coastal share. Keeping in mind that coastal provinces contributed a much larger share to the central government revenue than they received in central government investments, the central government's regional investment policy was evidently highly redistributive, taking from the coastal region with the left hand and then giving to the interior with the right hand.

The impact of the central policy on spatial disparities is also reflected in the shift in the center of economic activity. Chinese geographers calculate that in about two decades, from 1952 to 1971–75, this center for China moved inland by 395 kilometers or 245.5 miles. In comparison, it took eight decades (1880–1960) for the center of population in the United States to move 250 miles (Lu Dadao *et al.* 1990: 32–33).[4]

Finally, the impact of the redistributive investment efforts is also reflected in the pattern of provincial output changes from 1952 to 1979 (Table 2.3). Between 1952 and 1979 the per capita industrial output of five of the 11 coastal provinces declined, compared with five out of 18 in the interior.[5] The interior's gain was clearly made at the expense of the coast through the central government redistribution of revenues. While Shanghai (20 percent in 1959; 10 percent in 1972) and Liaoning (18 percent in 1972) kept only a small portion of their revenues, the poorest provinces (including Xinjiang, Qinghai, Tibet, Gansu, Yunnan, Guizhou, Guangxi and Ningxia) not only retained all their revenues but also received government subsidies (Riskin 1987: 212; Lardy 1978).

Yet, despite the central government's redistributive investment policy which reduced the coastal region's share of total fixed assets from 72 percent in 1952 to just 43 percent in 1983, the coastal region still produced nearly 60 percent of the national gross industrial output value in 1983 (Table 2.2). Figure 2.1 plots the regional shares of national income over 1961–79. While the coastal share declined swiftly during the first phase of the third-front program, it managed an upturn during the Cultural Revolution and by the mid-1970s had again returned

Table 2.2 Distribution of industry by region (1952 and 1983)

	Amount		% of total	
	1952	1983	1952	1983
Original value of fixed assets (Rmb bn)	14.88	476.78	100.0	100.0
Coast	10.71	205.97	72.0	43.2
Interior	4.17	270.81	28.0	56.8
National GVIO (Rmb bn)	34.33	616.44	100.0	100.0
Coast	23.81	366.75	69.4	59.5
Interior	10.52	249.69	30.6	40.5

Source: State Statistical Bureau 1984: 40.

Table 2.3 Distribution of per capita industrial output by province*

Province/Year	1952	1965	1974	1979
COASTAL REGION				
Liaoning	385	334	300	257
Beijing	481	385	617	513
Tianjin	1,112	572	663	498
Hebei	55	86	122	84
Shandong	62	58	77	87
Jiangsu	84	93	113	138
Shanghai	1,517	1,165	1,404	1,106
Zhejiang	76	72	58	85
Fujian	69	56	48	59
Guangdong	84	94	85	79
Guangxi	33	32	37	57
CENTRAL REGION				
Heilongjiang	222	195	127	141
Jilin	161	148	109	120
Inner Mongolia	60	251	187	63
Shanxi	92	—	72	91
Henan	30	41	43	50
Anhui	36	40	36	51
Hubei	74	64	58	86
Jiangxi	54	—	49	51
Hunan	40	41	44	63
WESTERN REGION				
Xinjiang	82	86	46	54
Gansu	51	87	100	92
Ningxia	10	24	35	80
Shaanxi	56	73	64	80
Qinghai	45	73	99	78
Sichuan	55	53	41	54
Guizhou	33	48	34	36
Yunnan	48	38	32	40
Tibet	7	13	14	11

Source: Riskin 1987: 226.
* Percentage of national average.

to more than 50 percent. In essence, the imbalance between coast and interior increased since the coastal region still produced the bulk of China's industrial output and national income but with much less investment. Two major reasons, one economic and the other political, account for this disjuncture between investment and regional output.

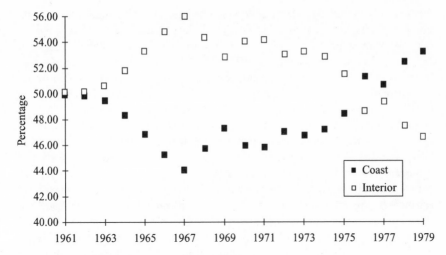

Figure 2.1 National income by region, 1961–79

Sources: State Statistical Bureau 1990: *ZGTJNJ* 1986: 56; 1987: 54; 1988: 55; 1989: 33; 1990: 39; 1991: 37; 1992: 37; 1993: 40; 1994: 38.
Note: National income figures at current prices are used because of the unavailability of GNP or GDP data for this period.

In economic terms, the coastal region enjoyed superior factor endowments compared with the interior. Coastal bases possessed an industrial labor force with many years of experience while the interior had workers who were mostly recent recruits from the peasant population (C. Cheng 1982: 435; Wei Wei, Wang Jian, and Guo Wanqing 1992: 140–97). Coastal industries also accumulated superior managerial skills compared with those in the interior. Moreover, the coastal region generally boasted better infrastructure than the interior. Finally, many of the third-front projects were so poorly situated and constructed that they might be said to have been born with severe congenital heart problems; their chances for survival became especially slim once the Chinese economy started out on the path of market-oriented reform. The Chinese government itself estimated that more than 30 billion yuan of the total third-front investment was wasted (Cong Jin 1989: 468; Naughton 1988; Xiao Min and Kong Fanmin 1989: 63–67, 40). Many of the remaining third-front plants could not operate without state subsidies and had to be relocated. According to a survey done in late 1987, only 30 percent of the equipment in third-front plants was put to good use (Jiang Baoqi, Zhang Shengwang, and Ji Bing 1988: 63). Moreover, because of the dominance of the "unit" mentality, which was strengthened owing to the military nature of most of the projects, most of these plants had few linkages with the local economy and contributed little to the development of these localities, including most areas inhabited by ethnic minorities. In light of these factors, it is hardly surprising that industrial productivity in the coastal region remained considerably higher than in the interior in spite of the shift in central investment to the interior (Rawski 1979: 160–64; Mao Zedong 1974: 67).[6] According to an estimate by Liu Zaixing, state enterprises in third-front areas in 1978 produced only 70.4 yuan worth of output for every 100 yuan of fixed-asset investment, compared with 141.4 yuan for the coastal region. The rate of profitability for state enterprises in third-front areas was 9.2 percent in 1978, compared with 23.4 percent for state enterprises in the coastal region (Liu Zaixing, Jiang Qinghai, and Hou Jingxin 1995: 19).

Politically, as Thomas Lyons (1987) has shown in his perceptive study, both the structure of China's planning organization and the procedures used to generate directives tend to produce disintegrative tendencies along provincial boundaries. These tendencies were further intensified by the emphasis on self-reliance in the aftermath of the Great Leap Famine (D. Yang 1996a). Each province had considerable power to direct local economic development and seek self-sufficiency, especially following the two waves of economic decentralization in 1958 and 1970, though after 1960 some recentralization occurred to deal with the post-Leap crisis. As a result, the coastal provinces had considerable leeway to take advantage of their superior factor endowments. Therefore, both China's economic system and the Maoist policy of self-reliance eventually served to undermine the policy of eradicating regional industrial imbalance through centrally directed investments. Within this political framework, higher productivity in the coastal region enabled the coast to outproduce the interior despite the higher proportion of government investment going into the interior.

Thus, the central government's attempt to spread China's industrial facilities more evenly produced paradoxical results. The improvement in equity came at the expense of efficiency since the national economy would have grown more rapidly had investment been made in terms of economic efficiency. While the conventional Chinese position holds that China's past investment patterns must be assessed in their proper historical context and that 30 years' economic construction had resulted in a more evenly spread industrial distribution (Wei Shi'en and Guo Zhiyi 1992: 6), even leaders of interior provinces that had benefitted from rising central investment had mixed feelings about the way regional equity was achieved, especially because many of the third-front factories have had great difficulty in adjusting to economic realities during the reform era. After all, the third-front projects were built under the direction of a small group of central leaders and with little regard to local interests.

Most significantly, however, was the policy backlash produced by the Maoist regional development strategy as influential Chinese economists and policy-makers drew lessons from the Mao era. Two major lessons from the 1953–80 experiences are especially worth noting.

First, not only was the interior-oriented investment itself regarded as poorly executed by Chinese leaders and scholars, it also occurred at the expense of the development of the coastal region, which was starved of funds for renovation and maintenance during the 1953–80 period. From 1950 to 1976, the industrial center of Shanghai remitted to the center an amount that was equal to 42 percent of total state investment. It also supplied many of the industrial plants built in the interior as well as hundreds of thousands of technical personnel (Liu Guoguang *et al.* 1984: 267). Meanwhile, the state of Shanghai industries showed little improvement, especially in light of developments in the rest of the East Asian region.

Citing Soviet and American experiences in expanding their industrial base from one part of the country into another as an extremely long-term and arduous process, Liu Guoguang and others concluded that "seeking to build up interior industries within a short time, without developing the old bases of coastal industry, was unrealistic" (Liu Guoguang *et al.* 1984: 269–70; Shao 1985: 100–108). Haste only made waste. The allocation of limited development funds essentially represented a zero-sum game. The rush to invest in the interior came at the expense of the transformation and modernization of coastal industries and therefore hindered the development of both and harmed the national interest. China had "paid a heavy price" for the pro-interior development strategy (Zhang Wenhe 1989: 71; Xia Yulong 1994). For Liu Guoguang and others, economic policy-making must follow certain "objective laws" of development. While it is not exactly clear what laws of development they were referring to, their critique evidently called for turning away from the headlong rush into interior development.

Second, Maoist development as well as self-reliance policies committed the sin of disregarding the basic idea of comparative advantage (Liu Guoguang *et al.* 1984: 270–72).[7] The eminent economist Xue Muqiao, for example, dismissed the [investment] construction policy as "erroneous."

> If the comparative advantages of [backward] regions had been systematically developed in the past 30 years, there would not have been such shortages of raw materials in the advanced industrial regions, and light industry would have developed to a greater extent. Income of backward regions also would have greatly increased.
>
> (Xue Muqiao 1982: 126)

In other words, Xue and others did not object to investment in the interior *per se*. What they regarded as problematic, however, was that programs such as the third front were wasteful and often counterproductive.

The attack on the Maoist regional development policy was intimately tied to the re-evaluation of China's overall development strategy under Mao. That strategy combined features of a Stalinist heavy-industrial development strategy with Maoist ideals of egalitarianism and self-reliance but ended in the worst of both worlds. Both became discredited in the 1980s. Dong Fureng and other Chinese economists concluded that the Maoist development strategy had seriously compromised the improvement of economic results in China by consuming excessive amounts of inputs, by causing serious disproportion in investment at the expense of light industry and services, and by retarding technological progress (Dong Fureng 1988: 235–41). In reaction to the Maoist legacy, the Dengist era has been engaged in a constant battle to improve the Chinese economy on all these fronts. In regional terms, as the next section will show, the new development strategy has meant emphasis on comparative advantage and especially the development of the coastal region. It is a recipe for unbalanced regional development.

THE DENGIST REGIONAL DEVELOPMENT STRATEGY

Whereas it is conventional to use the year of 1978, especially the third plenum of the 11th CCP Central Committee held in December 1978, as the starting date of the post-Mao reforms, in reality a significant shift in China's regional development strategy had started to occur by 1972. The death of Defense Minister Lin Biao, Mao's heir apparent, and the thaw in Sino-American relations led the Chinese leadership to scale back the third-front program, which continued on a reduced scale because of sheer momentum and enthusiasm on the part of some local leaders. With China's strategic reorientation, the Chinese government imported much capital equipment from the West to deal with various bottlenecks in the economy. The imported projects of 1973–77, approved by Premier Zhou Enlai, emphasized petroleum, petrochemicals (including chemical fibers and fertilizers), and electric power, and cost just under US$4 billion. After Mao's death, Hua Guofeng called for learning from foreign countries and launched another wave of imports that again put emphasis on capital equipment, including petroleum processing and metallurgical plants.

While the import programs, particularly Hua's Great Leap Outward, have been criticized for causing economic imbalances, the spatial distribution of the imported projects nevertheless showed a marked contrast to the third-front program. Of the 47 projects, 24 were located along the coast, 12 were in the central region, and 11 were situated in the western region, especially Sichuan (Lu Dadao *et al.* 1990: 28–29). Even when they were located in the interior, they were situated close to water transportation. There was also some clustering of interconnected projects to take advantage of agglomeration effects. In short, even though investment in the third front continued to loom large through the mid-1970s, the import programs suggest that Chinese planners had already learnt lessons from the third-front program and begun to steer China's regional development in a different direction. Moreover, the imports point to a willingness to engage in the world economy. The same willingness was also shown in the drive to boost exports through export production bases in the early 1970s, particularly in Guangdong. Indeed, as was shown in Figure 2.1, the coastal region's share of national income steadily rose throughout the 1970s. Thus, as far as the orientation of regional development was concerned, the Deng Xiaoping–Chen Yun coalition that took over power from Hua Guofeng did not herald a radical break from the past.

Nevertheless, by pushing a tentative reorientation into a fully-fledged development program, the post-Mao era deserves its own appellation. Since Deng has been much more audacious than Chen Yun in emphasizing an imbalanced development program between the late 1970s and early 1990s, I shall refer to China's regional development strategy during this period as the Dengist regional development strategy.[8]

Like other aspects of the post-Mao reforms, the Dengist regional development strategy must be appreciated within the context of China's re-engagement with the world economy and Chinese leaders' realization that the country they were leading was lagging behind in economic development, particularly in light of the rapid rise of Japan and other newly industrialized economies in Asia, including old nemesis Taiwan. The crucial issue for Chinese leaders and scholars alike has been how to increase efficiency and innovation in every aspect of the economy ("to enliven the economy," as the Chinese are fond of saying) so as to enable China to catch up with her burgeoning neighbors. To attain the goal of catching up, the Chinese leadership has opted to favor growth at the expense of some equity, at least in the short and intermediate run. In regional development, the concern with efficiency and rapid growth led the Chinese leadership to emphasize the allocation of limited economic and human resources to the development of the more developed coastal region in order to maximize national economic growth and national economic strength (Hu Xuwei 1989; Deng Xiaoping 1993 [1983]: 23). The coastal region, as then Premier Zhao Ziyang explained in 1984, would "radiate both inward and outward (*duinei fushe he duiwai fushe*)" and become a pivot in developing the whole country (Zhao Ziyang 1986a: 26–27).[9] The center was unable to invest large amounts in areas such as Xinjiang (in the western region) in the short term; these areas would have to wait until at least the 1990s (Zhao Ziyang 1986b: 18). As one Chinese scholar put it: "it is impossible to eliminate these disparities within several decades. . . . A relative preference for the developed regions may be necessary to ensure national growth" (Shao 1985: 107).

Theoretical justification

Chinese economists have generally taken two different positions on regional development in recent years: the "ladder-step doctrine (*tidu lilun*)" and the "anti-ladder-step doctrine." According to the ladder-step doctrine, the different regions are like steps on a ladder;[10] the coastal region is akin to a higher step. Since the three regions differ considerably in economic efficiency, national development strategy should first concentrate on developing the more advanced coastal region by providing it with adequate capital, energy, and foreign currency. This is necessary if China is to modernize and catch up with its neighbors in economic development. Only after the coastal region has become sufficiently developed, will attention be turned to the central region. Eventually development will reach the western region after the coastal and central regions have attained relative prosperity (Yun Mei and Yi Xing 1987: ix–10; Yu Jianxun

1987: 686). The principle of comparative advantage is thus central to the Dengist regional development strategy and dovetails with Deng Xiaoping's call for some areas to become wealthy first.[11] On the one hand, it advocates that each region specializes in what it is most able to do. On the other, it advocates that "the whole country is but one chessboard," that is, the regional division of labor is in the national interest, even if one region gets ahead of the others (Xue Muqiao 1982: 125–28; Liu Guoguang *et al*. 1984: 275–76).

The logic of the ladder-step argument is as follows. The coastal region already possesses significant industrial qualifications; hence it is easier to turn the coastal region into a processing center for inland raw materials and China's export base. Moreover, since the coastal region already possesses higher levels of technology and managerial sophistication than the others, it would be easier for it to absorb the imported advanced technology and develop indigenous capabilities for technical and economic innovations. Then it will be able to diffuse that technology throughout the economy. Therefore, it is important to concentrate on developing the coastal region first. Some writers have suggested that this development philosophy should also be applied at the level of the province. In the case of Yunnan, for example, one proposal argued that the province should concentrate its limited resources on the development of the more developed eastern part and then promote the vigorous development of western Yunnan when the province reached a certain economic strength (Wang Zhiyong and Wang Xiaochun 1987; Peng Yong'an and Li Hongguo 1987: 8).

In essence, the "ladder-step doctrine" is akin to the liberal argument that development will diffuse gradually from the center to the periphery.[12] The many vibrant coastal cities are designated China's "engines of growth" or "growth poles," pulling the whole country along the paths of economic development. Advocates of this doctrine appeal to the national interest. While they emphasize development of the coastal region in the short term, they promise that in the future economic growth will diffuse or trickle down to the interior. For them, China's socialist system will make such a development process smooth and beneficial to all.

Regional policies and regional disparities

The ladder-step doctrine has clearly been on the ascendancy within the Chinese leadership since the 1980s. In essence, the Dengist regional development strategy may be interpreted as an application of the growth center doctrine within the context of international competition and an unbalanced development strategy within China. This was most evident in China's Sixth (1981–85) and Seventh (1986–90) Five-Year Plans for economic and social development. Both emphasized the different economic development levels in the coast and the interior (The Sixth Five-Year Plan 1983; The Seventh Five-Year Plan 1986). In the Seventh Five-Year Plan, the interior is further divided into the central and western regions.[13] In consideration of the underlying economic realities, the

Chinese leadership stipulated in these plans that China concentrate on developing the coastal region starting from the Sixth Five-Year Plan and up to at least the 1990s. The Seventh Plan clearly stated that the objective of regional development was "to speed up the development of the coastal region, to put the emphasis on energy and raw materials construction in the central region, and to actively make preparations for the further development of the western region" (The Seventh Five-Year Plan 1986: 91). Each region is assigned a special role to take advantage of each region's factor endowments (or comparative advantage in the static sense). The coastal region was urged to "strengthen the technological transformation of traditional industries and . . . develop knowledge- and technology-intensive and high value-added consumer products industries" (The Seventh Five-Year Plan 1986: 92). It would gradually transfer high energy-consuming and high pollution-producing factories to the less developed regions that had more resources (Chen Minzhi 1985; Shijie xinjishu 1986; Guangdong jingji 1986). The central region should concentrate on producing energy and raw materials, certain machinery and electrical products, and agricultural produce (The Seventh Five-Year Plan 1986: 95). Finally, the western region was directed to emphasize agriculture, forestry, animal husbandry, and transport, and selectively develop its energy and mineral resources and certain local processing industries (The Seventh Five-Year Plan 1986: 98). In short, the emphasis is on efficiency through regional complementaries rather than regional self-sufficiency.

The emphasis on coastal development is evidenced in the reversal of the central government investment bias towards the interior that characterized regional development during the Maoist era. Symbolic of this shift has been the center's sustained and successful effort to attract foreign investment, transforming China from one of the most autarkic economies to a leading destination for foreign direct equity investments. Part of China's success in attracting foreign investment and increasing exports is due to a series of policies and institutions that offer foreign investors a relatively desirable investment environment. In 1979, the year China's first law on Sino-Foreign Joint-Venture Enterprises was promulgated, central authorities, including Deng Xiaoping, approved a proposal from Guangdong and soon established four special economic zones (SEZs) in Guangdong (Shenzhen, Zhuhai, Shantou) and Fujian (Xiamen).[14] In addition to tapping the goodwill and resources of overseas Chinese to introduce foreign technology and promote Chinese exports, the zones also acquired the additional function of facilitating China's national unification with Hong Kong and Macao (Vogel 1989: 81–83). Moreover, Guangdong and Fujian were allowed to set up the special zones partly because the two provinces had been starved of investment under Mao; granting them special policies was a sort of compensation for past neglect (Fujian 1990: 55–56). Finally, they were relatively small in the planned economy and failure would have a limited impact on the Chinese economy as a whole.

The special economic zones offered foreign investors special incentives, including lower tax rates, foreign exchange retention privileges, and lower land use fees. Meanwhile Guangdong and Fujian were also given greater autonomy in managing the economy. Originally modelled upon export processing and free-trade zones in other countries, the special economic zones have also become pioneers in various reform experiments such as labor management, housing, and foreign trade. These special zones grew at a torrid pace and prompted Deng Xiaoping to urge, in early 1984, that more coastal cities be given various special policies. Fourteen coastal cities (Dalian, Qinhuangdao, Tianjin, Yantai, Qingdao, Lianyungang, Nantong, Shanghai, Ningbo, Wenzhou, Fuzhou, Guangzhou, Zhanjiang, Beihai) were given the status of coastal open cities for foreign investment that year.[15] In spite of a controversy in 1985 over the performance of the special economic zones, the trend toward opening up continued and in early 1985 the Lower Yangtze Delta, the Pearl River Delta and the Xiamen–Zhangzhou–Quanzhou Triangle were designated as Coastal Economic Development Zones (CEDZs). In early 1988 Hainan Island (formerly part of Guangdong province) became a separate province as well as China's largest special economic zone. Finally, Shanghai was authorized in 1990 to launch the development of Pudong (East Shanghai) New Area and has since been treated as a special economic zone and given a host of special policies (Huang Qifan 1992).

Besides the major development zones and areas, a myriad other categories of special areas have also come into being since the mid-1980s. Those that are approved by the central government include free-trade zones, economic and technological development zones, and high and new technology industrial development zones, as well as open provincial capitals, border region open areas, and state tourist vacation zones (see Table 2.4). In addition, lower levels of governments have set up various preferential investment zones or districts of their own. The proliferation of different types of development zones is a remarkable manifestation of the various interests at work within the Chinese political system. These interests include different levels of government as well as different government departments. Besides the State Council itself, major government ministries such as the Ministry of Foreign Trade and Economic Cooperation, the State Science and Technology Commission, and the Ministry of Finance each have their own category of development zones to enhance their administrative reach and advance their bureaucratic mission. The State Nationalities Commission and the State Commission for Reforming the Economic System have also designated experimental zones for local reform and opening up in ethnic areas (Zhang Nianhai 1995).

There are significant variations in the preferential policies offered to different types of special zones. In general, the SEZs, open cities, and CEDZs were granted expanded administrative and economic authorities. Firms located within these special areas, be they Chinese or foreign, enjoyed tax privileges (including import and export taxes) and other benefits. Most of the open cities listed above also opened up special technology development zones or districts to facilitate

Table 2.4 Centrally approved special development zones and areas, by region

Zone type	Coastal	Central	Western	National total
Free trade zones	13			13
Special economic zones	5			5
Economic and technological development zones	25	4	1	30
Coastal open cities	14			14
Coastal open areas (cities and counties)	260			260
River valley open cities		5	1	6
Border-region open areas	2	5	6	13
Open provincial capitals	2	8	8	18
High and new technology industrial development zones	29	14	9	52
State tourist vacation zones	10		1	11
Total	360	36	26	422

Source: Guo Kesha and Li Haijian 1995: 67.
Note: Data were current as of 1995 and did not include the Shanghai Pudong New Area and the Taiwan Investment District in Xiamen, Fujian.

research and development as well as production (Waiwen Chubanshe Zhongguo Qingkuang Bianjishi 1987: 294–99). Perhaps the most radical experiment has been in Hainan province. Though a late starter, it has acquired a reputation for being the most free-wheeling special economic zone, particularly because of the real estate boom and speculation that seized the island in the early 1990s and the rampant presence of prostitution there. Much less noticed has been the island province's radical experiment to reduce government interference in the economy under the premise of "small government, big society." Companies simply register with the relevant government department rather than apply for permission to get started. Moreover, the province has promoted a series of policies promoting the free flow of people, funds, and production materials.[16] Foreign travellers may get a visa upon landing; employees can change jobs freely; and all barriers and toll stations have reportedly been removed from highways in Hainan (Ruan Chongwu 1994).

Until the mid-1980s the location of special zones was confined to the coastal region (especially the southeastern coastal provinces). Since then special zones have spread throughout the country (see chapter 3). Nevertheless, the figures in Table 2.4 show clearly that the coastal region has remained the primary beneficiary of preferential territorial treatment. It should be kept in mind, however, that the more developed coastal provinces would still have benefitted more than the land-locked interior from China's opening up simply because of their proximity to major international markets such as Hong Kong, Taiwan,

Japan, and South Korea as well as Southeast Asia and beyond. These markets serve both as the destination of Chinese export products and as sources of direct equity investment coming into China. In other words, even had the central government not given preferential treatment to the coastal region, that region would still have received more than its share of direct foreign investment. The presence of preferential investment policies has thus served to accentuate the coastal region's existing advantage and enabled it to take a commanding lead in attracting foreign investment, along with the advanced technology and management skills embodied in such investment. By the end of 1995, China had approved 258,903 foreign investment projects and the actually utilized amount of foreign investment had reached US$133.372 billion. A number of localities soared on the wings of the preferential policies. Shenzhen, in particular, transformed itself into a major metropolis and manufacturer in just a decade; it produced a quarter of the world output of clocks and bicycles in 1995 and was also a leading producer of various other consumer electronics products in China (*RMRBO* 3/26/96: 1). In the 1990s, the Shanghai Pudong New Area has defied skeptics to become a major manufacturing and financial center. In contrast, the 18 provincial units comprising the interior regions (central and western) had attracted only US$10.421 billion in foreign investment, or less than 10 percent of the total (*RMRBO* 4/22/96: 1). Moreover, the size of the average overseas investment project in interior regions is far smaller than the national average and tends to be technologically less sophisticated as well. A mere five of the 200 largest overseas invested enterprises in China as of the mid-1990s are located in the interior regions (Zhao Wei and Sun Yuxia 1996).

The Chinese government has recently sought to encourage foreign investment in interior regions, but it seems that foreign investment is spreading more to other parts of the coastal region, especially Shanghai, Tianjin, and Dalian, than to the interior. The Shanghai Pudong New Area, complete with an export processing area and a free-trade area, has become a major destination for new foreign investment since its inauguration in 1990. In 1995, Pudong alone took in a total of US$4 billion and set up 838 foreign-funded enterprises, bringing the total to US$14 billion and 3,501 enterprises (Xinhua 1/8/96 in FBIS-CHI–96–013 1/19/96: 35–36). Overall, 2,880 foreign-funded enterprises registered for operation in Shanghai in 1995, with an estimated total investment of US$10.5 billion. This brought the number of foreign-funded firms in Shanghai to 14,500 and raised the amount of overseas investment to US$68 billion (Xinhua 1/19/96 in FBIS-CHI–96–013 1/19/96: 36). While the amount of foreign investment going to interior regions is likely to rise substantially over time, it remains to be seen whether the relative regional shares will be altered significantly.

The proliferation of foreign investment zones and areas in China should be viewed as the manifestation of an overall drive toward international engagement.[17] Starting from a few tentative steps toward opening to the outside world in the 1970s, China is but one more in the expanding group of countries to embrace the doctrine of export-oriented development that has become, in the

Table 2.5 Foreign investment by province and region (actually used)

Province/Region	1985 % of total	1986 % of total	1987 % of total	1988 % of total	1989 % of total	1990 % of total	1991 % of total	1992 % of total	1993 % of total	1994 % of total
COASTAL										
Beijing	6.74	8.60	5.75	15.98	9.31	8.12	5.53	3.18	2.44	4.12
Tianjin	4.24	2.95	7.23	1.94	0.91	1.07	3.00	0.98	2.24	3.05
Hebei	0.63	0.65	0.56	0.61	1.27	1.29	1.28	1.03	1.45	1.57
Liaoning	1.86	2.77	4.94	4.14	3.67	7.49	8.19	4.69	4.68	4.33
Shanghai	8.16	8.55	11.63	7.40	12.28	5.06	3.28	4.49	11.56	7.44
Zhejiang	2.02	1.42	1.97	1.39	1.57	1.43	2.09	2.18	3.77	3.44
Fujian	9.00	3.59	3.01	4.62	10.13	9.31	10.65	12.94	10.51	11.16
Guangxi	2.33	2.83	2.45	0.66	1.54	1.04	0.72	1.65	3.24	2.51
Jiangsu	2.54	1.94	4.69	3.98	3.69	3.90	4.95	13.30	10.40	11.31
Guangdong	49.42	49.53	40.04	39.72	38.50	46.05	43.90	33.63	27.63	28.45
Hainan	n/a	n/a	n/a	3.73	2.76	3.00	3.99	4.11	2.59	2.76
Shandong	2.70	3.77	6.66	2.85	4.75	5.40	4.89	9.12	6.85	7.67
Coastal total	89.63	86.59	88.93	87.02	90.39	93.17	92.46	91.30	87.37	87.83
CENTRAL										
Inner Mongolia	0.20	0.43	0.27	0.20	0.13	0.31	0.04	0.05	0.31	0.12
Shanxi	0.04	0.01	0.27	0.21	0.29	0.10	0.09	0.49	0.32	0.10
Heilongjiang	0.30	1.41	0.76	2.20	1.67	0.83	0.47	0.66	0.85	1.05
Jilin	0.37	1.39	0.40	0.31	0.29	0.51	0.71	0.68	1.01	0.73
Anhui	0.23	2.02	0.18	0.89	0.25	0.39	0.24	0.50	0.94	1.11
Jiangxi	0.80	0.52	0.29	0.28	0.27	0.22	0.44	0.91	0.76	0.79
Henan	0.63	0.61	0.74	2.04	1.34	0.33	0.86	0.48	1.12	1.16
Hubei	0.61	0.71	1.41	0.71	0.83	0.92	1.05	1.85	1.98	1.81
Hunan	2.07	0.56	0.16	0.41	0.68	0.41	0.57	1.21	1.60	1.00
Central total	5.24	7.66	4.47	7.24	5.74	4.03	4.48	6.82	8.88	7.85
WESTERN										
Sichuan	2.18	1.83	1.32	1.28	0.38	0.71	1.83	1.02	2.09	2.77
Guizhou	0.74	0.70	n/a	0.31	0.37	0.31	0.32	0.18	0.16	0.19
Yunnan	0.12	0.22	0.34	0.26	0.23	0.21	0.08	0.26	0.35	0.20
Shaanxi	1.18	2.13	3.96	3.55	2.83	1.38	0.72	0.41	0.86	0.72
Gansu	0.04	0.07	0.01	0.07	0.03	0.04	0.11	0.00	0.04	0.26
Qinghai	0.01	n/a	n/a	0.09	n/a	n/a	n/a	0.01	0.01	0.01
Ningxia	0.02	0.00	0.00	0.01	n/a	0.01	0.00	0.00	0.04	0.02
Xinjiang	0.83	0.80	0.96	0.16	0.03	0.16	0.00	n/a	0.19	0.15
Western total	5.13	5.76	6.60	5.73	3.87	2.81	3.06	1.89	3.75	4.31
Total amount (US$bn)	1.32	1.74	1.84	3.15	3.44	3.44	4.43	11.00	27.34	33.26

Sources: *ZGTJNJ* 1986: 583; 1987: 605; 1988: 735; 1990: 655; 1991: 631; 1992: 643; 1993: 650; 1994: 530; 1995: 557.

words of Jagdish Bhagwati, "the new economic orthodoxy" in development studies (Bhagwati 1987: 257). Capping the trend toward outward orientation, the Chinese leadership formally launched its own version of export-oriented development strategy in early 1988, officially christened the "outward-oriented development strategy in the coastal areas (*yanhai diqu waixiangxing fazhan zhanlue*)," or coastal development strategy (D. Yang 1991).

Briefly put, the coastal development strategy was intended to allow the more prosperous coastal provinces to participate more fully in the international economy through the development of labor-intensive processing industries that import raw materials from abroad and then export the finished products, namely, to use imports to support exports. In reality, fuelled by rising foreign investment, export growth has expanded beyond labor-intensive processing to higher value-added products (Encarnation 1992). Instead of development through self-reliance, trade has provided a major engine for China's economic growth, just as it did for China's East Asian neighbors. Needless to say, because of its geographical location, abundant overseas linkages, superior economic fundamentals, the coastal region has been the engine as well as the main beneficiary of China's export-led growth.

While the coastal region has dominated China's international economic interaction, its position in domestic investment has been no less impressive. Indeed, under the condition of decentralized development and given the coastal region's lead in technology, management, and human resources in general, the coastal provinces have compounded their commanding position in domestic investment as well. Table 2.1 reveals that the coastal region's share of total investment in fixed assets of state-owned enterprises has increased gradually since the late 1970s. Table 2.6 updates the data series to the 1984–94 period and shows that the coastal share further expanded by 8.5 percentage points to 59 percent of the total by 1994. Although this does not mean that the center is taking money from elsewhere in order to invest in the coastal region, it does indicate that central investments and policies have allowed the coastal region to sharply increase its share of investment in the state sector.

The regional breakdown of total investment in fixed assets shows an even more impressive rise of the coast (Table 2.7). As is well known, economic decentralization has not only allowed lower administrative levels to retain more revenue but has also encouraged the establishment and expansion of private and collective businesses, which have been particularly vigorous in the coastal region. If investments by lower levels of government and the private and collective sectors are included, the coastal region's share of total investment in fixed assets rose to just under 66 percent of the total in 1994.

In short, while the coast and the interior were more or less equal in aggregate economic terms at the start of the reforms, the coastal region has undoubtedly become far stronger than the interior since then and has taken a commanding lead in the investment race with the interior. Since it is known that the coastal region has also enjoyed superior returns to investment relative to the interior

Table 2.6 Total investment in fixed assets of state-owned units by region (in 100 million yuan)

Year	National total	Coast		Interior	
		Amount	% of total	Amount	% of total
1984	1,102.99	558.15	50.60	544.84	49.40
1985	1,554.85	812.81	52.28	742.04	47.72
1986	1,793.24	971.02	54.15	822.22	45.85
1987	2,156.46	1,189.35	55.15	967.11	44.85
1988	2,615.56	1,481.17	56.63	1,134.39	43.37
1989	2,378.41	1,322.94	55.62	1,055.47	44.38
1990	2,750.56	1,541.72	56.05	1,208.84	43.95
1991	3,403.58	1,895.12	55.68	1,508.46	44.32
1992	4,994.26	2,877.73	57.62	2,116.53	42.38
1993	7,193.91	4,172.76	58.00	3,021.15	42.00
1994	8,705.96	5,142.91	59.07	3,563.05	40.93

Sources: ZGTJNJ 1985: 414; 1986: 443; 1987: 469: 1988: 561; 1989: 479; 1990: 155; 1991: 145; 1992: 147; 1993: 147; 1994: 142; 1995: 138.

Table 2.7 Total investment in fixed assets by region, 1981–94

Year	National total	Coast		Interior	
		Amount	% of total	Amount	% of total
1981	408.20	207.93	50.94	200.27	49.06
1982	790.67	401.80	50.82	388.87	49.18
1983	1,303.21	688.76	52.85	614.45	47.15
1984	1,750.69	925.24	52.85	825.45	47.15
1985	2,417.57	1,274.83	52.73	1,142.74	47.27
1986	2,887.44	1,566.96	54.27	1,320.48	45.73
1987	3,499.34	2,020.22	57.73	1,479.12	42.27
1988	4,349.34	2,591.92	59.59	1,757.42	40.41
1989	3,980.64	2,380.59	59.80	1,600.05	40.20
1990	4,281.21	2,525.68	58.99	1,755.53	41.01
1991	5,284.28	3,142.15	59.46	2,142.13	40.54
1992	7,575.61	4,689.55	61.90	2,886.06	38.10
1993	11,993.80	7,688.78	64.11	4,305.02	35.89
1994	15,753.82	10,370.10	65.83	5,383.72	34.17

Sources: ZGTJNJ 1985: 414; 1986; 443; 1987: 469; 1988: 561; 1989: 479; 1990: 155; 1991: 145; 1992: 147; 1993: 147; 1994: 142; 1995: 138.

regions, we can expect the coastal region's dominance in investment to propel the coast to pull further ahead of the interior. A look at the regional GVIO shares confirms this proposition (Table 2.8). Despite some economic cycle fluctuations, this data series clearly establishes the trend that the coastal region's share of the national GVIO has steadily increased over time.[18] In an ironic twist of history, the regional proportions of industrial activity as of the mid-1990s have reverted back to those that prevailed during the early years of the communist takeover (Table 2.2). Data on regional shares of gross domestic product show similar trends (Table 2.9). Moreover, since the regional population shares have seen little change over the period covered here, the discussion is also true in per capita terms. In short, the coastal region has over the past two decades recovered its commanding lead in the Chinese economy and played a pivotal role in fulfilling the Chinese leadership's ambition of making China into a global economic power. In the meantime, under China's unbalanced development strategy, the disparities between the coast and the interior regions have also risen sharply.

Before we shift our attention to the political economy of regional relations and disparities in the following chapters, it is important to keep in mind that the rising coast–interior disparities have occurred against the background of significant economic growth in all regions during the reform period. In the meantime, there has also been substantial spatial change within each region. Within the coastal region, for instance, all areas have not grown equally well and pockets of poverty frequently coexist side by side with locales of much prosperity. Moreover, as in a marathon, various provinces have taken the lead at different time periods. Guangdong and Fujian were the early beneficiaries of the Dengist regional development policy. By 1988, more than 10,000 enterprises were already processing materials supplied by foreign businesses for export in Guangdong (Gao Shangquan 1988), prompting observers to refer to Guangdong as Asia's "fifth dragon" (de Rosario 1988: 62; see also Vogel 1989). Since the late 1980s, Hainan, Jiangsu, Shandong, and Zhejiang have also basked in the limelight for their robust growth records, as has Shanghai in the 1990s. Indeed, when overseas investors decide not to invest in the special economic zones, they usually choose to go to another area in the coastal region, such as Jiangsu's Suzhou Industrial Park, rather than venture into the interior.[19] Built with Singaporean assistance and modelled upon Jurong town in Singapore, the Suzhou Industrial Park was launched in 1994 but had already attracted US$1.4 billion in investments within a year of its founding (Luce 1996).

CONCLUSIONS

The four and a half decades of Chinese regional development policies and practices surveyed here are marked by the giant swings to the interior and then back to the coast. The Maoist development strategy emphasized regional industrial balance and sought to correct the inherited coast–interior "imbalance" by directing a large portion of industrial investment into the inland area. As a result, the interior's share of industrial assets increased rapidly. However, the lop-sided emphasis on inland investment was marked by gross inefficiency. Despite its growing share of industrial assets, the interior continued to be out-produced by the coastal region in the late 1970s. This was an important reason behind the central government's switch to the Dengist regional development strategy.

Table 2.8 Share of gross value of industrial output (GVIO) by region, 1981–94

Region	1981	1982	1983	1984	1985	1986	1987	1988	1989	1990	1991	1992	1993	1994
Coastal	60.49	59.97	59.49	59.78	59.39	60.41	61.21	61.97	62.21	62.73	63.84	65.71	67.1	67.01
Central	27.25	27.61	27.62	27.31	27.58	27.34	26.55	26.24	25.93	25.36	24.27	23.28	22.34	22.60
Western	12.26	12.62	12.89	12.91	13.03	12.25	12.24	11.79	11.86	11.91	11.89	11.01	10.59	10.39

Sources: ZGTJNJ 1988: 258; 1990: 417; 1991: 397; 1992: 409; 1993: 415; 1994: 376; 1995: 378.
Note: Data for 1993 have been adjusted on the basis of provincial figures.

Table 2.9 Gross domestic product by region (in 100 million yuan)

Year	National total	Coast Amount	Coast % of total	Interior Amount	Interior % of total
1980	4,470.00	2,264.68	50.66	2,205.32	49.34
1981	4,773.00	2,467.78	51.70	2,305.22	48.30
1982	5,193.00	2,727.28	52.52	2,465.72	47.48
1993	5,809.00	3,026.03	52.09	2,782.97	47.91
1984	6,962.00	3,622.26	52.03	3,339.74	47.97
1985	8,557.60	4,402.59	51.45	4,155.01	48.55
1986	9,696.30	4,984.70	51.41	4,711.60	48.59
1987	11,301.00	5,931.29	52.48	5,369.71	47.52
1988	14,068.20	7,519.08	53.45	6,549.12	46.55
1989	15,606.14	8,490.26	54.40	7,115.88	45.60
1990	17,226.21	9,263.54	53.78	7,962.67	46.22
1991	21,142.09	11,642.94	55.07	9,499.15	44.93
1992	25,794.29	14,593.28	56.58	11,201.01	43.42
1993	34,227.68	19,810.50	57.88	14,417.18	42.12
1994	45,586.40	26,607.90	58.37	18,978.50	41.63

Sources: State Council Development Research Center 1992; *ZGTJNJ* 1990: 38; 1992: 30; 1994: 35; 1995: 33.
Note: Data for 1990 and later are gross domestic product. Gross national product figures are used for 1989 and before. Chinese figures for the two sets of data show only minor differences before 1990. Gaps in data for Jilin and Guangxi are estimated from national income figures.

Based on the idea of comparative advantage, the Dengist regional development strategy represented a radical reorientation from the Maoist era. It calls for differential development among the regions. Indeed, the leadership accepted the idea of uneven growth and granted preferential policies to the coastal region so that it might develop faster and become the engine of growth for China. The result of the new strategy, as is revealed through data presented here, is that both domestic and international investments in the coastal region have risen dramatically since the early 1980s, propelling the coastal region back to economic dominance by the mid-1990s.

One could argue that, given its superior geographical location and reservoir of human resources, the coastal region would still have gained over the interior once China started to leave the command economy behind and move toward the market, even if the center had not offered it preferential policies. Moreover, there would most likely still be a regional development gap in China even if market conditions had prevailed in the past four decades or more.[20] First, the process of modern economic growth in China, rooted in the expansion of foreign trade, originated and was concentrated in the environs of the coastal cities (Rawski 1989). Second, unlike sectoral imbalance, unbalanced regional growth tends to persist; growth, as Albert O. Hirschman noted, not only has the tendency to be concentrated around some starting points, it also has the ability and tendency "to round itself out for a long time within some subgroup, region, or country while backwardness retains its hold elsewhere" (Hirschman 1958: 184; Hirschman 1986: 26–33). In the US, for example, despite the existence of conditions for factor mobility, the industrial belt stretching from the Atlantic coast to the shores of Lake Michigan accounted for 75 percent of all manufacturing at the turn of the century and 68 percent as late as 1940 (Agnew 1987: 110–111; World Bank 1990c: 182–3). Thus, the increasing regional development gap in post-Mao China appears to represent a return to the path that would have prevailed had the central government not been as intrusive as it was during the Maoist period.

A crucial difference exists, however, between the post-Mao pattern of regional development and the hypothetical case of regional development under market conditions, though both involve issues of power. This difference came to my attention during interviews with Chinese scholars and policy-makers and a broad-gauged reading of relevant Chinese publications: interior interests are not discontented with the gap between the coastal region and the interior regions *per se*. They understand very well that no development process is even. What interior interests intensely dislike in the post-Mao period are the preferential policies for the coastal region and the distorted price structure, both of which are due to central government policies and would be mitigated if market forces prevailed in China. For interior interests, these two factors constitute an inequitable institutional structure which favors the rich and serves to widen the coast–interior development gap. In the next two chapters, I discuss how the interior provinces have responded to this challenge and interacted with the central government as well as the coastal region.

Part II

Regional relations amid economic liberalization

3 The dynamics and progression of competitive liberalization

A number of developments during the post-Mao period have accentuated cleavages between the coast and the interior regions. Specifically, the introduction of a limited market sector alongside materials allocation by planners has served as a poignant reminder to interior leaders that, under central planning, interior producers were not adequately compensated for exporting resources at state-set prices. Adding insult to injury, the central government has switched from an interior-oriented development strategy to one that favors the economically more advanced coast by adopting a series of preferential policies for the coastal region while reducing the share of investment funds allocated to the interior. To cope with the changing policy environment, leaders of interior provinces have engaged in policy *panbi*, lobbying central leaders for the extension of preferential policies to the interior. In the meantime, interior localities have taken matters into their own hands by processing the raw materials *in situ*.

In this chapter and chapter 4, I analyze the dynamics and consequences of these two types of local behavior and discuss the evolution of regional cooperation and cleavages under the reforms. This chapter will discuss the spread of preferential policies under conditions of fiscal decentralization. After a brief review of the trend toward decentralization, I introduce a simple game-theoretic model to explicate the dynamics of competitive liberalization. Next the predictions from the model are empirically substantiated through a discussion of the spread of preferential policies throughout the country. Finally, I point out the implications of competitive liberalization for macroeconomic control and inter-regional relations.

FISCAL DECENTRALIZATION

As numerous Chinese and Western commentators have pointed out, a key feature of China's post-Mao reforms has been the ongoing realignment of central–local relations, especially in terms of fiscal arrangements. In an acceleration of a trend that began long before the reform era, marginal increases in fiscal resources have been increasingly decentralized from the central government to local authorities.[1] Moreover, in tandem with the downward shift of fiscal resources is the transfer of spending responsibilities for public works, education, and welfare subsidies to local governments.

The transfer of both resources and obligations to lower levels of governments has created powerful fiscal incentives for these governments to promote local economic growth in order to raise revenue and create employment. David Granick has argued that regional governments in China acquired *de facto* property rights in economic agents (such as individual state-owned enterprises) by historical tradition or investment in the fixed capital of the agent or both and that this system of multiple principals, with property rights belonging to different levels of government, distinguished China from the Soviet or East European centrally planned economies (Granick 1990; see also Qian and Xu 1993). The trend toward fiscal decentralization under the reforms has only served to accentuate the tendency of local principals in the hierarchy to pursue their own interests (Eggertsson 1990: 40–45). The fact that as many as half of all county-level governments suffered from budgetary deficits as of the late 1980s and early 1990s served to accentuate the revenue imperative, whether through development or sometimes development-cum-predation (Byrd and Gelb 1990).[2]

THE DYNAMICS OF COMPETITIVE LIBERALIZATION

The theory of agency predicts that once local governments are given *de facto* possession of property rights, including part of the fiscal revenue stream, they would pursue local interests. Nevertheless, the center may use other mechanisms, such as a tightly controlled nomenclature system, to moderate and curb localist behavior. Christine Wong (1991) has argued persuasively that fiscal direction from the center has been quite substantial during the reform era. Indeed, the severity of the economic austerity program of 1988–91 underscored the degree of central discretion. A recent study by Yasheng Huang (1996) has produced similar conclusions on the implementation of macroeconomic policies.

Yet the theory of agency does *not* predict why local governments must pursue reform and/or development even though a number of authors have provided strong empirical evidence that the local government in China is developmentalist, particularly in prosperous localities situated in the coastal region (see especially Oi 1992, Zweig 1995). The interests of local governments (staffed by cadres who are of course not above pursuing personal interests) may be met in a variety of ways and economic development is only one of a choice set. In this subsection, I suggest that a simple model could account for why there has been a tendency on the part of local governments to compete and emulate each other in adopting certain policies of economic liberalization. While the actors in this model are local and especially provincial leaders, the interaction of their decisions results in the extension of territorially based preferential policies within the coastal region and to the interior.

Theoretically, it is possible that all the local units can get together to coordinate the economic activities in the country and strive for macroeconomic stability. However, leaving aside the issue of inadequate information, each local government has strong incentives to be the first to pursue policies of liberalization once liberalization is deemed politically desirable. This can be illustrated by the following example.

Suppose there is a country comprised of two adjacent local governments A and B, with relatively porous borders between them. Both have to pay out considerable amounts of subsidies to urban consumers who purchase rationed grain from government stores at fixed (and lower than market) prices. The government in turn procures grain from farmers at a state-set price that is lower than the market price but higher than the price that it resells the grain to urban consumers. In light of the fiscal pressure the subsidies exert, leaders in both administrations consider whether to liberalize grain prices (assuming that the central government encourages but does not dictate the decision and that consumer protest is minimal). There are four possible choice combinations in this case.

(a) Both decide, whether independently or jointly, not to liberalize grain prices at the present time. The fiscal pressure remains.
(b) Both decide, whether independently or jointly, to liberalize grain prices at the same time. The price paid to farmers and by consumers soon reaches the market price. Both local governments encounter some complaints from urban consumers but are no longer burdened by grain subsidies.
(c) In two other choices, however, either A or B liberalizes grain prices before the other does and, assuming that there is a considerable time-lag before the other liberalizes, then obviously grain will move from the subsidized area to the liberalized area as farmers and grain traders seek to take advantage of the price differentials in A and B. As a result, the late liberalizer faces procurement problems as well as the loss of subsidized grain to the other area. It adopts administrative measures such as border blockades to stop the grain from being taken out but this is far from successful given the porous borders. In consequence, it is not only still burdened with the price subsidies that it pays urban consumers but is also confronted with a shortage in grain availability that threatens to become a source of social instability. In other words, the late liberalizer is the sucker in a competitive policy game.

In summary, both A and B will have strong incentives to avoid being the sucker. As the formal discussion in the appendix shows, if the provinces fear punishment by the central government for liberalizing, then their choice will depend on their sensitiveness to the punishment relative to the cost of maintaining subsidies. Once the provinces know that they will not be punished by the central government for pursuing liberalization, they will rush to liberalize. In consequence, outcome (b) will be the result of this two-player game, leading to a rush to liberalize. The moral of this simple model can be extended to a country comprised of a multitude of local governments endowed with a certain degree of autonomy: It does not pay to liberalize later than one's neighbor. In the real world, however, the rush to liberalize will likely initially be less strong than indicated by the model because local leaders may be held back by ideology as well as lack of information. It is likely that the initial trend toward liberalization will start tentatively. Once the benefits enjoyed by the early liberalizers are demonstrated, others will want to climb on the bandwagon of liberalization, eventually producing the liberalizing rush.

The above discussion does not just apply to the liberalization of prices but can, with some adjustment, also be applied to other policy arenas such as investment. In the case of investment, the long-term differential impact on early and later liberalizers can be particularly significant given the path-dependent nature of investment decisions. Theorists of regional change from Hirschman to Krugman have emphasized that regions which come to dominance in earlier periods tend to retain their preeminent positions for long periods, despite the existence of the countervailing effect of trickle-down (Hirschman 1958; Myrdal 1957; Richardson and Tonwroe 1986: 647–78; Krugman 1991b; Krugman 1993: 293–98). If one area (such as a special economic zone) in a country adopts preferential policies toward investors ahead of other areas of the country, then this one area will probably get a disproportionately large share of the total investment and remain ahead for a long period to come. Investors are unlikely to simply pack up their factories and move when another area catches up in liberalization. Because of the dynamics described here, localities are expected to emulate and compete against each other to liberalize and to offer more preferential policies as long as they are politically and ideologically permitted to do so. The competition to offer ever more attractive terms will tend to make the entire country a giant special economic zone, making no area more attractive than the others in policy terms (investors will also consider other factors such as the quality of the local labor force and access to transport facilities). Though this will make China a more attractive investment target compared to other countries, this may result in more concessions being made to investors than if the process is centrally coordinated. Furthermore, the dynamics of competitive liberalization lead to bandwagons that exacerbate the difficulties of macroeconomic management in a transitional period and thus invite administrative intervention, leading to cycles of decentralization–centralization.[3]

Overall, the above model of competitive liberalization describes the trend of China's opening up quite well. In the early 1980s political and ideological concerns about the spread of liberal policies were strong among some members of the top elite, constraining the progress of liberalization. As these concerns were gradually eased, the dynamics of competitive liberalization came to predominate, producing a rush to establish special investment zones and programs throughout the country in the 1990s. Seen from a regional perspective, the various special policies spread from a few coastal cities to other areas along the coast first and then throughout the coast and finally reaching into the interior. Moreover, the pace of the spatial transmission appeared to accelerate over time.

INTERIOR INTERESTS AND TERRITORIAL PREFERENTIAL TREATMENT

In a limited way in the early 1980s, interior interests that relied on the planned economy and central budgetary transfers were likely to seek to limit the scope of preferential policies extended to selected areas in the coastal region. In this endeavor, these interests had their advocate in patriarch Chen Yun, whose emphasis on economic adjustment gave the special economic zones a slow start (Ruan Ming 1991: 58). The incidence of smuggling in Shenzhen also invited criticisms from communist party stalwarts. At the Conference of First Provincial Party Secretaries held in December 1981, it appears that inland leaders supported patriarch Chen Yun in emphasizing that the number of special economic zones should be limited to the four then in existence even though other parts of Guangdong and Fujian also sought to be designated such zones (Zhonghua 1987: 449). Chen Yun believed that the experiences of the existing special economic zones had not been adequately reviewed. He was also afraid that export processing by the special economic zones might wipe out domestic products and mentioned that provinces such as Jiangsu should not establish special economic zones (Chen Yun 1981: 276–77). By limiting the scope of zonal development, planners stood to benefit from foreign investment but had no fear of losing control of the developmental process.

By 1981, various central leaders had expressed their strong support for the special economic zones. On each of their visits to Shenzhen, Vice-Premiers Bo Yibo and Gu Mu were at pains to stress that central policies toward the special economic zones would not be reversed (Shenzhenshi Dang'anguan 1991: 22, 28). Yet in spite of the support from these central officials, SEZ leaders were not sure that the zones would be allowed to continue as long as Chen Yun was not on board. Indeed, the remarks by Bo and Gu highlighted the pervasive skepticism and uncertainty then surrounding the future of the special economic zones, which were criticized for spreading bourgeois influence and breeding economic crime.[4]

Relief came on October 30, 1982, when Chen Yun read the preliminary review that the Guangdong leadership had submitted to the center on the zones. Chen commented that "The special zones should be built. [We must] continually sum up experiences and strive to run the special zones well" (Shenzhenshi Dang'anguan 1991: 36). As soon as He Chunlin, head of the State Council Office of Special Zones, saw Chen's comment, he called Guangdong leaders to inform them of the good news. By now, the zones had also been made test sites for domestic reforms in housing, labor management, and other practices. Shortly after Chen Yun's comment was made, General Secretary Hu Yaobang made well-publicized visits to the Xiamen and Shenzhen special economic zones in December 1982 and February 1983. Hu reiterated Chen Yun's message and reaffirmed the central leadership's determination to develop the special economic zones using special and flexible policy measures.[5] Then in early

1984, amid a conservative campaign against spiritual pollution, Deng Xiaoping made an inspection trip to Shenzhen. Deng praised Shenzhen's achievements and concluded that the decision to establish special economic zones had been correct.

INTERNAL LINKAGES

Since most provinces were prohibited from establishing their own special economic zones at this time, it was natural for enterprises from these provinces to seek to profit from the preferential policies that the four special economic zones in Guangdong and Fujian enjoyed; the tax rate for companies in Shenzhen was set at only 15 percent and zone companies retained most of their foreign exchange earnings.[6] There was soon a proliferation of what has been called "internal linkages (*neilian*)," that is, cooperative relationships within China. Provincial and local governments established their links with Shenzhen and other special zones by opening representative offices, branch companies, and joint ventures in the zones, which served as China's windows and bridges to international markets. For example, Hualian Textile Corporation was founded in Shenzhen in December 1983 with the participation of textile bureaux from 18 provincial units (Shenzhenshi Dang'anguan 1991: 59).

For their part, the special economic zones faced many obstacles in their early years and eagerly sought cooperative relationships with non-zone areas for both economic and political reasons. Economically, the cooperative projects brought in human talent, investment funds, and technology and often led to sales for products produced in or going through the zones. Bao'an county, which became Shenzhen, had only six engineers on its payroll at the start (Liu Zhigeng 1991: 199). Once it became a special economic zone, it was able to attract thousands of technical personnel from around the country. Indeed, much of the investment funds in the special zones in the early years came from within China rather than abroad.

Politically, leaders of the special economic zones sought to enhance linkages with interior provinces in order to garner political support, particularly because the zones were not very successful in attracting foreign high technology in the early 1980s (Kleinberg 1990: 74–75). Being officially "special," leaders of the zones could not be sure whether the zones were experiments to be terminated or popularized. Because the zones were the closest places to capitalistic practices within China, they became easy targets for politically motivated attacks whenever the political environment became ideologically charged. Ever since their establishment, the special economic zones have periodically faced criticisms, including charges of selling out to foreign interests and internal exploitation, as well as rising corruption, smuggling, and trade deficits (Crane 1990; Kleinberg 1990: 71–96). By building cooperative ties with interior interests that were likely to feel disadvantaged and resentful toward the SEZs, the special zones sought to improve their image, deflect domestic criticisms, and broaden their base of political support.

While cooperative ventures appeared in the special economic zones from early on, the number of such ventures rose sharply beginning in 1983. While there were a total of 29 cooperative projects over 1979–82, 969 such projects were reportedly planned in 1984. Of the 969, 395 came from 27 provincial authorities and 236 were sponsored by lower-level governments (cited in Crane 1990: 88). This was partly because the status of the zones had become more certain following Chen Yun's 1982 comment and Hu Yaobang's visits. Moreover, the Shenzhen government convened its first meeting on enterprises built on internal linkages and approved a set of highly attractive policy measures for such enterprises. Besides tax and import duty privileges, enterprises based on domestic linkages could lease land in Shenzhen for 30 percent less than the going rate for foreign investors and retain 20 percent more in foreign exchange earnings (Shenzhenshi Dang'anguan 1991: 50). These preferential policies for domestic investors signalled to interior interests that the special economic zones cared for them and treated them more favorably than overseas investors. In short, as far as laterally linked enterprises were concerned, the interests of coastal special economic zones and interior governments seemed to converge. This was the honeymoon period for inter-regional cooperation.

Since the mid-1980s, Shenzhen has redoubled its efforts to stabilize and consolidate its domestic linkages when the political climate turned gloomy, as in 1985–86 and 1989–90. During the storm of criticism that raged over SEZ performance in 1985, Shenzhen was attacked for relying on "state blood transfusions" and "only making money out of the interior." To burnish Shenzhen's image, its leaders launched a shrewd publicity campaign. In November 1985, Deputy Mayor Zhou Xiwu talked about strengthening Shenzhen's linkages with the rest of China in order to make its industry become outward oriented. The next month Mayor Li Hao stated that "Shenzhen needs continual support from the rest of the country and Shenzhen must serve the rest of the country better" (Shenzhenshi Dang'anguan 1991: 169, 174; Li Hao 1986). Soon the Shenzhen leadership decided to adopt the slogan of "The whole country supports Shenzhen; Shenzhen serves the whole country" as the centerpiece of its publicity campaign (Liu Zhigeng 1991: 200).

To fulfill the pledge of mutual support, the Shenzhen municipal authorities sought to soothe the grievances of the enterprises based on internal linkages. During 1986–87 they cracked down on excessive levies and fees and strove to treat these enterprises on the same footing as local ones (Liu Zhigeng 1991: 200–201). In May 1987, the municipal government established an office of economic cooperation and also issued a set of interim regulations for further promoting internal linkages. By mid-1986, 27 central ministries and 27 provinces had established 2,300 cooperative enterprises and institutions in Shenzhen with total pledged investment of 5.6 billion yuan. More than 500 cooperative industrial enterprises produced 170-plus kinds of export products (Shenzhenshi Dang'anguan 1991: 217–18). Many third-front enterprises in the interior set up branches in Shenzhen in order to gather market and technical information and exploit market opportunities (Vogel 1989: 142). Moreover, a growing number of Shenzhen-based enterprises were setting up plants in the rest of China.

THE BANDWAGON OF SPECIAL ZONE CREATION

Once central leaders unanimously supported the special economic zones in Guangdong and Fujian, leaders in other parts of China abandoned their wait-and-see attitude and lobbied central leaders to request that similar zones be established in these provincial units as well. In the words of Chen Yun, "Every province wanted it and sought special treatment" (Chen Yun 1982: 280). In the meantime, provincial officials from all over the country began to make visits to Shenzhen to take a first-hand look at China's leading special economic zone and discuss the establishment of cooperative ties. The Shenzhen official chronology lists only provincial delegations led by first party secretaries. Between December 1983 and January 1985, eight such top-level provincial delegations, from Henan, Tibet, Sichuan, Hunan, Guizhou, Jilin, Shanxi, and Shanghai, toured Shenzhen (Shenzhenshi Dang'anguan 1991).

While Chen Yun approved the decision to establish special economic zones in 1982, Chinese authorities deferred to his earlier injunction on limiting the number of special economic zones and did not designate new special economic zones until 1988, when Hainan, which had been a leading candidate since the early 1980s, was finally made the fifth special economic zone as well as a separate province. Instead, reformers seeking to expand the reformist coalition and garner political support for economic liberalization came up with new appellations to differentiate the newly designated areas or zones from the four special economic zones.

Most of the newly designated zones were granted preferential treatment to foreign investors but on terms that were less generous than those in SEZs. Shortly after Deng Xiaoping's 1984 visit to Shenzhen, for example, the State Council approved the extension of the open policy to 14 coastal cities and Hainan Island and others were added to the list in later years. The open coastal cities also set up Economic and Technological Development Zones. The following year, the open policy was extended to the Yangtze, Pearl River, and South Fujian deltas. By now, the coastal region had become dotted with one or another sort of development zones. The ground was already laid for the coastal development strategy that was formally promulgated in 1988 (D. Yang 1991).

As the earlier discussion of the dynamics of liberalization suggested, as the benefits of becoming a special economic zone became clear, there was growing demand for territorially based preferential policies. Shanghai, for example, felt threatened by the rise of Shenzhen and asked for preferential policies and got some in the form of the Shanghai Economic Zone in 1983, which accorded the city greater leeway in managing international economic interactions (Crane 1990: 39). This fell far short of special economic zone status, however, and

Shanghai officials complained bitterly (Shirk 1994: 39). During his 1992 tour of the south Deng Xiaoping realized that Shanghai should have been made a special economic zone from very early on and regretted that the delay caused the city to lag behind in reforms. Yet the case for making Shanghai a special economic zone was extremely difficult to make in light of the elite cleavages and China's fiscal situation in the early 1980s (White 1989). On account of its disproportionate contribution to state revenue, it was difficult for planners to relax their grip on Shanghai at the time. On the other hand, by giving it some preferential policy treatment, reformists in Beijing at least tempered the resentment in Shanghai. Indeed, over the 1980s, the resentment in Shanghai grew steadily as Shanghai watched Shenzhen and other cities in the southeast leap forward with more favorable policies.

While groups of visitors toured Shenzhen, leaders of inland areas also began to turn from complaining about the preferential policies for coastal areas to actively seeking those policies for their own turf in the mid-1980s, having seen the growing amount of foreign investment being attracted to the special economic zones and open cities in the coastal region (*JJRB* 6/3/85 in FBIS 6/12/85: K5–6). After Deng affirmed the success of the SEZs and suggested that 14 coastal cities be given preferential treatment, 24 inland cities reportedly asked for the same privileges (Howell 1993: 23). In the case of Yunnan, Yan Liankun and Chen Zhi (1985: 8) not only advocated that it improve its infrastructure and adopt preferential policies to attract foreign investment but also asked the central government to make Yunnan an interior trading port and offer it more favorable policies than those enjoyed by the coastal open cities.

Broadly speaking, two types of argument were used to justify the adoption of preferential policies in interior regions. The first type of argument claimed that the establishment of special zones in the interior was a natural extension of China's opening. Indeed, one article published in a Yunnan economic journal contended that the existing special zones were too isolated (*gu lingling de*) and not well integrated with the Chinese economy. The authors of the article proposed that special economic zones be established in interior provinces to form a cluster of special zones across China and link up the national economy with the world economy (Wu Jixue and Yang Linjun 1985). The second type of argument pointed to the special conditions in parts of the interior regions, particularly the backwardness and political importance of ethnic minority areas. It was argued that areas inhabited by ethnic minorities were special and should not be governed with universal policies. Instead, they needed special preferential policies to attract technology, capital, and human resources (Xu Jingjun 1987: 19).

While it is difficult to quantify the impact of local demands on national policy, it is certain that the many demands for preferential treatment from the provinces reinforced the trend toward decentralization and liberalization. By mid-1986, many provinces had been allowed to offer tax exemptions, reductions, or holidays to targeted foreign ventures (Harding 1987: 167; *CBR* 1986).

This interior effort at joining the bandwagon of "opening up" reached a climax following the promulgation of the coastal development strategy in early 1988 and the decision to make Hainan a separate province and China's largest special economic zone (D. Yang 1991; Shirk 1994). For example, the group of special open zones authorized by the State Council after the promulgation of the coastal development strategy included Sanwan, Ya'an, and Suining in Sichuan, whose leaders had complained about the preferential policies for Guangdong in 1987 (*Inside China Mainland* 1988: 29). These open zones typically offered various enticements to foreign investors, including tax breaks and other kinds of sweeteners. In the meantime, the central government sought to be more regionally balanced in initiating a program of high and new technology industrial development zones. Many of the zones so designated were located in interior cities such as Wuhan, Xi'an, Chengdu, Changchun, Changsha, and Chongqing. Started in 1988, these zones were part of the State Torch Plan for technology development that was under the auspices of the State Science and Technology Commission.

The spread of various types of zones and increasing local discretion in setting investment policies served to intensify competition among local governments to attract foreign capital. In order to compete with southern cities, the city of Dalian in Liaoning offered Canon factory land for free in 1989. Other companies, such as Toshiba, basically determined their own land prices when they chose to invest in Dalian in 1991 (Thornton 1994: 56).

Competition with the southeastern coastal provinces, especially Guangdong, was the most important reason behind the drive for open-zone status in a number of adjacent interior provinces. Amid the fanfare for the coastal development strategy, landlocked Henan announced the establishment of two open zones for foreign investment in June 1988 despite higher-level disapproval (Lam 1989: 249). The policy of the leaders of Hunan and Jiangxi, two of Guangdong's inland neighbors, in dealing with the coastal challenge was to "counter openness with openness, dynamism with dynamism (*yifang duifang, yihuo duih uo*)," as our game-theoretic model predicts – after all, if you can't beat them, join them. Such a strategy led Wu Guanzheng, then governor of Jiangxi, to announce new preferential measures to attract outside investment, make southern Jiangxi an experimental zone for reforms, and abrogate all barriers to commerce between Jiangxi and the coast (i.e., Guangdong and Fujian) in the late 1980s (Lam 1989: 248; Wang Guoxing 1991: 31). The competitive dynamics also affected Jiangxi's price policies because its richer neighbors, Guangdong and Fujian, tended to purchase agricultural and raw materials from it at higher prices than its government offered. In order to compete, the Jiangxi government had repeatedly to raise its procurement prices for agricultural and raw materials before eventually freeing up prices (Li Xianghua and Wu Shaohua 1990: 44).

In Hunan, the provincial government maintained cooperative ties with its Shenzhen counterpart. In July 1987, for example, then Hunan governor Xiong Qingquan led a delegation for economic cooperation to Shenzhen and signed agreements on the production and supply of agricultural and sideline products, the development of export products in textiles and food production, machinery, chemicals, and electronics, and for the promotion of trade and tourism (Shenzhenshi Dang'anguan 1991: 268). Meanwhile, faced with the repercussions of Guangdong's reforms, which led to rising prices and labor costs, and following pressure from residents asking for more autonomy to compete with Guangdong, Hunan petitioned the State Council and received permission to make the municipality of Hengyang and two adjacent prefectures in southern Hunan an open economic zone (Zhang Ping 1988; E. Cheng 1989: 46; Liu Qingxuan and Zhang Jianping 1995).[7] In effect, for the Hunan leadership, the southern Hunan zone was designed to act as a buffer between rapidly liberalizing Guangdong and the rest of Hunan. Gradually, however, the Hunan leadership (and new leaders) called on Hunan to actively develop in concert with Guangdong. In the 1990s, Hunan has worked under the motto of "Hunan will do whatever Guangdong does" and has used the southern Hunan zone to integrate the Hunan economy with the Guangdong economy in order to gain better access to the Guangdong market and attract capital and technology from there (Zhang Annan 1996).

FROM TIANANMEN TO ZONE FEVER

The political crisis within China and in other socialist countries stimulated a drive by the central leadership to become more balanced in treating different regions and thus broaden the territorial base of their support. While they did not scrap the special economic zones, as some had feared, the central leaders nevertheless increased demands for financial contributions from Guangdong and Fujian (Chang Mu 1991). Moreover, the introduction of a unified foreign exchange system in preparation for China's entry into GATT curbed the foreign exchange privileges of the special economic zones.

Yet even while the central leadership emphasized that no new special economic zones were to be created, all attention was on Shanghai's Pudong (eastern Shanghai) New Area, which in 1990 came to enjoy practically the same preferential policy treatment as the special economic zones and was designated to become China's financial center. The central government's support for Pudong generated fears in the existing five special economic zones; they were afraid that Shanghai, with its entrepreneurial tradition and strong pool of human resources, would steal the show. The fact that Shanghai's leaders took every opportunity to trumpet Shanghai's technical depth and financial ambitions did little to allay the anxiety in the southeastern provinces.[8] Competition within the coastal region thus served to enhance the center's political leverage over each locality.

Interior lobbying for preferential policies continued after the Tiananmen crisis of 1989 and was especially visible in connection with the discussion on the Eighth Five-Year Plan at the Seventh Plenum of the 13th CCP Central Committee held at the end of 1990. As Jia Zhijie, then governor of Gansu which is one of the poorest provinces in the western region, pointed out, by giving preferential policies to the coastal region, the center was adding flowers to the brocade and making it more difficult for the western region to stay in the competition. For Shaanxi (another poor province in the western region) Governor Bai Qingcai pleaded the case that the interior provinces should be allowed to emulate the successful experiences and policies of the coastal provinces (Cheng Mu 1992: 12; see also Xu Changming 1989: 23). Even though interior provinces were not permitted to establish Shenzhen-style special economic zones, these provinces exploited the general relaxed policy environment to their advantage. Anhui, for example, designated five cities as open cities for foreign investment in April 1991 (Radio Beijing 1991). For its part, the central leadership in the aftermath of Tiananmen also sought to garner the support of interior leaders and to moderate the impact of the sanctions being imposed on China by governments in OECD countries. Interior regions such as Xinjiang demanded that they not only be allowed to open up their border areas but be permitted to establish free-trade zones and economic development zones in order to promote industrial development, enhance China's full opening, and alleviate the rising disparities between east and west (Tang Lijiu and Hu Ye 1991). In early 1990, the central leadership advocated China's all-round opening that would span the coastal rim as well as the western region. Thus it was natural to open up China's frontiers along the western borders. Within this context, Deng Xiaoping's much publicized 1992 tour of southern China provided the stimulus for the climax of China's opening.

Deng Xiaoping went on his highly symbolic southern tour and put his prestige behind faster economic growth because he had become impatient with the limited reform measures that had been adopted after the Tiananmen crisis and sought to set the agenda for the 14th Party Congress to be convened in fall 1992.[9] In his remarks on the tour, Deng emphasized that economic development was vital to the legitimacy of the Chinese Communist Party and called for bolder reform experimentation. For Deng, the economic austerity program of 1988–91 was necessary but insufficient. It only served the goal of stability and did not adequately promote economic growth.

Deng gave special encouragement to local initiatives:

> Areas with adequate conditions should try to grow faster; as long as they emphasize efficiency, quality, and outward-oriented economy, [we] should not worry about them [growing too fast]; slow growth [in the context of faster growth rates by China's neighbors] is tantamount to stagnation, even retrogression. [We] must seize the opportunity and the present is a good opportunity.
>
> (Deng Xiaoping 1992: 207)

In particular, Deng pointed out that Guangdong, Shanghai, and Jiangsu should grow faster than the national average. Indeed, Guangdong "should strive to catch up with the Asian 'four little dragons' in twenty years" (*Ibid.*). Rather than the 6 percent growth rate Premier Li Peng had stipulated in his government report to the National People's Congress, Deng reportedly called for China's GNP to grow by 10 percent per year (Saich 1993: 22–23).

The Deng line soon dominated the political agenda and his southern tour became the start of a new wave of reform euphoria in China. In effect, Deng, like Mao had done on numerous occasions, allied himself with the provinces while the central government had been trying hard to rein in the provinces to prevent a repeat of high growth–high inflation. Deng's clamoring for growth upset a precarious balance that had coalesced in the aftermath of the Tiananmen crisis. On the one hand, provincial authorities could now invoke Deng and justify highly expansionary policies (Yuan Shang and Han Zhu 1992: 102–41), thereby precipitating an intense round of emulation and competition among the provinces in adopting "innovative" policies such as development zones. The party secretary of Hainan, for example, called for making the island a "socialist Hong Kong." More generally, provincial leaders from across the country advocated more reform and opening up. On the other hand, as central leaders jumped on the bandwagon of bolder reforms one after another, there was no longer any serious effort by central leaders to exercise macroeconomic control and prevent economic overheating from recurring until things threatened to get out of hand. Words of caution might easily be interpreted as political disloyalty. Indeed, Deng had reportedly stated that anyone who obstructed the reform campaign ought to be removed (Goldstein 1991; D. Yang 1996a).

The balance thus tipped toward the localities, particularly after the issuance of Central Document No. 4 in June 1992 that extended the policy of opening up from the coast to the rest of China. During the year, five cities along the Yangtze River and 18 provincial capitals in the interior were granted the same treatment as the coastal open cities (Zhongguo gaige yu fazhan baogao zhuanjiazu 1994: 3). Finally, interior provincial units bordering on foreign countries, including Heilongjiang, Liaoning, Jilin, Inner Mongolia, Xinjiang, Yunnan, and Guangxi, were given permission to designate border open cities, each of which also set up a border economic cooperation zone. The 13 border zones so designated by the State Council enjoyed lower tax rates and special import privileges to attract investment from the rest of China and encourage export processing and trade with all of China's neighbors, including bustling border trade with erstwhile enemies Vietnam and the republics of the former Soviet Union (Wang Sanmin, Xu Fan, and Huang Deli 1993: 517–699).

Each of the border provinces adopted a variety of flexible strategies to open up to the outside. For example, Heilongjiang advocated "opening up to the north and linking up with the south"; Xinjiang published eight preferential policies and measures for opening up and emphasized "linking up with the east and going out to the west"; and Yunnan proposed "linking up with the coast and turning to South Asia in the west." One study even suggested that Yunnan should make use of its extensive border openings to create a "little Hong Kong in the interior" (Xiong Siyuan 1993: 59). This new round of opening gave a boost to the border provinces. Xinjiang, which also benefitted from the opening of the Second Eurasian Continental Bridge (railways), saw its trade volume jump from US$459 million to US$750 million in 1992. The number of foreign-invested enterprises rose from 46 to 164 in the same year (Chen Guojun 1995). For the 1993–95 period, the average annual economic growth rate of the border open cities was 17 percent, several percentage points higher than the national average (Zhang Jinsheng 1996).

The opening up of border areas in the interior provinces signified the completion of the process. While initially the open policy was confined to a few special economic zones, by the early 1990s, China's opening had become multi-dimensional both geographically and economically. Yet the political momentum for reform in 1992 was far more than the opening up of border regions. Fundamentally it empowered localities to pursue local interests through the offering of various preferential policies and the designation of special zones.[10] As can be expected from our model of the dynamics of competitive liberalization, once the center gave the signal that all localities could set up development zones, a race to establish such zones ensued across China. It was common for localities to disregard central government edicts in their scramble for outside investment. Localities set up such zones by offering preferential policies to attract outside investment. Since the amount of such investment was not infinite, inevitably localities competed against each other to offer more favorable terms, such as low tax rates (Zhang Nianhai 1995). Moreover, the rush to develop real estate and processing industries also had the effect of diverting much-needed funds from infrastructure and basic industries such as mining, raw materials, and energy (Liu Li 1993: 4). Usually overseas investors setting up shop in the zones were free of income tax for the first two years and enjoyed tax reduction during the next three. Some areas, such as a Guangxi city, even eliminated the land-use fees charged to investors in violation of China's Law on Land Management. In consequence, the number of development zones shot up in a matter of months. Whereas China had only 111 development zones (including 27 that were approved by the central government) at the end of 1991, by the end of September 1992 the number of development zones had jumped to 1,951. One report revealed that the total number of various types of development zones designated by authorities at the township government level or above reached about 8,700 (*CD* May 24, 1993: 4). The dynamics of competitive liberalization had reached its logical conclusion. Even the most geographically isolated areas in China, such as Tibet, were not left untouched by the march of global capitalism. In the words of a prefectural official there, Tibet should not only make full use of the special policies authorized by the central government, but should adopt other flexible policies and measures and encourage people to try such policies and measures as long as they benefitted Tibet's economic construction. In establishing cooperative ventures with other areas, the regional government should "offer low taxes and tax exemptions whenever they can" (Zhu Yaoping 1993: 56). For Qinghai, another landlocked province that also lacked international borders, the provincial leadership called for establishing windows along the coast and in border areas in order to "sail with borrowed boats, exit through others' borders, sing on rented stages, and make money on foreign land" (Yan Zhengde 1993: 6).

The scale of the land enclosure into development zones was astounding. According to one estimate, by May 1993, the total size of development zones in China had reached about 15,000 square kilometers, an area larger than the country's 517 cities combined (about 13,000 square kilometers). One official from the Ministry of Construction admitted, however, that 98 percent of the zoned areas remained to be developed (Wang Yong 1993: 8). Much of the outside investment that did come went into real estate rather than industry and the rampant real estate speculation in the early 1990s was a major source of corruption. Most importantly, because each locality strove to grow faster than average, macroeconomic stability soon became the casualty of uncoordinated local actions.

REINING IN THE LOCALITIES

The zone fever thus became both cause and symptom of China's macroeconomic difficulties in 1993. It was high time for the central government to standardize the rules and their implementation. In doing so, the center sorely needed the cooperation of localities. Yet the task of gaining local compliance had been made difficult by Deng's encouragement of local initiatives in 1992. Whereas during 1988–89 the center tightened control and put a premium on provincial compliance with central policies, by 1992, it was precisely the provinces which disregarded the austerity program and pursued growth policies such as Guangdong and Shandong, that received praises from Deng and central leaders. This sent a powerful signal to local leaders that in spite of central policies the most important criterion for evaluating performance was rapid growth.

The central leadership thus had a credibility gap with local leaders who sought to blunt the punches from the center and protect local initiatives with greater verve than they did during the last austerity program in 1989–90. Indeed, the perception of economic overheating was largely confined to the center. Virtually no local leader admitted that his province or locality had become overheated. Whereas leaders in more developed coastal provinces called for full-throttle growth to catch up with the four little dragons in Asia, their counterparts in interior regions were concerned about lagging behind the coast. "Sichuan says it's backward, it needs to develop; Hainan says it's lagged behind; Jiangsu says it's not overheated. No one thinks the message applies to them" (quoted in K. Chen 1992). All (including central leaders) justified their pro-growth attitudes by conveniently invoking the authority of Deng (Yi Shuihan 1993: 50–51; Goldstein 1993: 21).

The central leadership recognized the difficulties of eliciting local compliance with its policies. It had to adopt various administrative measures and replace the head of the central bank in order to impress local leaders that it was serious about fighting inflation (D. Yang 1993). After issuing documents that sought to restrain the stock-issuance fervor in April, the State Council in mid-May issued a circular which reasserted its veto power over the establishment of local economic development zones. Noting that local governments had competed among themselves to set up such zones with preferential policies to attract outside investment, the circular concluded that the development had resulted in the loss of large tracts of farmland and aggravated the shortage of funds going into energy, communications, transport, and raw materials. The circular decreed that only the provincial-level administration and above had the authority to set up development zones. Moreover, after an examination of the zones set up without proper approval, those that lacked adequate infrastructure and funding must be suspended (*CD* 5/17/93: 1). By August 1993, it was reported that provincial authorities in the coastal region had eliminated 1,000 of 1,200 economic development zones set up by local officials without proper authorization, most of which had been established in name only (UPI 1993).[11] However, in an apparent gesture or nod to interior interests, the center indicated that it wanted to promote development zones in inland and riverside areas to bridge the growing gap between the wealthy coastal areas and the rest of the country and to make exceptions for some provinces such as Guizhou (Zhu Ling and Wang Yong 1993; DJN 8/17/93). Vice Premier Zhu Rongji reportedly gave his backing to the impoverished province of Guizhou's attempts to catch up with its prosperous neighbors by sparing it from the national austerity drive and allowing it to develop overheated sectors that others were being advised to cool down, such as real estate and tourist facilities (Kwan 1993). Jiang Zemin and Zhu Rongji also gave Shanghai – where both Jiang and Zhu had served before moving to the center – generous credit targets and other exceptions in order to keep it growing at high speed (Zhong Xingzhi 1993: 19).

CONCLUSION

In this chapter, I have argued that the patterns of the spread of preferential policies across China can be understood in terms of the dynamics of competitive liberalization. As the constraints of ideology and lack of information are reduced over time, the model of local competition accounts for the rush toward the adoption of reformist policies in localities and underscores the need for central coordination and guidance. While the Chinese opening up started slowly, it culminated in the zone rush in the 1990s. Indeed, leaders of interior provinces have recognized that they are lagging behind in liberalizing. Yan Haiwang, party secretary of Gansu province, summed up well the race to liberalize: "Practice has led us to an increasingly deeper understanding that early opening up results in early development, late opening up results in late development, large-scale opening up results in large-scale development, and small-scale opening up results in small-scale development" (Ma Zhiqiang 1995: 42).

The preferential treatment given to the more prosperous coast was fundamentally an unstable policy and unjustified over the long term because in the early years the preferential policies benefitted the already more developed (southeastern) coastal region almost exclusively and thus constituted a major source of interior dissatisfaction. Thus, while reformist leaders such as Zhao Ziyang used such pro-coast policies to solidify the reform coalition in place, they also planted the seeds for interior discontent, which Zhao's political enemies would seek to mobilize in the aftermath of the Tiananmen massacre. As Wu Ren (1990: 17) pointed out, the preferential policies accentuated regional inequalities which in turn threatened to undermine the economic development of the whole country. He argued that the preferential policies for the coast must be moderated and rectified in order to promote the harmonious development of regional economies. More concretely, Wu called for increasing investment in the interior regions, more uniform macroeconomic control, uniform foreign-exchange retention rules, and the abolition of special treatment for some areas.

Yet the interior regions wanted preferential policies of their own. This is because the creation of a policy disequilibrium had both a demonstration effect and a political effect. In the former, the success of the early liberalizers provided models for others to emulate. In the latter, efforts by the late liberalizers to jump on the bandwagon generated momentum for further liberalization. From this perspective, even though they did not begin with a theoretical model, Chinese reformers were logically and politically correct in emphasizing the implementation of reforms in specific regions, especially along the coast. By doing so, reformers reduced the political shocks simultaneous reforms throughout the country might cause – had they been able to overcome the objections of conservatives – but still started the disequilibrium process that would lead the entire country down the path of liberalizing reforms.[12] Indeed, because of the spread of preferential policies across the country, the special economic zones are far less special in the mid-1990s than they used to be. In spite of the central government's efforts to check the proliferation of special zones, the whole country is still dotted by thousands of them as this book goes to press.[13] Fujian province alone has three central government-authorized economic and technological development zones as well as two free-trade zones, two Taiwan investment zones, two state tourist zones, two high-tech industrial zones, and 101 other types of development zones (*QB* 5/9/96: 21). In a sense, China has become a giant special economic zone in order to compete with other emerging economies for overseas investment. In the meantime, interior elites have less reason to think that their regions have been treated like stepchildren by the central government.

APPENDIX TO CHAPTER 3: A GAME-THEORETIC MODEL OF COMPETITIVE LIBERALIZATION

Let's say we have Γ (Ni, Ai, Ui), i = 1, 2, 3.

N1: the central government (CG);
N2: province 1 (P1);
N3: province 2 (P2);

A1: (Punish, Not Punish) or (P, NP);
A2: (Liberalize, Not Liberalize) or (L, NL);
A3: (Liberalize, Not Liberalize) or (L, NL).

U1 is not fully specified here because we are not interested in predicting the behavior of CG. Note here $-i$ indicates actions of all players except i.

U2: U2 = (A2, A-2);
U3: U3 = (A3, A-3).

Say if P1 and P2 liberalize while the CG playing P, the provinces incur costs from the punishment $Dj > 0$ $(j=1,2)$ for each period;

Say without liberalization, both P1 and P2 continue to subsidize grain purchases which costs $Sj > 0$ $(j=1,2)$ for each period;

Say both provinces liberalize, they no longer need to subsidize but grain price rises above the state set price. With higher price for grain on the free market, both P1 and P2 may face some pressure from their constituencies and the cost for that is $Xj > 0$ $(j=1,2)$ for each period;

Say if Pj $(j=1,2)$ liberalizes unilaterally, Pj gets rid of the cost of subsidy, but the market price in Pj will be higher than before but lower than if both liberalize (grain supply from the other province will keep the price lower than otherwise). Let's denote the cost of inflation pressure as X'j, we know that $X'j < Xj$ $(j=1,2)$;

Thus we have a repeated game with unlimited time horizon starting from t = 0. Keeping in mind that U1 is not fully specified in the model, we have the strategic game form as depicted in Figure 3.1.

So far we have assumed that both P1 and P2 possess perfect information, i.e. one player always knows the structure of the game and the repertoire of moves by the other. This assumption is actually not necessary. In the following strategic form, we assume that P1 and P2 always knows the move by the central government, i.e. they know whether they are in the left or right part of the game.[14]

Let's first look at the right part of the game, i.e. when the CG plays NP. We

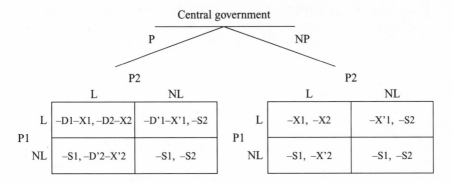

Figure 3.1 Incentives for competitive liberalization

Note: This form does not include payoffs for the CG.

know X'j < Xj for j = 1,2(defined). Assuming that Sj > Xj for j = 1,2, we know that L becomes the dominant strategy for both P1 and P2. Thus we know that (L, L) is the Nash equilibrium.

As mentioned above, assuming that the game is a repeated game with time represented by t > = 1 for each stage with discount rate $\delta = 1$ for both P1 and P2, we can show that (L, L) with t = 1 is also sub-game perfect as long as the CG plays NP (actually this is also true when $\delta j \neq 0$ for j = 1,2). This means the outcome predicted by the model is that both P1 and P2 will play L in the very first stage when the CG plays NP.

Things become a little bit more complicated in the left part of the game, i.e. when the CG plays P. However, the equilibrium can still be predicted once we know the relationship between Dj and Sj which may be different for P1 or P2 given their different sensitivity to the punishment by the central government.

Implication: Our game-theoretic model predicts that once the provinces know that the central government will not punish them for pursuing liberalization, they will rush to liberalize as soon as possible. However, if they know that liberalization will be met with punishment, their choice will depend on their sensitivity to the punishment relative to the cost of maintaining subsidies.

4   Resources, regional cleavages, and market integration

The bandwagon for competitive liberalization notwithstanding, it should be remembered that until the 1990s the liberalizing reforms have been far from complete. Overall the incremental nature of the Chinese reforms has been credited with helping China avoid a sudden collapse and sustain a healthy economic growth rate (Naughton 1995). Nevertheless, many of the incomplete reform measures were also destabilizing. They tended to accentuate existing tensions and generate new anxieties in the short run.

This chapter analyzes the impact of partial price reforms on inter-regional relations. Prior to the post-Mao reforms, the allocation of energy resources and industrial raw materials was undertaken through the planning and materials-distribution apparatus using state-fixed prices. In general, this state-administered economic system tended to underprice energy and raw materials and overprice manufactured goods. Meanwhile, the central government taxed the manufacturing industries at higher rates and then redistributed fiscal revenue to producers of energy and industrial raw materials. Because the interior regions were net exporters of energy and raw materials to the coastal region, which served as China's manufacturing belt, the price system discriminated against the interior while the tax system came down hard on the coast. While the interior received less from its exports made at state-fixed prices than would have been the case had market prices prevailed, it was compensated by the central allocation of investment funds and fiscal subsidies. In the meantime, the coastal region received underpriced inputs but had to surrender much of the profits to the central government treasury as fiscal revenue, which the center redistributed. This circular resource allocation system, coupled with an intensely political atmosphere, muted coast–interior cleavages during the Maoist era (Mao Zedong 1974: 61–83).

In the 1980s, however, the circular resource allocation system was steadily eroded as reforms were gradually introduced in the fiscal system, prices, as well as materials allocation. As state administration gave way to market-based transactions, the interests of various players that had been integrated through the central planning apparatus were unmasked, unleashing a flurry of local activities driven to the realization of their interests. The partial price reforms have especially constituted a major structural incentive for local governments to seek the establishment of local processing industries. In consequence, at the regional level there has been a dramatic display of inter-regional conflict and cooperation centered around the processing of scarce natural resources. This chapter argues that, even though the reforms were intended to enhance economic integration, incomplete price reforms actually led, in the short run, to backward specialization as evidenced in the duplication of industrial capacity across administrative boundaries, market fragmentation, and local protectionism.

More important, however, is the long-run effect of such localist behavior. Through an examination of more recent data, I shall suggest that there has been a substantial reversal of the earlier trend of backward specialization. Since the end of the 1980s, market competition has resulted in industrial consolidation and the coastal region has recaptured the market share it lost earlier.

PRICE STRUCTURE AND THE REGIONAL DIVISION OF LABOR

The development of the coastal region and the interior regions was interrelated through the allocation of resources such as energy and industrial raw materials by the materials bureax of the central planning apparatus.[1] The interior regions produce vast quantities of coal, crude oil, and other industrial raw materials that are transported to the coastal region for processing into manufactured goods. A major share of the finished goods manufactured in the coastal region is then shipped to the interior for sale.

In contrast to market-based transactions between buyers and sellers, however, China's regional division of labor was characterized by administrative intervention from the central government. To begin with, because of inadequate price adjustments, the state-fixed price structure that was introduced in the 1950s became increasingly artificial over time, especially in comparison with price movements on world markets. Until the 1990s, the post-Mao reforms had failed to address the distorted price structure systematically. Instead, a dual-pricing system in which production units were allowed to sell above-plan output at negotiated as well as market prices was introduced, which exposed the distorted price structure that had existed. This price structure generally assigned relatively high prices to manufactured and especially consumer goods and underpriced energy and raw materials. According to one estimate undertaken in the mid-1980s, combining both plan and market prices in China and taking world market prices as unity, then the Chinese prices for various products were: coal, 0.5; crude oil, 0.3; timber, 0.5, cement, 0.7; railway transport, 0.4; steel wire, 1.0; copper, 1.2; aluminum, 1.0; textiles and light industrial products, 1.1; machinery, 1.4; electronics, 2.0 (Tian Yuan and Qiao Gang 1991: 215).

As long as market competition was limited and demand was of little concern to producers, a situation that prevailed until the end of the 1980s, high state-set prices plus declining production costs ensured high profitability for manufacturing industries. In contrast, extractive industries were squeezed between low prices and rising costs and tended to suffer operating losses. In 1985, for example, the rate of profit plus taxes for extractive industries was 10.38 percent but that for manufacturing was 20 percent (Jiang Qinghai 1990: 12). In the iron and steel industry, there was in the mid-1980s practically no money to be made from iron ore and coal mining owing to rising excavation costs and low prices for iron ore and coal. Indeed, the coal industry has continually suffered losses since at least the 1970s (Lardy 1989: 292–93). In contrast, because of the high prices for steel and steel products, the rate of profit plus taxes was 15 percent of sales for steel ingot, 44 percent for rolled steel, and a whopping 68 percent for steel plates (Ding Xing 1985: 7).

The artificial price structure has had important implications for the development of different regions in light of the regional division of labor. The industrial structure of the interior regions is dominated by low-profit extractive industries which produce the bulk of China's energy (coal and crude oil) and other industrial raw materials, some of which were allocated to the coastal

Table 4.1 Profit and tax rates in state-owned industries (1986)

	Profit + tax	*Profit*
	Capital (%)	*Capital (%)*
ALL INDUSTRIES	15.4	7.9
EXTRACTIVE INDUSTRIES:		
Coal	−1.0	−2.0
Crude oil and gas	10.5	6.5
Ferrous metals	9.5	8.6
Nonferrous metals	5.5	4.5
Construction materials & other nonferrous metals	4.5	2.7
Timber	9.5	5.3
MANUFACTURING INDUSTRIES:		
Food	15.8	9.6
Cigarettes	179.7	7.6
Textiles	20.8	10.4
Petroleum	66.8	30.5
Chemicals	14.8	7.0
Chemical fibers	18.0	12.2
Rubber products	39.9	17.4
Plastics	15.2	9.9
Construction materials	16.2	10.0
Ferrous metals	16.8	9.6
Nonferrous metals	12.8	7.9
Machinery	11.9	8.1

Source: Wang Zhenzhi and Qiao Rongzhang 1988: 17.

region for processing.[2] As a result, the interior regions have received lower revenues than would have been the case had the state price structure not discriminated against raw materials industries. It was estimated that in 1989 the benefit derived by coal consumers from low coal prices amounted to 25 billion yuan and the inter-regional transfer from coal producers to coal consumers in that year alone was about 2 billion yuan (Rajaram 1992: 13).

The coastal region tended to specialize in both light and heavy manufacturing industries that enjoyed relatively high profit rates. The coastal region in turn exported manufactured products to the interior at high mark-ups.[3] In short, the interior regions were shortchanged twice in China's regional division of labor. They were first underpaid for the energy and raw materials they produced and then they had to overpay for the manufactured products and consumer goods.

The state-set price structure and the prevailing regional division of labor were sustained through and indeed, as one analyst from the State Price Bureau pointed out, required, the heavy (fiscal) hand of the central government. As mentioned in chapter 2, the center has relied on taxing the more profitable coastal region for its revenue. In the meantime, the center redistributed its revenue regionally. It not only invested heavily in the interior through the third-front program but has also provided fiscal subsidies to most interior provinces. It has also urged coastal provinces to enter into horizontal ties with poorer interior provinces to provide technical and financial assistance (Dong Fan and Cheng Yaoping 1990: 37).

Yet as long as the circular resource allocation system was not fundamentally altered, a vicious cycle in interior development was perpetuated (Jiang Qinghai

Table 4.2 Composition of gross value of industrial output (GVIO) by region (1989)

Region	Light industry %	Heavy industry %	Total %
Coastal region	52.48	47.52	100.00
Interior regions	42.94	57.06	100.00

Source: ZGTJNJ 1990: 60.

Table 4.3 Industrial energy production and consumption by region

	Energy output (1989)				Industrial energy consumption (1988)	
	Coal (mil. tons)	% of total	Crude oil (mil. tons)	% of total	Amount (mil. tons)	% of total
China	1,054.14	100.00	137.64	100.00	577.75	100.00
Coast	236.73	22.46	58.58	42.56	276.70	47.89
Interior	817.42	77.54	79.06	57.44	301.05	52.11

Source: ZGTJNJ 1990: 467, 504.

1990: 12). With low state-set prices for energy and other raw materials, the more the interior provinces expanded their extractive industries, the more they lost money and needed subsidies from the central government as though they were unproductive and poor. It was, as some Chinese academics put it, a sort of "blood transfusion economy" and "outside assistance economy." But the regional division of labor did not just produce accounting losses for the interior; it had real consequences for interior development. More concretely, the emphasis on producing a certain quantity of coal and other resources has served to distort the incentives of interior producers, leading them away from the pursuit of profits and thus reinforcing the popular and somewhat self-reinforcing perception that people in the interior were less entrepreneurial than those in the coast region. Most importantly, the incentive structure facing the interior has made it difficult for interior provinces to accumulate the local funds needed for investment, miring many interior provinces in ties of dependence upon the central government and what might be termed a poverty trap (State Planning Commission 1989).

RESOURCE PRICING AND REGIONAL CLEAVAGES

With the introduction of liberalizing reforms, the system of circular regional resource flows became strained. First, decentralization and the intensification of market competition reduced the share of economic resources under the direct command of the central government. Persistent fiscal deficits weakened the central government's ability – in terms of shares of the total – to redistribute resources, including investment funds, across regions (Naughton, 1987, 1992; D. Yang 1990). Toward the end of the 1980s, the center even stopped the automatic upward adjustment in subsidies to ethnic minority areas.

Second, while the introduction of dual-track pricing eased some distortions in the pricing system, it also revealed the hidden losses that the resource-exporting provinces were taking and created strong incentives for interior provinces to process their resources locally or otherwise to sell their resources at market prices rather than surrender them to plan agents. Between 1984 and 1988, the divergence between state-set and market prices increased significantly owing to rising demand for raw materials; the ex-factory price for all raw materials rose by 9.3 percent per year, but the prices at which those raw materials were purchased by downstream enterprises rose by 14 percent per year. It was estimated that the differences between state-set and market prices amounted to 150 billion yuan in 1988 (Wang Haibo and Li Shijin 1991). The arbitrage activities to capture the difference between state-set and market prices became quite extensive and spawned tens of thousands of "briefcase" companies, becoming a hotbed of corruption (Tian Yuan and Qiao Gang 1991: 224–26).

There are no systematic estimates of the losses the interior has sustained for supplying energy and other natural resources at state-set prices. However, rough estimates for two provinces indicate that these losses amounted to more than half of the provincial income from industry as of 1987–88. Gansu province was estimated to have been underpaid 3.3 to 3.6 billion yuan a year supplying nonferrous metals at state-set prices in the 1980s. For Yunnan, the amount was estimated to be about 3.8 billion per year for supplying seven types of raw materials and the total amount was some 5 billion yuan per year in the late 1980s (Xia Hanxing, Feng Dengkun, Cao Jianfang, and Sun Guoqi 1989: 59; Yang Jisheng 1989a: 16; Wu Ren 1990: 14). While it is unclear how reliable these figures are, they nevertheless point to a major political issue: both provinces are among the poorest and the majority of the counties in both provinces have suffered from extreme fiscal difficulties, yet these provinces have sustained huge financial losses by exporting resources at state-set prices. As Zhu Houze, then the party secretary of China's poorest province (Guizhou), told a senior Chinese economist in 1984: Guizhou province would not mind exporting its resources had the prices been "right." But the province was placed in an unfavorable situation in having to export "rocks" (mineral resources) at state-fixed prices.[4]

With the share of state investment going to interior regions being reduced, the continued central allocation of raw materials from the interior to the coastal region at low prices set by the central government has proved to be particularly galling to interior interests. Indeed, even before the introduction of dual-track pricing, provinces that exported underpriced raw materials already chafed at the price structure and repeatedly demanded that the price system be rationalized to rectify the unequal exchanges between the regions.[5] Some authors pointed out that the superior performance of the coastal region would have been less stellar had the price system been less favorable to processors of raw materials (see, e.g., Liu Jinwen, Wang Yiwu, and Zhang Xiusheng 1985: 41). Interior interests demanded that some of the profits that accrued to processors of low-priced raw materials be shared between the processors in coastal cities and the exporters in underdeveloped regions. One author concluded that only by sharing the profits "could the interests of both state and locality be protected, thus benefitting the development of backward areas" (Hu Tongyuan 1982: 27–28).[6]

The introduction of higher market-based prices alongside state-set prices in the mid-1980s was partly intended to provide some relief to producers of products then in scarcity but it had the ironic effect of serving as a constant reminder to energy and raw materials producers – in our case, the interior provinces – that their resources were being taken away through the central planning apparatus without adequate compensation. In short, inter-regional resource allocation and preferential treatment for the coastal region have been the two most prominent sources of coast–interior cleavages and interior–central government ill feelings during the reform era.[7] As Pan Danke (1987) pointed out with poignancy, Yunnan province not only received little revenue from these industries that exported raw resources but actually lost the top soil through exploitative development. "Resources are taken away while pollution is left behind" (Wang Dingchang, Long Liqing, and Wei Fengxian 1989: 27). Pan concluded that the centrally directed export of raw materials deprived Yunnan of its basic right to process its own resources and build up its own industries. In consequence, the province was made dependent on fiscal subsidies. He contended that the Yunnan economy could not expand further because of this and called for a readjustment of the interests affected.

THE PURSUIT OF LOCAL MANUFACTURING

Even though the state-administered allocation of resources as a proportion of the total has steadily declined in the reform period after the introduction of the dual-pricing system, the central government has for a variety of reasons continued to allocate substantial amounts of key materials, especially coal and crude oil. In 1988, the planning apparatus still allocated 43.5 percent of the coal output, 46.8 percent of steel products, and 25.9 percent of timber (down from 57.8 percent, 74.3 percent, and 80.9 percent respectively in 1980) (Xie Minggan and Luo Yuanming 1990: 107–108; World Bank 1990a: 61). While most consumer prices in China had been freed up by the 1990s, roughly 20 percent of production materials continue to be subject to central government price control and allocation. As long as centrally directed resource allocation remains, the interior provinces will continue to harbor grievances and complain about resource exploitation.

Some of the grievances have been translated into efforts to build local processing industries in the interior. This is because progressive fiscal decentralization has increased the share of resources under local discretion and thus provided local authorities with the wherewithal to build local factories. Meanwhile, local governments have strong incentives to build such factories because they rely on local enterprises for fiscal revenues and to generate local employment.[8] In this context, the distorted price structure has served as a powerful incentive and arbitrage opportunity for interior resource producers to develop local processing in order to avoid the price losses that arise from central resource allocation. As Pan Danke concluded in the case of Yunnan, the province should shift from exporting raw materials to local processing so that it could not only capture the monetary profits that might be derived from the processing of underpriced raw materials but also develop indigenous industries that would generate fiscal revenue for local governments as well as employment (Pan Danke 1987). There is thus a symbiotic relationship between fiscal decentralization and local developmentalism.

While it is rational for interior localities to invest their limited resources in manufacturing to process locally produced raw materials, this effort nevertheless pits the newly constructed factories, often built with second-hand equipment, against established producers in the competition for raw materials and consumers. In spatial terms, producers in a region that is a net importer of raw materials find it more difficult to obtain raw materials even though factories in these areas already have excess production capacity and may be more efficient than those being erected in the interior. The tension between the raw materials-producing region seeking to keep the materials for local processing and the importing region working hard to import the materials is thus a major reflection of the cleavages between the interior and the coast, each pursuing its own economic interest (Ni Shidao and Wang Yang 1989: 53).[9] As competition heats up, it is expected that local authorities will seek to protect their local producers whenever possible by adopting administrative measures such as embargoes on the export of scarce raw materials and bans on imports of competing products. Many of the widely reported roadblocks of the late 1980s were thus the concrete manifestation of regional economic cleavages.

Sufficient evidence already exists about the efforts of localities to develop their own resources. Such localist behavior intensified from the mid-1980s to the late 1980s, when fiscal decentralization accelerated and when the unified purchasing of grain, cotton, wool, and other products was relaxed or even abolished. During the 1988–90 austerity period, for example, local governments imposed high taxes as well as limits on profits in order to prevent local commercial departments from selling popular goods from other areas (such as bicycles and soft drinks from Guangdong). Yunnan led the trend by prohibiting the importation of 19 types of outside goods in November 1989. Guizhou and Sichuan prohibited the importation of bicycles, televisions, and refrigerators from other provinces in 1990. Xinjiang reportedly banned the "importation" from other provinces of 48 kinds of products ranging from color televisions to soap and bicycles. More informal types of local protectionist behavior were found in many other localities (*The Economist* 1996; Kristof 1990: 2; Li Zhengping 1990: 13–14; *Shijie ribao* 1989: 17; 1990: 17; Wedeman 1995). As can be expected, raw materials purchasers responded with countermeasures of their own. In one highly publicized case, some Guangdong companies used monetary inducements and even army vehicles to transport raw silk out of Sichuan, in the western region, where the various levels of government had issued decrees to prohibit such outflow (Xia Yang and Wang Zhigang 1988: 3).

The most dramatic outcome of the localist behavior is the widely publicized "commodity wars" over such raw materials as cotton, wool, silk, and tobacco leaves. Watson and others have undertaken a detailed study of the "wool war," a phrase they used to describe the situation "where growers dispute their contracts with the state purchasing system, where local levels of government have instituted their own controls over the decentralized wool marketing system and where merchants and processors compete for supplies in a market full of speculation and profiteering" (Watson, Findlay, and Du 1989: 216).[10] In response to the profit structure and changes in price and marketing, the governments of the main wool-producing areas, including Gansu, Qinghai, Xinjiang, and Inner Mongolia, adopted a policy of "local production, local use, and local sales (*zichan, ziyong, zixiao*)."[11] As a result of such a policy, processing capacity in all these areas expanded substantially in a relatively short time period, leading to local reluctance to supply outsiders. The same was true of cotton (Xinjiang, Henan, Shandong), beans (Heilongjiang), and coal (Shanxi), and other commodities.

Table 4.4 Percentages of main industrial products produced by region

Year	Chemical fibers	Wrist watches	Motor vehicles	Cement	Caustic soda	Chemical fertilizer	Tractors	Mini- tractors	Metal- cutting machines	Wool fabric	Knitting wool	Silk	Sewing machines	Bicycles	Pig iron	Steel	Finished steel products	Cigarettes
1978	80.57	90.45	45.27	49.99	70.14	48.92	51.78	49.53	64.68	75.69	67.20	75.85	83.14	93.52	57.72	62.79	64.10	44.66
1980	72.73	85.00	44.40	49.56	69.66	48.10	53.18	60.85	64.00	74.32	65.39	74.86	77.51	88.21	57.16	59.95	62.97	43.43
1981	73.05	82.55	37.19	51.17	69.38	47.24	59.84	61.27	69.40	75.21	65.38	70.18	73.59	83.14	57.04	60.41	62.99	42.37
1982	72.63	83.16	36.12	50.78	68.39	45.96	64.97	60.67	69.34	75.46	63.91	66.31	72.03	78.73	56.63	58.56	61.75	40.29
1983	75.25	82.89	36.32	50.55	67.96	45.22	67.51	55.41	68.10	72.82	65.20	64.53	78.85	78.61	55.59	57.84	60.72	37.76
1984	75.17	81.83	37.99	51.19	67.43	43.97	64.54	53.11	67.72	71.23	65.65	66.83	85.86	80.07	55.16	57.11	59.67	37.32
1985	76.36	76.70	42.45	51.47	66.66	42.72	69.89	51.67	66.57	69.89	67.97	67.62	83.80	78.81	54.23	56.51	58.41	35.80
1986	76.93	83.07	47.90	52.03	65.64	43.11	60.56	55.32	69.09	70.48	68.56	68.30	82.70	76.02	54.34	58.61	58.07	35.26
1987	76.98	86.73	49.49	52.90	65.18	43.16	59.93	54.37	71.18	69.52	72.51	67.91	82.40	73.67	54.40	58.79	58.14	33.88
1988	77.79	86.73	49.60	52.96	64.48	41.86	62.00	58.49	69.59	71.32	73.33	65.80	80.59	74.70	54.75	58.44	57.99	32.67
1989	76.35	87.05	49.72	53.55	65.13	41.30	71.96	57.40	70.79	72.13	74.99	66.22	80.80	77.21	54.15	57.54	58.00	32.35
1990	76.39	87.55	51.36	54.01	65.30	39.80	58.03	55.78	72.70	71.95	80.00	66.33	83.96	83.24	54.49	58.02	59.35	31.69
1991	75.62	84.57	54.47	55.21	65.81	38.30	60.72	56.84	74.28	72.98	84.57	65.52	84.45	80.64	55.37	58.76	60.64	30.73
1992	76.75	89.86	55.00	55.55	65.47	38.03	64.16	60.69	74.14	76.61	86.74	67.25	82.77	81.68	55.32	59.27	61.30	31.31
1993	78.74	95.04	51.92	56.88	64.36	37.32	72.41	62.67	75.39	79.15	88.79	68.44	74.35	84.93	52.64	59.30	62.03	30.56
1994	78.81	96.90	51.95	58.15	64.00	35.85	67.74	59.61	77.15	81.87	89.14	58.95	87.37	87.76	52.39	60.08	63.74	29.93

Sources: ZGGYJJTJNJ, 1991: 171–81; ZGTJNJ 1992: 448–55; 1993: 454–61; 1994: 401–411; 1995: 408–415.
Note: Only data for the coastal region are presented. The interior share = 100 − coastal share.

The conflict over raw materials supply was exacerbated by the different foreign exchange retention rates and the dual foreign exchange rates that were introduced in the early 1980s (Wu Ren 1990: 16). In the 1980s, special economic zones retained 100 percent of the foreign exchange they earned and coastal provinces generally retained 30 percent. In contrast, interior provinces were permitted to retain only 25 percent of the foreign exchange they earned. Because foreign currency was worth far more on the black market than the official exchange rate, the special economic zones could afford to pay higher prices to purchase raw materials for export than those areas that retained a smaller percentage of foreign exchange, thus intensifying the scramble for raw materials such as silk cocoons and tea and prompting raw materials-producing localities to impose trade restrictions. In the 1980s, in Qinghai, the outside purchasing price for wool was bid up to 50–70 percent higher than the local purchasing price, making it difficult for local producers to buy wool and yet still make a profit. This prompted local government to set up road blockades to prevent wool outflows and resume forced procurement at low prices (Gong Yu 1989: 16). In a sense, the relaxation of central control led local governments to strengthen their own ability to intervene in the economy, leading some Chinese economists to refer to China as a "feudatory economy."

The drive by the interior regions to develop local industries led to shifts in the regional distribution of major industrial production. Table 4.4 shows the coastal region's shares of output of some major industrial products.[12] We find that, with a few exceptions such as cement, chemical fibers, and machine tools (metal-cutting machines), the interior's share of the output of most industrial products rose in the first half of the 1980s, with some of the increases continuing into the late 1980s.[13] The interior's share of the following products expanded by especially big margins: wool fabric, silk, silk fabrics, caustic soda, chemical fertilizers, pig iron, steel, finished steel products, sewing machines, bicycles, wrist watches, motor vehicles, and, of course, cigarettes, production of which has enjoyed the most handsome profit and tax rate possible. In some cases, such as silk production, the increase in the interior's share of output followed a trend that had begun before the post-Mao reforms started. Not only did the interior regions increase their share of China's industrial production, but enterprises in the interior also enjoyed an upswing in economic returns. Between 1978 and 1985, the ratio of profits plus taxes to capital for state-owned independent accounting enterprises rose 3.6 percentage points for Sichuan, 7.07 for Guizhou, 11.99 for Yunnan, 0.38 for Shaanxi, and 0.31 for Gansu, suggesting that interior industries benefitted from price improvements and the turn to local manufacturing.

BACKWARD SPECIALIZATION

It should be obvious to the reader that the exceptions to the trend identified above were to be expected. The production of machine tools had relatively high barriers to entry in terms of investment and human capital and it was expected that the more developed coastal region would retain its dominance. As for cement production, transport costs made it difficult for the interior regions to expand their market share nationwide and the coastal region relied on the expansion of local production to meet the construction boom of the reform era. What was puzzling was the interior's growing output share in products ranging from textile products and color televisions, to refrigerators and motor vehicles (some of these are not included in Table 4.4). While the barriers to entry in textiles are relatively low and thus easy for the interior regions to enter into, the same cannot be said of a variety of other manufactured products, although the case of motor vehicles could be explained by the location of major state factories in Hubei and Jilin.

In reality, the rapid growth in the number of automotive factories and other types of manufacturing and assembly plants throughout the country to more than 100 provides evidence for the thesis of price-distortion-induced duplication. Price distortions and local government intervention led to the proliferation of manufacturing enterprises that would have found it impossible to survive had these enterprises competed in a market economy. The overall trend was that the interior regions intensified their efforts at processing their own raw materials. But effort at indigenous development was of course not limited to the processing of local materials. Local governments also rushed to mobilize scarce resources, to import assembly lines for consumer products such as color televisions, washing machines, refrigerators, tape recorders, and electric fans in order to derive revenue from these high value-added products. As a result, each province acquired several assembly lines and, as the market quickly became saturated, few of the assembly lines operated at full capacity.

As local governments rationally responded to the price structure and mimicked each other to build up duplicate manufacturing plants that were of low quality, small scale and high energy consumption, the industrial structure of the different regions converged rather than diverged during most of the 1980s.[14] In fact, there was a steady decline in the rate of fulfillment of deliveries of energy and industrial raw materials within the plan as producers either sold their output at market prices or processed them locally. Instead of integration and comparative advantage, the trend went temporarily toward duplication and fragmentation, or backward specialization. This phenomenon not only intensified local protectionist behavior and trade frictions but also served to harmonize the economic cycles across the regions and thus served to magnify the fluctuations in the Chinese economy (Sai Feng and Zhu Mingchun 1990; Yang Jianrong and Yao Xiaobo 1993: 9–16).

INTER-REGIONAL COOPERATION AND BARTERING

While the drive by interior provinces to process their own resources caused tension between the coastal and interior regions, it also demonstrated the interior's importance as supplier to coastal producers and enhanced the interior's bargaining power *vis-à-vis* the coastal region as far as raw materials were concerned. Many interior producers would not release their raw materials at state-fixed prices without some kind of side-payments to compensate for the difference between plan and market prices.

Coastal producers faced three choices: curtailing production, turning to foreign suppliers, and paying side-payments to interior suppliers. All three occurred. By the late 1980s the coastal region became more dependent on the world market for certain primary materials than was the case a decade earlier. The rapid growth of wool imports was one case in point. One main reason for Zhao Ziyang's adoption of the export-oriented coastal development strategy in 1988 was to urge the coastal region to use more primary materials from the world market and thus lessen the coastal region's dependence on resources from the interior and also alleviate the inter-regional resource conflicts (D. Yang 1991).

More interestingly, there was, amid the commodity wars, actually a steady rise in efforts by local authorities to enhance inter-regional cooperation. Much as in countries dealing in barter trade, special economic coordination offices were established in each provincial unit to coordinate resource flows and jointly invest in the production of raw materials. In order to obtain the raw materials they need, most coastal provinces have entered into cooperation agreements with interior provinces. Shanghai, for example, earmarked hundreds of thousands of its bicycles and later passenger cars to trade for raw materials such as coal and wool from the interior. In 1986 it started to invest 110 million yuan in an iron mill and six nonferrous metals mines in Liangshan Yi autonomous prefecture, one of China's least developed areas, in Sichuan province, in return for supplies of pig iron, zinc, and copper (Xinhua 12/5/86 in FBIS-CHI 12/12/86: K4–K5). Shandong and Qinghai entered into 33 cooperation agreements over the 1987–90 period. Qinghai has provided Shandong with wool and other raw materials in exchange for assistance in developing Qinghai's own industries.

The most interesting case of such interprovincial relations is that of Guangdong, which perhaps has the dubious honor of being the most envied and resented by other provinces during the past decade. (Under Jiang Zemin, will that honor now go to Shanghai?) It also devoted more energy to smoothing its relations with other resource-rich but capital-scarce provinces by investing in coal mines in Shanxi, hydro-electricity projects in Guizhou and pig breeding in Sichuan (de Rosario 1989: 62). In 1988, Hunan and Guangxi separately concluded cooperation agreements with Guangdong. (Though Guangxi officially belongs to the coastal region, Chinese scholars have sometimes classified it in the western region.) Hunan was to supply grain and other essentials in return for Guangdong investment in infrastructure development. Guangdong would provide Guangxi with technological expertise in return for the right to exploit mineral resources (E. Cheng 1989: 45–46).

The cooperative agreements are generally non-exclusive. For example, since the late 1970s the provincial government of Yunnan has entered into cooperative agreements with most provinces, particularly coastal areas such as Shanghai, Tianjin, Beijing, Jiangsu, Fujian, and Shandong. In a cooperation fair held in May 1982, the amount of funds raised from outside reached 460 million yuan, which was equal to 50 percent of the province's local fixed-asset investment in 1981. Rather than allocation by planners, the cooperative projects were based on mutual benefit. Yunnan supplied raw materials such as tin, lead, zinc, aluminum, timber, rubber, and coal while the other sides helped the province set up factories and provided technical assistance (Li Qiaonian, Qian Desan, and Huang Qiuyan 1982).

Some Chinese commentators have suggested that the increasing inter-regional cooperation was the inevitable outcome of regional competition (Zhang Yungang and Zhu Xinkun 1993: 265). This is not true. In theory, economic relations among competing localities may degenerate into a spiral of localism and autarchic economic policies. What distinguishes the Chinese case, however, is the fact that the central government has been deeply committed to promoting such cooperation and thus offered local governments a quick exit out of a downward spiral. In the meantime, local government officials in some regions, such as the southwest, have also gathered together to tackle common economic problems.[15] Unlike nations that may be concerned about relative gains, these local governments have been more easily persuaded of the virtues of trade.

REVERSAL OF BACKWARD SPECIALIZATION[16]

Throughout the 1980s and early 1990s, the central government repeatedly sought to crack down on the localist behavior that manifested itself in the duplication of industrial plants across the Chinese landscape. The center also issued a series of injunctions calling on local authorities to break regional barriers, such as road blockades, and promote inter-regional trade and cooperation.[17] Yet these injunctions to promote integration had little effect on local behavior as long as serious distortions afflicted the economic system. The incidence of local protectionist behavior became widespread and attracted much attention among both Chinese and Western commentators in the late 1980s.[18]

In a fundamental sense, the resort to local protectionist behavior during a period of market transition was the instinctive response of governments that had previously known only central planning. But many Chinese commentators used the highly evocative term *zhuhou jingji*, literally fiefdom or feudatory economy, to describe the phenomenon, arguing that the Chinese economy was being fragmented along administrative lines just as in ancient China the dukes and princes under the emperor each set up their separate kingdoms. As one of the most widely cited papers put it: "China's thirty provinces, autonomous regions and municipalities are big dukedoms; the more than 300 prefectures and cities are medium-sized dukedoms, and the 2,000-plus counties (cities) are small dukedoms. Each focuses on its own economy, has its own territory, and makes its own policy" (Shen Liren and Dai Yuanchen 1990: 12). The notoriety of the term *zhuhou jingji* contributed to the widely held perception that fiscal decentralization was leading to increasing economic fragmentation and regionalism which in turn could contribute to political fragmentation within China. Writing in the worst moment – the bottom of the austerity program in 1989–90 – of local protectionism, Chinese and Western commentators clearly saw the signs of a fundamental process at work. But they issued the wrong prognosis. For the intense efforts by local governments to protect local economic interests were as much the signs of protectionism as they were indications of the forces of market competition. While the "commodity wars" and blockades reflected the local governments' desire to control economic activities, they were indicative of the intensity of growing market competition for raw materials and in product markets.

In theory, each local government faces powerful revenue and welfare incentives to engage in protectionist behavior even though trade would improve collective welfare. It is thus possible that decentralization in a command economy of few local units may easily be turned into domination by local governments and economic fragmentation along administrative boundaries.[19] But the same is much less likely in an economy of numerous local governments with porous borders and governed by a central government intent on encouraging horizontal linkages and breaking down inter-regional barriers.[20] As of the end of 1993, China had 30 provinces (average population: 39.5 million), 570 cities, 2,166 counties, and 48,200 town and township governments. Each of these governments was also an investor. In this continent-sized economy, a local government, be it a township or province, that is bent on market expansion outside and protectionism at home must contend with the existence of other localities with similar aspirations.[21] As Naughton writes of rural industry, although each of the local governments

> may have originally tried to operate a miniature state-run economy, the fact was that ultimately producers in each were subject to competition from thousands of other villages. In this fundamentally competitive environment, each township or village found that it faced a relatively hard budget constraint, and had to make its own enterprise economically successful. Rural enterprises created competition for state firms, but they were themselves ultimately shaped by the competitive process as well.
>
> (Naughton 1995: 158)

Because China made the transition from the plan to the market gradually rather than in a bang, we would expect to find that local government behavior would rush to invest as market forces grew stronger. Initially local governments newly permitted to enter various industries rushed to invest in high mark-up industrial sectors, particularly sectors with low barriers to entry such as textiles and light industry. In the textile industry, for example, the number of enterprises rose from 12,145 in 1978 to 19,681 in 1984 and 48,747 in 1989 (*Zhongguo fangzhi gongye nianjian* 1986–91).

As new capacity went into production and competition heated up, one would expect that local governments would instinctively turn to bureaucratic protectionist behavior, which they knew best from having functioned in a command economy. Thus it appears that the cries of local protectionism, which rose to a crescendo in the late 1980s, can be better interpreted as indicators of intensifying market penetration and competition. The spread of capitalist competition has never been a neutral process (Polanyi 1957).

Over time price reforms have curtailed opportunities for local rent-seeking activities. In the meantime, competition has brought down profit margins (Naughton 1992) and forced factories to become either competitive or extinct. Indeed, as long as the central government persevered in its commitment to the market (Circular 1991), the logical outcome of 2,000-plus localities each seeking to keep the local market to itself, while seeking to sell to the outside, is the Smithian world of market competition. For no local government has a monopoly on production and factories in each locality have to face competition from the outside. As the "commodity wars" escalated, local cadres soon realized that their administrative measures to keep raw materials from flowing out and outside products from coming into the local market were futile (Zhang Yungang and Zhu Xinkun 1993: 265). By the turn of the 1990s, local governments found that it no longer made sense to keep local factories afloat if these factories could not compete and make money. Some of them soon decided to join the bandwagon of consolidation and cooperation. They induced mergers in sectors suffering from excess capacity and, in the case of the textile industry, signed inter-regional agreements to transfer production capacity from high-cost coastal cities to Xinjiang, China's leading cotton-exporting area (*RMRBO* 9/30/95: 2). For among local governments, the chief concern is about absolute rather than relative gains and local governments can set up institutions for inter-regional trade and cooperation much more easily than among nation-states. Thus the worst of inter-regional trade restrictions occurred during the 1987–90 boom–bust cycle owing to the adoption of various transitional measures, including partial price deregulation and large differentials in regional terms of trade. Because most of these transitional measures have since been removed in favor of market mechanisms, the tide of local protectionism has clearly subsided in the 1990s. While some efforts to keep products from the outside may still be seen (Xin Xiangyang 1995: 588–96), they are no longer as prominent as they once were.

By the end of the 1980s, most enterprises could no longer rely on low input prices to make money. Rising costs of production were putting most Chinese enterprises under pressure and a lot of factories were operating well under capacity. As the economic environment worsens, it is expected that the better-managed enterprises will do better than average. Given the technical and managerial expertise in the coastal region, we expect that enterprises in that region will generally cope with the worsening operating environment more successfully. This leads us to expect the coastal region to recover some of the economic territory it has lost to the interior regions.

The empirical data in Table 4.4 support such a hypothesis. There has indeed been a significant reversal of the earlier trend in the regional distribution of industrial outputs. In the production of various products, including wrist watches, motor vehicles, wool fabric, knitting wool, sewing machines, bicycles, steel, finished steel products, the coastal region's share of output first declined in the 1980s but then gradually recovered toward the late 1980s and early 1990s. The major exception is knitting wool. The coastal region actually increased its share of this product by six percentage points in spite of interior efforts at local processing as coastal producers turned to the international market for raw materials by importing mostly Australian wool. In short, the interior's gains in output shares proved to be short-lived for most products. With industrial consolidation in recent years, the coastal region has been able to reinforce its dominant position in the national economy.

CONCLUSION

Even though the post-Mao reforms were intended to enhance economic integration, incomplete reforms actually led to duplication and convergence in industrial structure among the localities and temporary tendencies toward market fragmentation along administrative lines (Lyons 1987). While the central government may have decided to use a high tax rate on a certain product to limit production and consumption, local governments in the meantime decided to produce that product in order to capture part of the high taxes being levied, thereby thwarting the plans of the central government. This produces the perverse consequence of high taxes encouraging local government investment in certain industries that the center wanted to restrict. Thus, in spite of the call for industrial rationalization, local behavior tended toward the opposite direction. More specifically, we find that the interior regions were able to increase their share of the output of a variety of major industrial products before the late 1980s. Yunnan, in particular, has been especially successful in developing its tobacco industry.

The rush by local governments to build processing plants made it difficult to control the scale of capital investments and was a major contributor to macroeconomic difficulties. Fortunately for China, the simultaneous pursuit of local industrial development by thousands of local communities made it difficult for any single community to derive super-rents for long. The time series data for regional shares of various products suggest that by the beginning of the 1990s consolidation had set in as consumer demand slumped following a spate of panic buying in 1987–88 and the imposition of tight liquidity in 1988–90. The interior's gains proved short-lived. Since the late 1980s, the coastal region has been able to recapture the output shares it lost in the first half of the 1980s and more.

Indeed, the coastal region's return to economic dominance in the Chinese economy is not limited to industrial production but can also be seen in other areas of the economy, including services and the media. While a number of publications from the interior were popular in the 1980s, China's publishing media (including newspapers and journals) are now dominated by productions from major coastal cities such as Guangzhou, Shenzhen, Shanghai, and Beijing (*QB* 5/13/96: 27).

In short, while the interior's efforts at self-development had a stabilizing effect on coast–interior disparities in the early 1980s, they did to a much lesser extent by the late 1980s. In the meantime, progressive price reforms have sharply alleviated price distortions and the regional cleavages those distortions gave rise to. By 1992, only 10 percent of the sales volume by state materials enterprises were still subject to the plan (Yu Meng 1993). While some Chinese writers have advocated continuing price reforms to alleviate the friction and contradictions between the coast and interior (Che Guocheng 1995: 82), such reforms, as well as the extension of liberal policies to the interior (as discussed in chapter 3), are likely to have only a very limited impact on alleviating inter-regional disparities. By the late 1980s, interior interests were increasingly turning to the central government for help to alleviate these disparities.

While price rationalization has removed a fundamental cause of regional cleavages, the resource issue will remain a focal point for inter-regional relations for the foreseeable future. One estimate suggests that by the early twenty-first century, more than 50 percent of the electric power and more than 60 percent of the raw materials needed in the eastern region will come from the interior (Hua Hua 1996). The removal of price distortions is expected to enhance regional cooperation in investing in infrastructural projects in the interior that might provide the coastal region with much needed power and raw materials while speeding up interior development (Wang Qingyun 1993; Yukawa 1992).

Part III

The reorientation of regional development

5 The politics of regional policy reorientation

The adoption of different economic development strategies has important political implications. As I have shown in chapter 2, while the Maoist development strategy was heavily redistributive and interior-oriented, the Dengist development strategy has been biased in favor of the coastal region. Indeed, under the post-Mao reforms, even if the interior had been granted the same preferential policies as the coastal region, owing to variations in regional conditions, the interior would not have fared as well as the coastal region without the visible hand of the center. The central government had assumed that growth along the coast would diffuse into the rest of the country. But as years passed by, nagging questions began to be asked about how soon and to what extent the trickle-down process would occur.

It must be recognized, however, that the complaints about uneven development notwithstanding, so far the reforms have created benefits for most people and most provinces. Economic growth has been widespread all over the country. It is true that the interior has registered a lower growth rate relative to the coastal region, but this should not obscure the fact that the interior, including those areas inhabited by ethnic minorities, has also experienced rapid economic growth in the post-Mao period. Thus the euphoria and rapid growth generated by the early reforms made it possible to delay the contentious issue of redistribution. Moreover, even if only the coast had benefitted, the "hope" factor, or tunnel effect, could still have kept the interior quiescent for a fairly long period of time.[1] As a result, like the United States in the first decade and a half of the post-war period (Cumberland 1971), the Chinese government in the 1980s was at best half-hearted in promoting economic development in lagging regions.

Yet, by the end of the 1980s, it was becoming ever more evident that the interior was lagging behind the coastal region. With their low starting level in economic development and the power of the compound-interest rate, the less developed areas need to have a high growth rate just to stay even with their more prosperous peers. Suppose a poor province starts with a per capita income of 500 yuan and a relatively well-off province starts with a per capita income of 1,200 yuan. Also suppose both grew at 15 percent per year over 15 years. Then at the end of this period per capita income in the poor province will have risen to 4,068.5 yuan. In the rich province, per capita income will have risen to 9,764.5 yuan. The relative proportions have not changed, but the absolute gap between the two provinces has increased from 700 yuan to 5,696 yuan! Thus, even though many interior provinces were growing at the national average growth rates, their absolute gaps with the richer provinces were nevertheless widening rapidly.

Had the central government been even-handed in its regional development policy, then the growing regional disparities between coast and interior might still be interpreted as a necessary evil – politically undesirable but economically unavoidable during the early stages of a market economy.[2] For interior leaders, however, what has been hard to swallow is that the central government advocated and practiced a regional policy that put priority on coastal development during the Sixth and Seventh Five-Year Plan periods (1981–90), each time asking the interior to wait and promising that development would be brought to the interior once the coastal region became relatively prosperous. Whereas initially such a regionally slanted policy could be justified on the ground that the coastal provinces had been neglected during the Maoist period and that it was imperative for China to catch up with its neighbors, as the gap between the coast and the interior became larger and the complaints from the interior became more vociferous, it became harder and harder for central leaders to justify an unbalanced regional development strategy and sustain and promote preferential policies for the already more prosperous coastal region.[3]

The drive to develop industries by interior localities suggests that local authorities were taking matters into their own hands in industrial development, but the central government's designation of development zones in the interior since the late 1980s suggests that the central government was promoting growth centers in the interior. Both the spread of development zones across China and the emphasis on local industrial development, as discussed in the last two chapters, were thus indications of a real, if still limited, shift toward more balanced regional development by the late 1980s. These changes also had the effect of soothing the grievances of interior interests and thus of ameliorating the major sources of cleavages that bedeviled relations between coast and interior. Unfortunately, these developments were too little and too late to turn back the trend toward widening coast–interior disparities. What had been an issue in development strategy was increasingly being thrust onto the political agenda.

In this chapter, I discuss the currents of intellectual and public opinion that paralleled the shift in development strategy. This discussion points to the growing strength of opinion in favor of more central government action to deal with the growing regional disparities. Then I discuss the factors that led the central leadership to place the issue of regional disparities on the political agenda and provide an overview of the shifting regional policies intended to alleviate regional disparities.

THE EVOLVING INTELLECTUAL CLIMATE

As was mentioned in chapter 2, although the Sixth Five-Year Plan called for the development of both the coastal and the interior regions, it stipulated that the interior regions should "speed up the development of energy, transportation, and raw materials industries, so as to aid in the economic development of the coastal region" (The Sixth Five-Year Plan 1983: 110). The Seventh Five-Year Plan for 1986–90 removed the politically charged provision that the poorer interior was to help the more prosperous coast to develop, but it nevertheless still detailed the center's rationale of emphasizing the development of the coastal region for the moment and only gradually pushing economic development into the interior (The Seventh Five-Year Plan 1986: 91–100).

The Sixth and Seventh Five-Year Plans were based on the assumption that economic development tended to diffuse spatially. They called for emphasizing the development of the coastal region first but promised that economic growth would gradually spread from the more developed coastal region to the interior regions. In practice it meant that the focus of regional economic development policy was to proceed, generally speaking, one step at a time, from the coastal region to the less developed central region and finally to the least developed western region.

As has been the case with many major policy initiatives in China, adoption of the coast–interior regionalization and the prioritization of coastal development in national planning in the 1980s were made with few deliberations and no serious policy study (Lin Fatang and Ling Chunxi 1986: 123). As China's intellectual climate became more relaxed, however, the pro-coast regional development strategy became a subject for heated debate in tandem with the rising conflict over regional resource allocation. Critics of the strategy charged that the development of interior regions was not given due consideration in national planning (*Ibid.*) and questioned the theoretical underpinnings of the official policy. A growing number of people, especially policy-makers and economists in interior regions, became palpably disenchanted with the official policy of giving priority to the development of the coastal region. Interior scholars commented extensively on the inequitable nature of the existing institutional structure and central policies and helped turn the intellectual climate against the pro-coast development strategy. By the end of the 1980s, the pro-coast regional development strategy had become intellectually and politically unsustainable without modifications.[4]

One of the first major publications challenging the pro-coast orthodoxy came from a 1984 article written by the Office of Policy Research of the Inner Mongolia Communist Party Committee and published in the *World Economic Herald* in Shanghai. Under the pretext of supporting the new technological revolution, the article countered that the "ladder-step theory" was one-sided in emphasizing the transfer of technology according to the existing level of regional technological development. Instead, the article argued that the less developed regions as late industrializers could jump-start the development process and leap forward by directly absorbing advanced technology from abroad and could then even transfer such technology to the more developed regions in China. There was thus no need for the sequential development of different regions. All should develop simultaneously (Strategy Group 1984; see also Yi Jun 1984; Zheng Hongliang 1990: 277).

By 1985, a western school (*xibu xuepai*) on regional development had coalesced. At the Symposium on the Reform of Economic Structure held in the coastal city of Tianjin in April 1985, proponents of this school surprised the other participants by presenting a set of comprehensive indicators which put a number of inland provinces such as Shaanxi, Xinjiang, and Inner Mongolia well ahead of most other provinces. Moreover, they bolstered their argument by pointing out that industries in the western region were plagued by central policy-induced losses while those in the coastal region benefitted from policy-based subsidies and argued that the usual perception that the coastal region was more efficient than the interior regions should be discounted (He Bochuan 1990: 140).

In any case, as the economist Feng Bin suggested in a separate setting, the ladder-step doctrine had serious pitfalls in an era of new technological revolution because less developed areas could make leaps in absorbing new technologies from other countries rather than wait for diffusion from the more developed regions within China (Feng Bin 1985). The western region should also be allowed to open up. Indeed, some argued that the adoption of the ladder-step doctrine was making it difficult for underdeveloped areas to realize their potential. Asking the underdeveloped western region to wait for trickle-down to occur would only condemn the development of the western region to a vicious circle (He Bochuan 1990: 140). According to Wang Wenchang and Meng Yanyan (1988), the central government's emphasis on coastal development was leading even the border areas in the western region to look to the east rather than take advantage of their border locations and open up to both the eastern areas and the countries beyond their borders. This led to the shrivelling of border trade, which urgently needed revival. Finally, Feng Bin warned that Deng Xiaoping's goal of quadrupling China's GNP would be unrealistic without the economic development of underdeveloped areas (Feng Bin 1985; see also Yan Liankun and Chen Zhi 1985). Some writers also claimed that the under-development of some areas affected the development of the prosperous regions. It would therefore be in the interests of the more developed areas to support the underdeveloped areas in technology, human talent, finance, and so on, so that the latter areas could help the former to use their resources (Liu Jinwen, Wang Yiwu, and Zhang Xiusheng 1985: 41).

Soon some regional economists began to point out that the ladder-step theory was merely one perspective on regional development. While acknowledging real differences between the coastal and interior regions, Wang Zhiyuan and Zeng Xinqun (1988) suggested that the prevailing regionalization scheme was too broad to capture the wide dispersion of industrial production in China and the very significant variations within each of these regions. This led them to conclude that the ladder-step theory was simply too crude as *the* foundation for China's regional development strategy. The major alternative for Wang and Zeng, as well as other regional economists-cum-policy advocates, was locational analysis that drew attention to central places, growth poles, and growth points throughout the country. As one writer based in Sichuan pointed out, interior cities such as Xi'an, Chongqing, and Chengdu already served as the growth poles or points for the interior regions and it was thus unjustified to confine China's development to one single regional theory that had limited applicability (the ladder-step theory) (Chen Jiaze 1987). For Chen, because the ladder-step theory relies on inter-regional exchanges, the promotion of the application of this theory in turn exacerbated the tendencies toward local protectionism during the reform era. In contrast, the promotion of growth poles and growth centers nationwide would lead to an emphasis on the development of large and medium-sized enterprises and central cities in the western region and help break the dualistic configuration of economic development in China and tend toward the eradication of obstacles to market integration.

The tide was turning against concentrating on coastal development. Perhaps the most forceful presentation of the argument against the ladder-step theory and for equal emphasis on interior development, especially in the poorer areas, was made in a book by Guo Fansheng and Wang Wei (1988: 55–86). Proceeding from the assumption that every aspect of the development of the western region should be based on considerations of economic efficiency, they suggest that the so-called industrial inefficiency in interior regions was calculated on the basis of state-fixed prices which depress those of extractive industries. Despite such policy distortions, however, Guo and Wang point out that from 1978 to 1983, while the ratio of profit and taxes to capital declined by 11.66 percent in Beijing, 2.51 percent in Tianjin, 11.72 percent in Shanghai, and 15.21 per cent in Liaoning, it increased by 86.44 percent in Inner Mongolia, 79.31 percent in Yunnan, 58.44 percent in Guizhou (Guo Fansheng and Wang Wei 1988: 112). Their favorite example is the Yi League Woollen Sweater Factory (and the wool-processing industry in general) in Inner Mongolia. Supplied with imported equipment in the early 1980s, this factory soon surpassed its coastal competitors by becoming the most efficient and profitable enterprise in China's wool-processing industry (Guo Fansheng and Wang Wei 1988: 37). For Guo and Wang, these facts constitute the most powerful argument for developing both the coastal and the interior regions simultaneously. Indeed, in an apparent reference to the preferential policies for the coastal region, people in the interior region are fond of saying: "[We] want policy, not subsidy." They believe that with the right policy, the interior can take off on its own.

Thus by the late 1980s little support existed among scholars and policy-makers for relying on the policy of diffusion in the interior, particularly the western region. As one article put it: "We had the illusion of solving the problem of east–west economic gaps by relying on the strategy of 'ladder-step development.' Yet, the actual development situation of the past few years demolished that illusion mercilessly. The gap between east and west not only did not narrow, but is still growing" (Dong Fan and Cheng Yaoping 1990: 37). Similarly, a writing group from Yunnan asked readers to reflect on whether the transmission of development from the east to the west was an inevitable law and ponder when the turn would come for the western region, and especially Yunnan, to catch up, if at all (Wang Dingchang, Long Liqing, and Wei Fengxian 1989). The authors of the writing group called for changing the existing regional development strategy, arguing that the strategy not only did not seek to rectify the historical legacy of coast–interior disparities but in essence served to enlarge them. Instead, they argued that it should be a goal of socialist development to limit the widening regional disparities and even narrow them (Wang Dingchang, Long Liqing, and Wei Fengxian 1989).[5]

In short, on the eve of the Tiananmen crisis, continuation of the pro-coast regional policy had already become suspect – intellectually, morally, and politically. It was widely recognized that the pro-coast regional policies had become excessive and neglected the coordination of inter-regional relations. Focusing on the policy-induced distortions, this argument, and the sense of fairness that went with it, won allegiance not only among scholars and policy-makers in the interior, but also among some of those on the coast (Yang Jisheng 1989b: 10). Even those who believed that regional imbalances were bound to increase under China's current circumstances recognized that the preferential regional policies in favor of the more developed coastal region ought to be moderated and that the relations between coast and interior should be harmonized under conditions of disequilibrium growth (Zhang Wenhe 1989: 75). The various attempts on the part of Guangdong, Jiangsu, and other coastal provinces to smooth relations with their interior neighbors were a reflection of the evolving perceptions. The ground was laid for the reassessment and reorientation of China's regional policy.

TIANANMEN AND THE MODIFICATION OF REGIONAL DEVELOPMENT POLICY, 1988–91

In all fairness, the post-Mao Chinese leadership had not been unconcerned about the cleavages in coast–interior relations prior to the Tiananmen crisis of 1989. While Deng Xiaoping emphasized the policy of letting some areas become rich first in the early 1980s, by the mid-1980s he had also started to promise that there would eventually be common prosperity after a certain time period (Deng Xiaoping 1993).[6] Even in the early 1980s, there was already a nascent effort by the central government to promote regional cooperation. Soon after the opening of special economic zones, the Chinese leadership urged consideration of an east–west dialogue in China. The 1981 joint directive issued by the Chinese Communist Party Central Committee and the State Council after a meeting of representatives from nine coastal provinces pointed out that the "correct handling of coast–interior relations was a strategic question in the socialist economic construction of our country." It urged "coastal areas, especially major coastal cities . . . to accelerate the economic development of coastal areas, while strengthening the economic alliance and technical cooperation with inland areas, and to effectively bring along the development of the inland economy" (Wang Hongmo *et al.* 1989: 485). Similarly, both the Sixth and Seventh Five-Year Plans made provision for inter-regional, especially inter-provincial cooperation and called for the development of lateral links centered on major cities.

Nevertheless, as was pointed out earlier, China's regional economic policy clearly favored the coastal region under the leadership of Hu Yaobang and Zhao Ziyang, two of Deng Xiaoping's lieutenants.[7] The hallmark of Zhao Ziyang's approach was not to seek balanced regional development but to urge the coastal region to minimize the adverse impact of coastal development on the interior. Zhao's coastal development strategy, for example, called on the coastal region to emphasize export processing by importing raw materials and semi-finished products, thereby reducing the competition for raw materials from the interior (D. Yang 1991). In the meantime, beginning in 1988, the center stopped the automatic upward adjustment in fiscal subsidies to provinces that depended on them, most of which were in the interior (Zheng Yan 1994: 24). Zhao was resigned to his pro-coast policy and fatalistic about the growing coast–interior inequality. When launching the coastal development strategy, he commented that "the disparity [between the coastal region and the interior] was unavoidable and conformed to the law of economic development" (Xinhua 1988: 11).

Yet it would be exaggerating to claim that Zhao's coastal development strategy represented a policy consensus. While some analysts did note that the coastal development strategy presented an opportunity for the western region to emphasize manufacturing and realize its potential (Wang Dingchang, Long Liqing, and Wei Fengxian 1989), the majority opinion was far more pessimistic. Instead of alleviating regional tensions, Zhao's promotion of the coastal development strategy in spring 1988 in fact caused those in the interior to worry that the coast–interior gap would become larger because the interior regions lacked the conditions for export-oriented development. They pointed out that the inland areas within the coastal region, rather than the real interior, would be the first to benefit from the relocation of traditional industries from the privileged coast. Moreover, the rise in raw materials imports for export processing might adversely affect the interests of some interior raw materials producers (Li Ke, Yu Senqing, and Wang Yuqi 1988). Regional economists at the State Planning Commission (SPC) shared the pessimistic assessment. In a study released in early 1989,[8] they pointed out that even if the emphasis on coastal exports provided some slack within the domestic market, it was likely that other companies from within the coastal region rather than companies from the interior would fill the slack (State Planning Commission 1989: 17). As the data presented in the last chapter indicate, this assessment proved prescient and the coastal region has in fact increased its share of China's industrial output since the late 1980s.

More significant, the SPC economists called on the central government to help the interior regions overcome the legacies of the past as seen in their heavy industrial structure and the segmentation between defense and civilian industries. In a critique of the official regional development strategy, they argued that the state "should not continue to relegate the western economy to a subordinate and passive position" as had been the case in the 1980s. The state should instead vigorously assist certain key industries and enterprises to foster their competitiveness through import substitution and thus help the western region to jump-start into a virtuous cycle of development. "In the future the issuance of any reform measure and regional policy should reflect the demands of western economic development," they concluded. Echoing a growing sentiment among interior writers, they warned that interior political grievances would "lead to future trouble that will be difficult to deal with" (State Planning Commission 1989: 20).

In any event, the political crisis of 1989, including the ouster of Communist Party General Secretary Zhao Ziyang, hastened the reorientation of the central government's regional development policies. Unlike Zhao Ziyang, who rode the reform tide beginning from landlocked Sichuan and was able to deflect some of the interior complaints about his pro-coast policy in an era when the rising tide of reform lifted every boat, Premier Li Peng and others associated with him were caught in the politics of hard times and did not have the same luxury. Instead, Li Peng had had to deal with an unruly economy even before the Tiananmen Incident. The political crisis of 1989 and the subsequent collapse of communist regimes elsewhere intensified the post-Tiananmen leadership's search for political support (Bachman 1989; Dittmer 1990). With Hu Yaobang and Zhao Ziyang, both champions of liberalization and coastal development, either dead or dismissed, the central government also removed close allies of these leaders, replacing Governor Liang Xiang and Party Secretary Xu Shijie of Hainan province as well as a host of lesser officials.

More interestingly, the Li Peng administration exploited Zhao's relative neglect of the interior for political benefit, so as to placate disgruntled interior leaders and garner their support. One indication of this tendency to please interior interests was an official report on a visit to the western region by Zeng Xianlin, the Minister of Light Industry. According to the report, the visit "resulted from a long considered concern of the nation's [present] leaders over the growing economic gulf between the east and west." The report praised the post-Tiananmen leaders for having "long planned to shift the economic focus by the turn of the century to the west and northwest" and commented with tongue in cheek that those areas had been "somewhat ignored in the nation's first burst of economic reform" under Zhao Ziyang (*CDBW* 11/6/89: 1, 3).

In the immediate post-Tiananmen period, two major policy strands had major implications for regional equity. First, the national political jitters and local political uncertainty undermined foreign investors' confidence and led to a temporary curtailment in foreign investment as well as trade. Since the coastal region was more dependent on foreign investment and foreign trade, the downturn in international interaction had a greater impact on the economy of the coastal region than on that of the interior. In this context, even though the center finally approved and Premier Li Peng personally announced the development of Pudong (Shanghai East) in 1990, the Pudong New Area found itself caught in a down draft and was slow to get started.

Against the background of international difficulties, the central government launched a reform of the foreign trade subsidy system in January 1991. Beginning on January 1, the State Council stopped subsidizing exports, which amounted to 4 percent of total exports in 1987, or US$1.4 billion (Liu Luyan 1991: 3). The foreign trade reform was ostensibly designed to reduce the growing state budget deficit and to introduce a unified trade policy for all regions. Yet the move also effectively trimmed the policy privileges for state enterprises in Guangdong, Fujian, and the special economic zones (E. Cheng 1991a; *Xingdao ribao* 2/4/91: 14). Because many products from inland areas were exported via foreign trading corporations in coastal areas, which, under the old policy that favored coastal areas, were able to offer higher purchase prices to domestic producers than inland corporations, the more uniform policy seemed to have, at least in the short term, boosted the amount of foreign trade handled by inland provinces (E. Cheng 1991b: 35).

Second, the State Council adopted the recommendation of the State Planning Commission to formulate China's industrial policy in terms of sectors rather than regions. In the Eighth Five-Year Plan (1991–95) and the 10-Year Program, the Chinese leadership explicitly de-emphasized the pro-coast slant and sought to gain interior support by stressing the importance of interior development. The State Planning Commission's guidelines, issued in late 1989, for drafting the Eighth Five-Year Plan put priority on reversing the emphasis on coastal development contained in the two previous five-year plans. Instead of using the regional classification of "eastern, central, and western" as in the Seventh Five-Year Plan, official news reports took pains to emphasize that the Eighth Five-Year Plan would emphasize particular industries rather than specific regions (*Wen Wei Pao* 1989). The new industrial policies emphasized the development of agriculture, energy, and other basic industries, which were believed to have lagged behind and become the bottlenecks for China's further development. Because the interior economies were more concentrated in these industries than the coastal economies, the emphasis on industrial policy was thus a *de facto* shift in favor of the interior regions, which had called on the central government to change from regional preferences to industry preferences (Zhang Wenhe 1989: 74; D. Yang 1995a).

Although the central rhetoric on regional balance had softened somewhat by 1991, the CCP's "suggestions" on the Eighth Five-Year Plan still called for "avoiding excessive gaps in regional income and distribution that might cause new economic and social problems." The state was to "correctly handle and coordinate the relations between resource-rich areas and resource-processing areas." Both types of areas "should enter lateral alliances and adopt ways that cater to the interests of both, combine the superiority of each and develop together" (ZZGZ 1991). Premier Li Peng's report on the Eighth Five-Year Plan was more specific about interior development. He not only stressed the development of resource industries in the interior, but argued that "places with rich resources should appropriately develop some processing industries" (Li Peng 1991). This might be read as a *post hoc* justification of what had actually happened in the interior in the 1980s, but it was certainly music to the ears of interior interests and in sharp contrast to the Sixth Five-Year Plan, which had stipulated that interior regions were to develop resources in order to help the coastal region. Moreover, Li Peng stressed that "the state and economically developed areas should work hard to help the economically underdeveloped areas to change their faces, so that all localities will make progress and achieve common prosperity" (Li Peng 1991).

THE RESURGENCE OF DENGISM: THE DENG WHIRLWIND

The emphasis by the Li Peng administration on the simultaneous development of the coastal region and the interior was evidently welcome news to inland interests. However, the Chinese leadership was better at enunciating general policies than at providing the tools to carry them out, especially in light of the weakening of the center's relative capacity to extract resources and redistribute investment (D. Yang 1990; Chen Yuan 1991: 18–26). In fall 1990, Premier Li Peng and his colleagues failed to push through a restructuring of the fiscal and tax systems that were designed to strengthen the central government's fiscal foundations (Baum 1992: 26–27). The setback in fiscal rationalization constrained revenue growth for the center and tied its hands in pushing for balanced regional development.

The coast–interior regional gap did show a little moderation around 1990 owing to tight economic stabilization policies. Yet by 1992, the central leadership's carefully calibrated appeal for interior development was blown away by the whirlwind of Deng Xiaoping's tour to various southern cities, including the special economic zones of Shenzhen and Zhuhai (Zhao 1993; Baum 1994: ch. 14). The tour became Deng's personal offensive for rapid growth and bold reforms. In talks during the tour, Deng argued that those areas that possessed the right conditions, such as Shanghai and Guangdong, should charge ahead. Even though the renewed commitment to Shanghai's Pudong New Area represented a significant shift (northward) away from the earlier emphasis on the four special economic zones in Guangdong and Fujian, it nevertheless served to accentuate, again, the emphasis on coastal development. More specifically, the Chinese government in 1992 issued a Yangtze development strategy calling for Shanghai Pudong's development and opening to be used as the spearhead to further promote the development and opening of the Yangtze River valley region (including Jiangsu, Zhejiang, Anhui, Jiangxi, Hunan, Hubei, Sichuan, and Shanghai). The offering of generous preferential treatment to Pudong energized overseas interest in the Yangtze river valley region. In 1991, the Yangtze river valley region utilized US$571 million in foreign investment or 4.9 percent of the national total. By 1994, the amount had risen to US$9.8 billion, or 29 percent of the national total. A study conducted under the auspices of the State Science and Technology Commission and the State Planning Commission forecast that by 2010 the region will account for 45 percent of China's gross domestic product, up from 39 percent in 1994 (*RMRBO* 1/4/96: 1).[9]

While the Yangtze River Valley Development Program was partly intended to help integrate the coast with interior regions, its immediate impact was in fact concentrated in the coastal areas, particularly Pudong. Both domestic policies and a sharp rise in overseas investment converged to produce a spectacular growth spurt for the coastal region, leading to a significant enlargement in coast–interior disparities (Yang and Wei 1996b).

Not every policy served to accentuate regional cleavages, however. Some new reforms, particularly price reforms, helped alleviate interior resentment. Taking advantage of the buyers' market created by the economic austerity program and the political shock of Tiananmen, the Chinese leadership steadily freed up various prices in the first half of the 1990s. As of the mid-1990s, the prices of most consumer goods are set by supply and demand rather than administrative fiat. Although the government continues to be involved in the pricing of various producer goods and basic materials such as coal, iron, and steel, there is indication that the central leadership has decided to end its control over the pricing and distribution of most production materials as well (Wu Zhong 1996). While the decision is intended to complete China's move to the market, it will finally end the distorted state price system which has been a major source of regional cleavages.

In sum, China's regional policy was caught in a crosscurrent in 1989–93. While the Li Peng administration sought a more balanced regional development strategy, Deng's southern tour added impetus to coastal development. In balance, the coastal region continued to reign supreme in China's economic development in spite of the shift to an industry-based policy and price reforms and was in fact the recipient of much investment from the interior. Fundamentally, whatever the shifts in government policies, the deficit-plagued central government lacked the muscle to bring about a major shift in regional development patterns.

BEYOND DENG: REGIONAL POLICY UNDER JIANG ZEMIN

Deng's southern tour proved to be his last hurrah.[10] While the Deng whirlwind temporarily overwhelmed the limited central government effort to reorient regional development, it did not silence the demands for redressing the rising regional disparities and the arguments against preferential treatment for the coastal region (see, e.g., Dong Fan 1993; Zuo Dapei 1994). Since Deng disappeared from public view, his successors led by President and General Secretary Jiang Zemin have been working hard to shore up their authority. In contrast to the dying Deng, however, Jiang's priority has not been the launching of another leap forward but the consolidation of his position and the foundations of the regime. While Jiang and his colleagues, including Premier Li Peng, are concerned about sustaining economic growth, they have also recognized the growing disparities between coast and interior as a major issue on their agenda. This poses a puzzle because of the dominance of coastal interests at the pinnacle of Chinese politics. What has made this coastal oligarchy pay serious attention to the plight of the interior regions?

To begin with, after 1991 coast–interior disparities jumped substantially amid the economic boom and it became evident that the post-Tiananmen regional policies did little to alter the pattern of changes in such disparities. In the words of Shanxi Deputy Governor Peng Zhigui (1996: 11): "Economic development in the central and western regions has become seriously retarded and underdeveloped relative to the southeastern coastal provinces and this not only implies income inequality across regions but has also become an obstacle to overall economic and social development." In consequence, interior demands for central government action to address the regional gap have also become more vocal.

More significantly, while interior interests point to economic numbers, their complaints about the growing coast–interior gap are frequently peppered with warnings of an impending socio-political crisis. There are two aspects to this issue. First, relative economic stagnation in the interior makes it difficult for the interior to create adequate employment opportunities. The resultant surplus labor has tended to search for jobs along the coast, contributing to the vast flow of migrant labor variously estimated at 60 to 100 million. Numerous Chinese commentators have viewed this transient population as a source of social problems and potentially political instability (He Xin 1990; Zhao Wei and Sun Yuxia 1996). Acccordingly, since at least the late 1980s, various interior writers have emphasized that persistence of the unbalanced regional development strategy "will very likely induce other economic and social contradictions and cause shocks to the whole national economy and society" (Dong Fan 1993: 15). In meetings held in August 1995 to prepare the ground for the Ninth Five-Year Plan, leaders from several interior provinces, including Sichuan, Shaanxi, Xinjiang, Gansu, and Guizhou, reportedly lobbied the central leadership to take concrete action to redress the regional economic imbalance through more central aid and preferential policies. They warned that otherwise their deteriorating economic situation might lead to more widespread outbreaks of crime and anti-government activities and cause them to lose control of law and order (Lam 1995f).

Second, domestic liberalization and the fallout from the collapse of communism in a number of China's neighbors have resulted in an increase in ethnic separatist activities in China's border regions, particularly in Tibet, Xinjiang, and Inner Mongolia (Baum 1994: 323–25; Gladney 1994). While the ethnic minorities as a percentage of China's total population are, at 8 percent, relatively small, the total ethnic population of around 100 million is obviously large and cannot be dismissed easily, especially in light of the prominent role ethnic cleavages played in the break-up of the Soviet Union.

On the surface, Chinese leaders on nationality affairs have insisted that the various ethnic groups live in harmony in China. According to Ismail Amat, Minister of the State Nationalities Affairs Commission, ethnic separatist activities are conducted by a very small number of people who lack support among the minority populations. Amat asserts that the economic and social gaps between the coastal and western regions will never lead to tension between different nationalities because the Chinese government's preferential policies for ethnic minority areas have successfully narrowed the economic gap between them and Han Chinese (Xie Liangjun 1996).

In reality, however, Chinese policy-makers and commentators have become extremely concerned about the potential for socio-political instability in areas inhabited by ethnic minorities. There is a widespread perception that increasing economic disparities between these regions and the more prosperous east coast have contributed to rising ethnic tension and separatist tendencies (Brauchli 1993). In a survey of provincial-level nationality affairs cadres on the economic gap between ethnic minority areas and the more developed coastal region, an overwhelming majority of the respondents believed that the gap had become excessively large (83.7 percent) and served to undermine social and political stability (84.8 percent). Close to 94.5 percent of the respondents believed that the widening gap had made the mentality of minority nationality cadres unbalanced or extremely unbalanced (i.e., upset). There was unanimous agreement among the respondents that the growing regional gap demanded urgent government action (Hu Angang 1994).[11]

While the nationality affairs cadres may have been self-serving in drawing attention to the political significance of their own work, numerous Chinese commentators have also argued that a thriving economy is crucial to social peace in places such as Tibet and Xinjiang, fearing that retarded development will cause minorities in these and other areas to join forces with their brethren living across the border and lead to social instability (Jiang Hai 1994; Liu Fayan 1995).[12] In the words of Che Guocheng:

> Stability is the first priority. Reform and development cannot proceed without a stable political and economic environment. This is especially important in the western region. Not only is the ethnic composition in the western region more complex than in the east, but various border areas share ethnic identities with neighboring countries. In consequence, the promotion of economic and social development and the realization of common prosperity of all peoples are crucial to the solution of ethnic problems and the preservation of political and social stability in the western region.
>
> (Che Guocheng 1995: 82)

The Chinese government has in fact consistently aided the ethnic minorities through fiscal subsidies and affirmative action programs. The ethnicity variable is a strong predictor of whether a provincial unit receives fiscal subsidies from the central government (D. Yang 1995b: 66).[13] The growing salience of ethnic issues and the availability of state aid tied to ethnicity have provided strong incentives for elites in the interior to couch their policy demands in ethnic terms particularly because Tibet and Xinjiang have enjoyed more financial subsidies from the central government than other provinces. One internal report submitted by the Guizhou Economic Reform Committee to the CCP Central Committee, for example, starts by saying that the size of the minority population in Guizhou is six times that of Tibet and thus deserves far more attention from the center than it has received. Similarly, officials from Qinghai complained that, even though Qinghai has a large ethnic population, the province had not received the same preferential policies for ethnic minority areas as Xinjiang, Yunnan, and Tibet (Cheung Lai-kuen 1996).

Since the end of the 1980s central leaders have apparently agreed that the widening gap between the coast and the interior regions needs attention and have obliged interior regions with more liberal policies. Pointing to the gap between areas inhabited by ethnic groups and the more developed areas, Buhe, a vice chairman of the NPC Standing Committee who hails from Inner Mongolia, urged all regions and government departments to pay more attention to the development of areas inhabited by ethnic minority groups "from the perspective of long-term stability and prosperity for all ethnic groups."[14] In the words of President and General Secretary Jiang Zemin, "If we allow polarization of minorities and regions then conflict between central government and provinces could burgeon and cause chaos" (Macartney 1995a).

I use the word "apparently" here with purpose. For the rebalancing of regional priorities has important political implications. While Jiang's comment has an element of truth to it, it is also plausible that he was using that sort of apocalyptic political rhetoric to cultivate the support of interior leaders while simultaneously enhancing the center's leverage over the increasingly influential coastal interests, especially since Jiang and his colleagues at the center do not possess the sort of authority Deng Xiaoping commanded. By arguing that more should be done to narrow the gap between the coastal areas and the poorly developed western and central regions and that this was in the interest of all, the central government has not only justified one dimension of its existence but has also put local authorities in the coastal region on the defensive. Indeed, some leaders from the coastal region have conceded that growth along the coast was to some extent achieved at the expense of interior regions. According to Shandong Governor Li Chunting, for a long time raw materials produced in the interior were deliberately underpriced to back the economic takeoff of the east. Li argued that in the long run, "only when the economies of the central and western parts are developed can the comprehensive national strength be enhanced and economic growth in eastern China be sustained" (Hua Hua 1996).

THE NINTH FIVE-YEAR PLAN AND THE SEARCH FOR REGIONAL BALANCE

Thus, while the interior regions are economically weak, their leverage over the policy agenda has nevertheless increased in recent years by virtue of a rise in their perceived negative power – the potential disruptions underdevelopment in these regions may cause to China's political stability, economic growth, and national unity (a point driven home by the bus bombings in Xinjiang and Beijing in early 1997). As President Jiang Zemin and his cohort of leaders emerge out of the shadow of Deng, they have paid more attention to interior development under the rubric of balancing reform, growth, and stability.

Much current discussion of the need to reshape China's regional development policies has centered on the policy measures to be taken during the Ninth Five-Year Plan period (1996–2000) and under China's Social and Economic Development Program for the period before 2010. In remarks to the central committee session that approved the guiding principles for drafting the Ninth Five-Year Plan, both Jiang Zemin and Li Peng called for serious attention to be paid to the widening disparities between coast and interior and stipulated that the narrowing of these disparities was an important and long-term principle (Jiang Zemin 1995b; Li Peng 1995). (This was clearly music to the ears of those members of the Central Committee who hail from the interior and whose votes Jiang needs.) Interestingly, probably as a concession to interior demands, Premier Li Peng (1996) moved the issue of regional disparities ahead of macroeconomic stability in his spring 1996 report to the National People's Congress on the outline of the Ninth Five-Year Plan. Thus, the Chinese leadership is making an effort to fulfill the promise, made in earlier five-year plans, of beginning to shift the emphasis of regional development policy to the interior in the 1990s.

Three components of the regional policy shift may be discerned. First, the center has indicated that it will gradually increase the proportion of centrally controlled state investment allocated to inland regions, continue to provide support for underdeveloped areas, and encourage the transfer of resource-intensive and labor-intensive industries from the coastal region to the interior. The fiscal reforms introduced in 1994, and to be discussed in chapter 6, promise to furnish the central government with more financial resources for transfer payments to localities and some of the increased transfer payments will probably be used to deal with rising regional economic disparities.[15] The newly created policy banks will gradually increase the amount of preferential loans to the central and western areas for infrastructural improvement by building power stations and railways.[16] The interior regions will also receive most of the development loans from foreign governments and international organizations such as the World Bank and the Asian Development Bank, a move that has received support from foreign donors.[17] The center will also continue its anti-poverty policy, announced in early 1994, which set the target of eliminating abject poverty for 80 million people by the year 2000 in China. This anti-poverty plan seeks to raise the annual net income of the majority of the poverty-stricken to 500 yuan (1990 prices) through the provision of infrastructure such as roads, drinkable water, electric supply, and improvement in education. The government has designated 582 counties, most of which are situated in the interior, as priority targets, and has decided to increase its investment in the Work for Food Program and in discount loans by one billion yuan each over 1994–2000 (Efforts 1994). Moreover, the China National Natural Science Foundation has indicated that it will grant most of its funds to the scientific development of the central and western parts of the country. Some 60 percent of a total of 400 projects to be financed will be in these areas to deal with urgent problems such as land deterioration, shortage of water, and ecological degradation (Xinhua 8/4/95, FBIS-CHI-95–151 8/7/95: 44). These changes will probably be of great significance over the long run, but in the short term the funds available are limited.

Second, since most overseas investment has so far flowed into the coastal region and become a major source of the regional imbalance, a major aspect of the recent central initiatives has been to promote overseas investment in interior regions. The Ministry of Foreign Trade and Economic Cooperation has promulgated a set of policy guidelines that are designed to boost trade and foreign investment in the interior by making foreign investment policies for coastal and interior regions converge, giving interior provinces equal authority to approve foreign investments in mid-1996. The center has especially encouraged the interior regions to introduce foreign capital for the joint development of natural resources (Policy 1995; *QB* 5/30/96: 4).

Prompted by government encouragement, rising production costs along the coast, and concerns about access to raw materials and markets, overseas investors have increased the absolute amount of investment in the interior in the 1990s (see, e.g., Liang Shutang 1995). In relative terms, however, the interior's share of overseas investment has changed little. It is now realized that the interior regions cannot copy the experiences of the coastal region in attracting overseas investment because these former regions lack the latter's geographical advantage and density of overseas linkages (*QB* 6/10/96: 12). The official policies for encouraging overseas investment in interior regions have partially reflected this reality and emphasized natural resource exploitation and the import of labor-intensive industries, including from the coastal region. Moreover, the Ministry of Foreign Trade and Economic Cooperation, the State Council's Office of Overseas Chinese Affairs, and other government agencies have organized trade fairs and trade and investment delegations to promote awareness of the interior regions so that overseas investors will consider it an option to invest there (*QB* 6/18/96: 1).

Finally, as in the past, President Jiang Zemin and other central leaders have urged the coastal provinces to increase the amount of assistance they provide for the development of the interior regions (*Window* 3/25/94: 5; *RMRBO* 7/15/94: 1). The center seeks to guide capital, technology, and managerial expertise from the coastal region and the world to the interior which possesses various natural resources, abundant labor, and a huge potential market. Provinces are paired together so that the richer partner can help the poorer one deal with the issue of poverty. These relationships combine central guidance with mutual interest. Nevertheless, while coastal cities such as Shanghai and Shenzhen could get back valuable commodities such as petroleum, cotton, and melons from Xinjiang, Yunnan, and Guizhou, Tibet has little to return to its benefactors. In consequence, the center has in the 1990s done quite a bit of arm-twisting to get coastal provinces and cities like Guangdong, Jiangsu, Zhejiang, Shandong, and Shanghai to help build 62 construction projects in Tibet that carry a total price tag of more than 2 billion yuan (Kwan 1994; Lam 1995b).

CONCLUSION

While the unbalanced regional development strategy has tended to reinforce itself economically, it has also produced its own discontents. By the late 1980s, the unbalanced strategy had been subjected to serious intellectual criticism in economic and ethical terms. As the coast–interior disparities have widened, it has become increasingly difficult to justify. Most important, changing domestic and international political contexts have led the Chinese leadership to associate the growing regional disparities with rising potential political costs, especially in light of the various peasant protests and Moslem rebellions that the interior regions have witnessed in the past. For their part, interior elites used the specter of instability to persuade the central leadership to purchase political stability. Whereas the Chinese leadership previously justified the unbalanced strategy in terms of China's national interests, it now argues that these same national interests call for the coastal region to make a greater contribution toward interior development (Ninth Plan Suggestions 1995: 14).

In the next two chapters, I examine the concrete manifestations of the regional policy reorientation by looking at the restructuring of the fiscal system, the effort to help the interior regions promote rural enterprise development, and the center's policies toward the special economic zones. Will the center get the funds it needs to help the interior? Does the reorientation mean that the center is turning its back on the coastal region?

6 The dilemmas of regional policy realignment

The reorientation of regional policy requires financial backing. Yet, by the late 1980s, China's fiscal system exhibited features common to most developing countries where "budget deficits have been financed to an excessive extent by money creation and borrowing abroad with consequent inflation and foreign debt problems. In principle, the deficit problem could be resolved by cutting expenditure and raising charges for services. But, with realistic allowances for expenditure economies and nontax revenue, it seems clear that many countries will need to increase tax revenue" (Goode 1990: 121; see also A. Lewis 1955). As I have discussed elsewhere, China's fiscal problems stemmed from a fundamental disjuncture between a set of economic institutions that were designed for a command economy and an economy that has become increasingly market-oriented (D. Yang 1994). While the fiscal contracting system adopted in the 1980s provided local governments with strong incentives to promote economic growth, it nevertheless capped the fiscal benefits the central government could derive from that growth. As a result, central government revenue as a share of economic activities, such as GNP, declined over time, making it difficult for the center to secure a stable macroeconomic environment and – even if it wanted to – increase support for interior development (D. Yang 1990).

While there was some recognition that the anachronistic fiscal and taxation system needed revamping, it was not until 1993 that a sweeping set of fiscal and tax reforms was adopted. This chapter discusses the politics of the fiscal rationalization and its implications for regional policy. It argues that the structure of the fiscal reforms makes it impossible for the central government to increase substantially the share of resources under its control in the short term. In consequence, in seeking to reorient the patterns of regional development, the central government is forced to promote policies that do not depend much on financial muscle. In the last chapter I mentioned a number of such efforts, including calling for more foreign investment in the interior and urging richer areas in the coastal region to "voluntarily" help interior areas. In this chapter, I shall provide a detailed examination of a regionally based rural enterprise development program.

RESHAPING THE FISCAL FOUNDATIONS OF THE STATE

Generally speaking, attempts to revamp a fiscal system and raise revenue are hampered by intellectual or analytical difficulties, political obstacles, and administrative and compliance weaknesses. While easy to adumbrate intellectually, systematic tax reform is especially unlikely to be accepted and carried out because of the resistance from the various interests it affects. Invoking the terminology of Albert Hirschman, Richard Goode suggests that "systematic tax reform may generally be classified as a 'chosen' problem selected by policy-makers for attention rather than a 'pressing' problem forced on the policy-makers by the pressure of interested or injured groups. The pressing problems are likely to be given priority" (Goode 1990: 124). Politicians are most likely to choose the path of least resistance first, that is financing budget deficits through money creation or borrowing. They rarely begin to perceive the need to strengthen the tax system until tolerance of inflation and opportunities for borrowing abroad have diminished. Frequently, it is perceptions of fiscal crises that serve to "concentrate the minds of government leaders and make them more receptive to new measures" (Goode 1990: 128). Even then, fiscal rationalization is neither inevitable nor guaranteed and its adoption and implementation depend on effective political leadership.

Analytically, Chinese economists-cum-policy advisers recognized the potential pitfalls of the fiscal contracting system soon after it was launched. As the economy shifted into high gear over 1983–88, however, concerns about the adverse consequences of fiscal decentralization receded (D. Yang 1994: 76–78). Those who called for fiscal rationalization had no immediate impact on policy in the 1980s; indeed, the central government even institutionalized fiscal contracting in 1988. Moreover, the central government gradually gave localities more leeway in setting tax rates for enterprises under their jurisdiction. In the meantime, throughout the 1980s, the central government regularly "borrowed" funds from the provinces to make ends meet but rarely bothered to repay its borrowing. The most prominent of such borrowing was Deng Xiaoping's direct intervention in securing a 2.5 billion yuan payment from Shanghai in early 1989 (Zheng Yi 1992: 179–80). But other provinces, including Jiangsu, Guangdong, Shandong, and Yunnan, have also been hit.

The central government's fiscal problems in the context of an economic austerity program and political crisis prompted numerous economists and policy-makers to demand fiscal reforms after 1988. For example, Xue Muqiao, China's senior statesman on economic policy, returned to his earlier concern about fiscal decentralization. At a meeting of the Central Finance and Economy Leadership Group held in April 1989, Xue vigorously argued for abolishing the fiscal contracting system that he deemed a major source of macroeconomic problems (Xue Muqiao 1990: 420–24). He was in favor of shifting to a tax assignment system (Xue Muqiao 1992: 91–92).

In the aftermath of the Tiananmen crisis, Premier Li Peng and Vice Premier

Yao Yilin made an attempt in 1990 to rationalize the fiscal system. This attempt faltered, however, for at least two major reasons. First, China's central leaders were timid about making major reforms amid political crises both in China and abroad that threatened regime legitimacy.[1] Second, the economic slowdown that resulted from the austerity program of 1988–90 not only dampened people's expectations but also sharply slowed down the expansion of both local and central revenue. In consequence, local efforts to fight for the fiscal *status quo* were much more determined than would have been the case had the economy been booming; and it was therefore more difficult for central leaders to negotiate a greater share of the revenue stream (Delfs 1991: 21–22).

Yet the delay in revamping the fiscal system and the continuing increase in government budget deficit fuelled a lively debate over China's fiscal situation and problems, providing the intellectual impetus for fiscal rationalization (Lu Dongtao and Xu Yan 1993: 250–87; D. Yang 1994: 79). There was widespread recognition that with the declining ratio of central government revenue to national income, China faced major fiscal problems. As Chen Yuan, a deputy governor of the People's Bank of China and the son of conservative patriarch Chen Yun, warned publicly in 1991, the decline of central revenue as a share of national income might lead to "the further loss of economic control and [even] economic disintegration" (Chen Yuan 1991: 18). The crisis rhetoric for fiscal rationalization was in full swing and would reach a crescendo in 1993, in anticipation of the Third Plenum of the 14th Central Committee. As one internal Chinese report speculated: "If a 'political strongman' [read Deng] dies, it is possible that a situation like post-Tito Yugoslavia will emerge" (Wang Shaoguang and Hu Angang 1993a; see also 1993b and 1994). Overall, there was broad agreement among Chinese economists that fiscal and taxation reforms were necessary for building a market economy, crucial to strengthening macroeconomic control, and fundamental to resolving the fiscal dilemmas facing the central government. Failure to strengthen the fiscal foundations of the state weakened the central government's ability to provide macroeconomic stability and deal with social inequality and regional disparities (Wang Xingyi 1993).

Western publications that had to work hard to grab the reader's attention did not mince words either. A report of November 6, 1993 in *The Economist* of London was entitled "China – Can the Center Hold?". It suggested that the center might be wobbling, lacking the courage to stand up to the boom provinces along the coast. The Tofflers, self-styled China-aficionados, were even more blunt. They claimed that the new elites in prosperous coastal provinces were already ignoring central government edicts and suggested that it would not be long before the coastal elites decided to "refuse to contribute the funds needed by the central government to improve rural conditions or to put down agrarian unrest." In a prophecy of apocalypse, the Tofflers concluded that unless Beijing granted the coastal interests "complete freedom of financial and political action, one can imagine the new elites insisting on independence or some facsimile of it – a step that could tear China apart and trigger civil war" (Toffler and Toffler 1993: 214).

As has been the case with reforms in other countries (Williamson 1994), while reform of the fiscal system was ultimately a political decision, the near unanimity with which analysts both in China and abroad dissected the country's fiscal situation undoubtedly helped strengthen the Chinese leadership's resolve to push through fiscal reforms in the early 1990s. By 1992 the psychology of the political participants had shifted with the reignition of the engine of economic growth and the apparent return of boom, especially after Deng Xiaoping's southern tour early in the year. The central leaders had largely steadied their nerves after the 1989 turmoil and the collapse of the Soviet Union and Eastern Europe. In the meantime, an unintended but nonetheless striking effect of the 1988–90 economic austerity program was to expose the weak foundations of China's fiscal system and help foster a perception of fiscal crisis among the top elite. Indeed, the concern about the rising budget deficit became so acute that the National People's Congress, in partnership with the Ministry of Finance, approved a Budget Implementation Law that stipulated that deficits be avoided in both central public expenditures and local budgets.

Against this background, Deng Xiaoping's ever-advancing age and feeble health appeared to have imparted a sense of urgency in rebuilding the fiscal foundations for the central government. In the words of one commentator, Deng's "personal agenda for [the Third Plenum of 1993] was to bolster the political and economic powers of the Party Center and to ensure that his anointed successor, President Jiang Zemin, can then hold the fort after [Deng's] rendezvous with Marx" (Lam 1993a). Besides the succession factor, the macroeconomic difficulties of 1992 and the limited success the leadership had with reining in economic overheating in 1993 also helped convince the leadership that speedy and fundamental changes were necessary to deal with the structural problems facing the economy (Chen and Leung 1993; D. Yang 1993). Finally, with the economy in upswing and expectations of brighter prospects, local officials tended to be more willing to make concessions in the bureaucratic wrangling involved.

The dynamics of central–local interaction

Since analysts had expected that the center would not be able to rein in the provinces and secure their agreement to fiscal rationalization, it is instructive to examine the factors that made it possible for the central leadership to bring sub-national officials onto the bandwagon of fiscal reform. Three factors are especially important. First, there is a strong Party norm against factionalism or the building of open alliances or blocs on specific policy issues. Thus organizationally, local officials can rarely present a united front against the center. Even if each of the sub-national officials had come to the conclusion that fiscal rationalization would be less advantageous to them, some of them might still be willing to agree with the center in order to curry political favor or obtain some other political goods in a clientistic manner. For a lower-ranked local official sitting face-to-face with a top-ranked central leader who has great resources and sanctions, the temptation to strike a deal with the center is especially strong even though, as in a prisoner's dilemma game, he and other local officials will have greater negotiating power if each of them sticks to a stronger stand than if some of them cooperate with the center. Not surprisingly, central leaders including Jiang Zemin and Zhu Rongji took advantage of their organizational advantage and made extensive trips to the provinces to convince local officials individually to accept the new tax and fiscal arrangements.

Second, while the fiscal reforms were intended to promote a sound macroeconomic environment, such an environment of macroeconomic stability was available to all localities as a public good. In consequence, each of the local players had incentives to contribute as little as possible to the making of that public good in the hope that others would still furnish it. But the effect of the fiscal reforms in terms of macroeconomic stability and regional policy has a differential impact on different localities. To begin with, all other things being equal and assuming an integrated economy, a high-growth and high-inflation environment means that faster-growing areas export inflation to areas that grow more slowly. In other words, officials in the interior, which has been growing less rapidly, would like the center to do more to establish macroeconomic order (He Ping 1995).

Overall, interior areas have been more likely to favor coordination in regional development and to call for treating the whole country "as a chessboard" through the subordination of local interests to national interests (Zheng Youjiong 1984: 17; Shirk 1985: 214). Because fiscal reforms would potentially give the center more resources for redistribution, it appears that many officials in the poorer interior would also welcome the reforms more than officials in richer coastal provinces so that the center might do more to alleviate the growing regional disparities. In the words of Qinghai Governor Tian Chengping, the center's inadequate capabilities to exercise effective macroeconomic control were detrimental to the improvement of income distribution and the narrowing of regional economic gaps (Deputies 1995). Thus the center could count on such regional cleavages in seeking support for fiscal reforms. Moreover, cleavages among local officials can also be found within certain provincial administrations. It is a well-known fact that the party secretary and the governor within a single provincial unit have tended to compete against each other, and a number of the personnel changes in recent years have been made to reduce such tensions within provincial administrations (He Pin 1993: 21–23). The lack of political cohesion within a locality has tended to undermine autonomy and administrative efficiency and invite central intervention.

Third, as adumbrated earlier, central leaders have powerful resources and sanctions in their hands for dealing with sub-national officials. It is generally recognized that Party norms and discipline have declined further under the reforms and that the legitimacy of Party rule has been severely eroded. Nevertheless, the Party center continues to hold serious cards *vis-à-vis* sub-national officials (Lieberthal 1992: 20). The most important of the sanctions is the power of appointment and removal of provincial-level leaders through the nomenklatura system (Burns 1989). The central leadership has from time to time rotated provincial leaders laterally to prevent them from becoming captured by parochial local interests. On fundamental issues, those local cadres who stick their necks out against the center may see their power reduced. For example, Guangdong Governor Ye Xuanping was kicked upstairs to a ceremonial post after he voiced strong opposition to fiscal rationalization in late 1990. Thus it is hardly surprising that in preparation for the Central Committee Plenum in 1993, the Party Center rotated and retired a significant number of provincial leaders and there was speculation that "quite a few regional politicians were dumped for rubbing up Beijing the wrong way" (Lam 1993a).[2] The most prominent case occurred in economic powerhouse Jiangsu, where Vice Premier Zhu Rongji reportedly had heated arguments with Shen Daren and Chen Huanyou about the shape of the fiscal reforms. Shen lost his job as Jiangsu Party Secretary in October 1993 (Lam 1993b).

In view of the three factors identified here, the central leadership may be expected to take a two-pronged approach to secure the cooperation of local officials and prevent them from pursuing collective action against the center.

1 Display unity; demonstrate resolve by removing recalcitrant local officials if necessary.
2 Divide and rule. This may be divided into two aspects.
   (a) Negotiate with local officials individually.
   (b) Target potential local resisters, especially those who are known to seek greater local autonomy, and persuade them to publicly support the center early, thus providing cues to officials in other localities suggesting the desirability of jumping onto the policy bandwagon.

Besides following tactics 1 and 2a virtually to the letter, as is apparent from our earlier discussion, the central leadership also adroitly applied tactic 2b. Early in fall 1993, some provincial officials had gone public in putting national interests above the specific interests of a province. For example, in an interview conducted in late September 1993, Zhejiang Party Secretary Li Zemin spoke of the need for all cadres to obey the overall situation, subordinating themselves to national interests as defined by the Party Central Committee. Echoing a refrain of central leaders, Li warned: "Serious consequences might result if everyone goes his or her own way, or if localities only attend to their own interests while disregarding national interests" (Wu Keqiang 1993).

The most stunning application of the center's divide-and-rule tactic occurred in Guangdong. In the early 1980s, a fiscal arrangement was concluded whereby Guangdong remitted 1.17 billion yuan per year to the center and retained the rest of the fiscal revenue; it was also given more autonomy to experiment with reforms. This arrangement was adopted because at the time Guangdong was relatively backward (especially compared to Shanghai, which remitted 10 times as much to the center) and had been starved of central investment throughout the Maoist era. After a decade of buoyant growth, however, Guangdong became the focus of jealousy from provinces that had been on other types of fiscal arrangement, especially Shanghai. Speculation was rife about Guangdong's growing autonomy even though the province had in fact increased its fiscal contributions to the central treasury. In 1990, for example, Guangdong remitted 3.83 billion yuan to the center; this meant that the growth of Guangdong's remittances to the center exceeded the rate of local economic growth. In addition, while at the beginning of the reforms enterprises in Guangdong under the jurisdiction of the center remitted only 0.44 billion yuan to the center, their remittances reached 10.96 billion in 1990 (Wang Zhigang 1993: 135). Altogether, Guangdong by the early 1990s was contributing just as much to the central treasury as did Shanghai (Jacobs and Hong 1994). But the perception of increasing local autonomy in Guangdong at the expense of the center persisted, as evidenced by the quote from the Tofflers cited earlier.

In preparing for the Third Plenum of 1993, central leaders apparently targeted Guangdong to provide an example for other localities. While Guangdong leaders Xie Fei and Zhu Senlin are well known for toeing the center's line, they reportedly were reluctant at first to meet the tax demands made by Vice Premier Zhu Rongji. Nevertheless, they agreed to the new plan when President Jiang Zemin met with them face-to-face (Lam 1993b). At the Plenum, Zhu Rongji reportedly praised Guangdong for having "played a great leading role in the current financial and banking structural reform" and for being a model "for submission by the part to the whole" (Chen Chien-ping 1993). Once the most freewheeling province agreed to the center's proposals for restructuring central–local relations, it was difficult for others to claim exemption.

The grand bargain and its implications for regional policy

Drawing on its organizational advantages and significant political resources, the central leadership pushed through an ambitious agenda geared toward transforming the Chinese economy into a market economy by the end of the twentieth century at the Third Plenum of the 14th Central Committee held in late 1993.[3] The central component of the policy package was a major fiscal rationalization program. As spelt out in Article 18 of the Plenum decision, the fiscal and tax reforms were intended to demarcate the tax control boundaries of local and central government and strengthen the central government's revenue base. This means shifting from fiscal contracting with the provinces "to a tax assignment system on the basis of a rational division of power between central and local authorities, and establishing separate central and local taxation systems."[4] In effect, with the institutionalization of the division of economic powers between the center and the local authorities, China is being transformed into a federal-style economic system.[5]

Though the full implications of the tax overhaul and fiscal restructuring may take years to be fully understood, the Chinese leadership hoped that the reform would "gradually increase the percentage of fiscal income in the gross national product (GNP) and rationally determine the proportion between central and local fiscal income."[6] According to Vice Minister of Finance Xiang Huaicheng, the center's share of state revenue should rise to 60 percent, with 40 percent as central expenditure and 20 percent as transfer grants to local governments (*CD* 11/25/93: 4). In time, this would not only allow the center to reduce its soaring budget deficits and strengthen macroeconomic control but would also provide more resources for transfer payments in order to "support the development of economically underdeveloped regions and the transformation of the old industrial bases."

In the process of negotiations leading to the final passage of fiscal rationalization, however, the center did have to compromise with local interests. In fact, the central–local negotiations took place with the understanding on both sides that neither excessive centralization nor excessive decentralization was desirable. Because most of the local expenditures were fixed for administrative expenses, subsidies, and other specific uses, it was difficult to redivide the existing pie (Huang Ming 1991: 12). Indeed, on the assumption that the pie would continue to grow rapidly, the center's strategy was not to redivide it but to capture more of the growing part of it. The center guaranteed the localities would receive all the money they already received (as of 1993) but claimed more of the marginal increase in revenue above the 1993 base. As Deputy Finance Minister Jin Renqing pledged, "the vested interests of these [coastal] provinces will be protected" and the fiscal reform "won't dampen their incentives" to expand their economies (Leung 1993).

Thus the grand bargain that resulted from the Third Plenum reflected the reciprocal interests of the center and the provinces. Even if the grand bargain is implemented to the letter and meets the specified revenue goals, it will not boost the central government's discretionary spending power immediately.[7] In consequence, the adoption of fiscal restructuring provides no immediate relief for interior demands for more transfer payments. Indeed, during 1994–95, local governments concentrated on the collection of local taxes ("Government Measures" 1995: 33) while widespread delinquencies in central tax collection occurred. Until the center sent out its tax inspection teams, the differential tax collection efforts had a corrosive effect on the central government's regional policy. This was because the Chinese fiscal system works by having the net revenue-contributing provinces, primarily coastal provinces, send money to the center which in turn helps the poorer provinces. The underperformance in central tax collection made it difficult, at least in 1994–95, for the center to provide funds to the interior in a timely manner.

RURAL ENTERPRISE DEVELOPMENT AND REGIONAL POLICY[8]

Because the fiscal reforms are not expected to produce a fiscal bonanza for the central treasury and for regional redistribution in the short run, the central leadership's rhetoric for balanced regional development has sounded somewhat hollow to interior interests. To at least partially meet the persistent interior demands for an activist regional policy, the central government has promoted a variety of policy measures that do not require much central funding. These measures include encouraging overseas investment to go to the interior and urging coastal provinces to do more to help poorer interior provinces. The rest of this chapter examines another major policy initiative, a program to speed up the development of rural enterprises in interior regions.

Given the coastal region's geographical advantage and superior human resources for business entrepreneurship, it should come as no surprise that in the reform era the non-state sectors have been more vigorous in the coastal region than in the interior, which has traditionally relied on government investment. During the austerity program of 1989, rural enterprises came under pressure as the central government focused its efforts on assisting state enterprises and treated the rural enterprise sector as "stepchildren." By 1991, however, central leaders such as Premier Li Peng had changed from skeptic to major supporter of the rural enterprise sector (D. Yang 1996a: chapter 8). Addressing the fifth session of the seventh National People's Congress in March 1992, Li Peng called on both central and local governments to vigorously support rural enterprise development in interior regions and other underdeveloped areas (Li Peng 1992: 829). In response to Li Peng's call, the State Council and the Ministry of Agriculture elicited studies from various government departments and convened a national symposium at the old revolutionary base Jinggangshan in June 1992. Symposium participants believed that the east–west economic gap was largely due to the regional disparities in rural enterprise development and called for strengthening rural enterprise development in interior regions.[9] Following a November 1992 national conference to exchange experiences in rural enterprise development in interior regions, the State Council formally issued its "Decision on Speeding Up the Development of Rural Enterprises in Central and Western Regions" in February 1993.[10]

The rural enterprise initiative was based on three major considerations. First, it was diagnosed that the growing gap between coast and interior regions was largely accounted for by the differential growth rates of rural enterprises. While the interior regions (central and western regions) had close to two-thirds of China's rural population (64 percent in 1993), their combined share of the national rural enterprise gross output value has hovered at just above one-third of the total, declining by more than three percentage points between the mid-1980s and 1992 (Table 6.1).

As can be expected, the growing gap in rural enterprise development between the regions is also reflected in per capita terms and especially measured in per

Table 6.1 Regional share of rural enterprise gross output value (%)

Year	Total	Eastern	Central	Western	Interior
1980	100	65.0	30.2	4.8	35.0
1985	100	63.2	31.9	4.9	36.8
1990	100	64.9	30.7	4.4	35.1
1991	100	65.7	30.1	4.2	34.3
1992	100	66.4	29.2	4.4	33.6
1993	100	64.2	30.6	5.2	35.8

Sources: Ministry of Agriculture 1993: 260 and 289; Ministry of Agriculture 1994: 19.

capita net income. Table 6.2 presents data on the economic gaps between the coastal region and the other two regions respectively. Item "c" (hereafter the c ratio) measures the per capita gross value of output gaps that are accounted for by the gap in rural enterprise development. Item "f" (hereafter the f ratio) is the gap in rural per capita net income that was accounted for by the gap in per capita earnings from rural enterprises (in percentage terms). For the coastal–central region comparison, the c ratio rose from 68 percent in 1980 to 85 percent in 1992, meaning that 85 percent of the per capita rural output gap between these two regions was accounted for by differences in rural enterprise output in 1992. In the meantime, the f ratio was at 40 percent in 1978, then fluctuated widely through the 1980s, only to rise to 43 percent in 1992, the same level as in 1985.

The most dramatic comparison is between the coastal and the western regions. The c ratio jumped from 60 percent in 1980 to 91 percent in 1992 and the f ratio increased from about 30 percent at the start of the reforms to 50 percent in 1992. In other words, fully 91 percent of the per capital rural gross output gap and 50 percent of the per capita net income gap between the coastal region and the western region may be accounted for by differences in rural enterprise development in 1992. Therefore, it was logical for the central government to hope that speeding up rural enterprise development in interior regions would help narrow the economic disparities between coast and interior and promote common prosperity.

Second, it was recognized that rural enterprise development had reached a new phase in the coastal region. Because of rising labor and land costs, shortage of energy and raw materials, and environmental degradation, it was argued that many enterprises in the coastal region had become ill-suited to labor- and resource-intensive processing industries and needed to move into more skill-based industries. In contrast, the interior regions still had cheap labor and abundant resources and could benefit from the relocation of labor- and resource-intensive industries from the coast. Because it may take a long time before such a spatial replacement and transfer process becomes significant, the central government decided to facilitate the process through policies that provided both

Table 6.2 Rural enterprises and regional gap (yuan, %)

	1978	1980	1985	1990	1991	1992	1993
Eastern–Central gap of:							
a. Rural GOV per capita	–	139	452	1,473	1,859	2,750	–
b. Rural enterprise GOV per capita	–	95	339	1,224	1,510	2,343	–
c. c = (b/a)*100	–	68	75	83	81	85	–
d. Rural net income per capita	20	37	107	266	332	370	532
e. Rural enterprise wages per capita	8	12	46	99	117	159	219
f. f = (e/d)*100	40	32	43	37	35	43	41
Eastern–Western gap of:							
a. Rural GOV per capita	–	207	621	1,864	2,247	3,340	–
b. Rural enterprise GOV per capita	–	124	464	1,659	2,018	3,046	–
c. c = (b/a)*100	–	60	75	89	90	91	–
d. Rural net income per capita	35	58	148	314	361	402	539
e. Rural enterprise wages per capita	11	16	64	140	161	199	292
f. f = (e/d)*100	31	28	43	45	45	50	54

Sources: Ministry of Agriculture 1993: 294–97; Ministry of Agriculture 1994: 19, 21; *ZGTJNJ 1994*: 278, 327; *Zhongguo nongcun tongji nianjian 1993*: 44, 55.

information and incentives for rural enterprises from the coastal region to move into the interior. The center has urged the regions to complement each other for "mutual economic benefit and common prosperity." The coastal region is encouraged to develop technology-intensive industries, promote exports, and transfer some labor-intensive production to the interior while the interior regions are asked to emphasize resource exploitation and processing (Ministry of Agriculture 1993: 21 and 62).

Finally, a major challenge facing all levels of Chinese government has been the creation of employment opportunities for a vast reservoir of rural surplus labor that was officially estimated at 120 million in 1994 and expected to top 200 million by the year 2000 (*CD* 2/9/95: 4). Most importantly, the interior regions have accounted for 65 percent of the total surplus labor force. In the past few years, millions of migrant rural laborers from interior regions have travelled to urban areas and the coast in search of employment opportunities. While the transient workers have made important contributions to economic growth, their sheer numbers, variously estimated at between 50 and 100 million, have posed a major challenge to public facilities in their host communities and are associated with a variety of economic and social problems.[11] A program aimed at promoting rural enterprise development in interior regions would serve to alleviate China's employment crisis and reduce the pressures from the flow of transient workers.

Key program components

The State Council decision of 1993 made rural enterprise development the strategic focus of the interior regions' economic development program. Besides signalling to domestic and foreign investors that investing in interior regions was an option for serious consideration, the central government also adopted a number of measures for the implementation of the government program, including increases in credit allocations and tax incentives and a project to promote inter-regional cooperation.

Credit policy

In 1992, the People's Bank of China authorized 2 billion yuan in bank loan quota and 3 billion yuan in rural credit cooperative loan quota to support rural enterprise development in interior regions. Anticipating the promulgation of the State Council decision, the People's Bank also decided in November 1992 to provide 5 billion yuan per annum from 1993 to 2000 in special loans for interior-based rural enterprises, to be disbursed through the Agricultural Bank of China (Ministry of Agriculture 1993: 70–71; State Council Office of Research 1993: 246). In September 1993, at the National Conference on Rural Enterprise Work, it was announced that the State Council had authorized a further 5 billion yuan per year in special loans to support interior-based rural enterprises over 1994–2000 (*Zhongguo xiangzhen qiye bao* 9/22/93: 9). In addition, at the end of 1992, the Agricultural Bank of China set up a 100-million-yuan special discount loan program for rural enterprises located in ethnic minority areas (*Ibid.* 11/16/92: 1).

Tax incentives

Besides the special loans, rural enterprises were also granted various tax incentives. Whereas China's fiscal reforms stipulated uniform taxes for enterprises of all ownerships, all newly established rural enterprises were to be exempted from income tax for three years in old revolutionary base areas, minority nationality regions, border regions, and poor areas. Provincial-level governments in Inner Mongolia, Xinjiang, Ningxia, Tibet, Guangxi, Yunnan, and Qinghai were also authorized to make special policies for rural enterprises in light of local situations (*Zhonghua gongshang shibao* 9/7/94: 6). In addition, rural enterprises in interior regions were exempted from the fixed capital investment orientation adjustment tax (Ministry of Agriculture 1993: 3; State Council Office of Research 1993: 5).

East–west cooperation

In his speech to the Xi'an conference on exchanging experiences in November 1992, Vice Premier Tian Jiyun called for promoting economic and technological inter-regional cooperation so as to speed up the development of rural enterprises in the interior. Following a study of the cooperative efforts between the eastern region and Shaanxi and Gansu provinces in rural enterprise development, the Rural Enterprise Bureau of the Ministry of Agriculture proposed an East–West Cooperation Project on Rural Enterprises at the 1993 national conference on rural enterprise work (subsequently renamed the East–West Rural Enterprise Cooperation and Demonstration Project) and secured the State Council's support in principle. Because of bureaucratic disagreement over financing and management, however, the project did not receive formal State Council approval until spring 1995.[12] Nevertheless, in the government's plans for agricultural and rural work in 1994, the CCP Central Committee and the State Council pointed to the need to "organize and implement the East–West Cooperation and Demonstration Project of Rural Enterprises and promote inter-regional economic cooperation" (Nie Xinpeng 1994: 10). By the end of 1995, the Ministry of Agriculture had approved 124 rural enterprise east–west cooperation demonstration zones (*RMRBO* 12/20/95: 4). As of mid-1996, 15 provinces have established leading groups in the cooperation program. The program is expected to generate 150 billion yuan in profits and taxes and create 5 million jobs in the interior over 1996–2000. The central government hopes that the eastern region will transfer one-third of its labor-intensive raw materials-processing industries into the interior (*QB* 6/17/96: 2).

Local government responses

The central government policy on promoting rural enterprise development in interior regions was announced amid a growing realization among interior leaders that rural enterprises could play a crucial role as an engine of economic growth and a major source of government revenue and rural income. Having lagged behind coastal provinces in rural enterprise development, the interior provinces were eager to do more to catch up. Thus the State Council decision on promoting rural enterprises in interior regions coincided with local impulses and quickly stimulated a range of local responses.

Most prominently, governments at various levels in the interior quickly sought to strengthen leadership over rural enterprise development. A survey by the Ministry of Agriculture found that most local governments in five provinces (Hubei, Hunan, Guangxi, Yunnan, and Guizhou) surveyed established a Leading Group on Rural Enterprises in early 1993. At the provincial level, the leading group, usually headed by the governor or chairman of the autonomous region and including the heads of various committees, bureaux, and offices concerned with rural enterprises, was to make major policy decisions on rural enterprises and coordinate various bureaucratic departments to support rural enterprise development. Indeed, Party Secretary Yue Qifeng of Heilongjiang gained national attention by calling on the province to shift its attention to the "second battlefield," i.e., non-state economic activities.

In a number of provinces the government bureaux overseeing rural enterprises were upgraded. In Hunan and Guangxi, for instance, the Rural Enterprise Bureaux of prefectures and counties were renamed the Rural Enterprise Economic Commission (Hunan) or Rural Enterprise Management Commission (Guangxi), attaining equal bureaucratic rank with similar commissions for Economy and Trade, Planning, and Agriculture (Special Investigation Group 1993: 103–104). Local cadres also devoted more attention to rural enterprise work. In Hunan, Hubei, and Guangxi, a majority of the township cadres had responsibility for rural enterprises.

The net effect of increased administrative guidance over rural enterprises is difficult to assess. Yet we have a sense that rising administrative involvement in rural enterprise development may have been a mixed blessing and will also have varied impact in different areas (Byrd and Gelb 1990: 358–87). Whereas it is probably necessary for local governments to strengthen leadership over and management of rural enterprises, if the local government involved seeks to replace the market with bureaucratic interference, the effect on rural enterprise development may in fact be undesirable. Studies have shown that undue administrative interference has undermined the normal operations of rural enterprises in some areas (Du Shiguo 1993).

The increased administrative involvement in rural enterprise development is also reflected in the choice of locations for priority development. Interior provinces have been less concerned about intra-provincial inequalities than about catching up with or at least not falling further behind the more prosperous coastal provinces (Ministry of Finance 1993: 1). In their drive to attain maximum economic growth, provincial governments in interior regions have generally laid more emphasis on supporting rural enterprises in relatively developed localities to make the best (economic) use of limited financial resources. This led to the establishment of 114 rural industrial zones by mid-1994 (Tian Fengshan 1994). Local governments also authorized various special policies for the rural industrial zones, including preferential policies in land use, finance, and credit, and household registration. These preferential policies were designed to enhance the attractiveness of rural enterprises as an investment vehicle as the preferential tax treatment accorded rural enterprises was to be phased out by the end of 1995.

Financing rural enterprise development

In spite of the official commitment to rural enterprise development in interior regions, financially strapped local governments have found it difficult to increase substantially the amount of budgetary allocations to the rural enterprise sector.[13] In Shaanxi province, fixed-asset investment in rural enterprises reached 2.6 billion yuan in 1993, of which only 58 million yuan or 2.2 percent of the total were supplied by local authorities (Zhao Tianzhen and Min Zhimin 1994: 37–38). As for provincial funds as a proportion of total investment in rural enterprises, Hunan had a target of 0.83 percent (50 million yuan), Hubei 0.44 percent (20 million yuan), and Guangxi 0.48 percent (30 million) in 1993 (Special Investigation Group 1993: 104–105). In light of the high hopes local governments had for developing rural enterprises, these percentages appear quite low and underscore the development dilemmas facing interior localities. As Byrd and Lin pointed out, local governments in poorer areas were more likely to be predatory (or rent-seeking) toward rural enterprises than their coastal counterparts (Byrd and Gelb 1990).

Unable to increase their own financial commitment to rural enterprises significantly, various local governments have invariably leaned on the banking sector to come up with extra credit. Under China's ongoing financial reforms, however, banks have become reluctant to fund projects with low economic returns. The Agricultural Bank of China in fact stipulated that special loans for interior-based rural enterprises must meet certain conditions, among which the ratio of overdue loans was not to exceed 10 percent and the ratio of non-performing loans was not to exceed 5 percent (State Council Office of Research 1993: 253–54). In reality, at the end of 1991, overdue and non-performing loans accounted for over 40 percent of Agricultural Bank and credit coops' loans to rural enterprises in these regions, much higher than the comparable figure for the coastal region. It is thus to be expected that the Agricultural Bank and credit coops would loan most of their funds (about 70 percent) to rural enterprises in the eastern coast (Ministry of Agriculture 1993: 314–17; State Council Office of Research 1993: 251). Improvement in inter-bank lending in recent years has facilitated such inter-regional financial flows.

While initial plans called for earmarking 5 billion yuan in low-interest loans to support rural enterprises in interior regions, the People's Bank decided later on in the same year that it could only provide ordinary commercial loans. Under commercial criteria, only 60 percent of the 5 billion yuan was disbursed by the end of the year in 1993 (Qi Jingfa 1994; authors' interviews). Similarly, the bulk of the special loans the State Council pledged were not disbursed in 1994 (Lam 1995e: 1).

Not only were the specially earmarked rural enterprise development funds not fully disbursed, but in some regions the amount of loans to rural enterprises from the Agricultural Bank decreased. In Guangxi, the Agricultural Bank's loan quota was reduced from 1.9 billion yuan in 1992 to 1.3 billion yuan in 1993; ordinary loans to rural enterprises fell from 200 million in 1992 to 66 million in 1993 (Special Investigation Group 1993: 107–108). In Anhui, rural enterprise loans accounted for 15.1 percent of the Agricultural Bank's loan portfolio in 1992 but merely 11.3 percent in the first half of 1993 (Anhui Shengwei Zhengyanshi 1993: 10–13).

In conclusion, in spite of strong official commitment to rural enterprise development in interior regions, local governments have found it difficult to channel the requisite funds to rural enterprises. Perhaps in recognition of this dilemma, the central government has started to steer more international aid from international organizations and bilateral programs into interior regions.

Inter-regional cooperation

In light of the limited funds available, the Ministry of Agriculture in 1994 launched the East–West Rural Enterprise Cooperation and Demonstration Project. Built on a long-standing government policy to enhance economic and technological cooperation between economically developed provinces and less developed areas, the inter-regional cooperation program seeks to set up 100 east–west cooperation and demonstration zones with 1 billion yuan of gross output value each and select 1,000 industrial demonstration projects in central and western regions by 2000. The Ministry of Agriculture also plans to assist 100 pairs of cities and counties in establishing bilateral cooperation in rural enterprise development and, together with the State Science and Technology Commission, to help train 10,000 backbone technicians and factory managers for interior regions in six years (Cheng Shan 1994: 1–3; Liu Jiang 1992: 662; *Zhonghua gongshang shibao* 9/30/94).

The Cooperation and Demonstration Project is still in its infancy. In August 1994 the Ministry of Agriculture authorized the first batch of 66 demonstration zones and 93 demonstration projects (*Zhongguo xiangzhen qiye bao* 10/13/94).[14] The demonstration zones, selected from a list of 120 submitted by interior provinces, included five high-technology demonstration zones, one agricultural and by-product processing demonstration zone, 14 suburban rural enterprise zones and 42 rural enterprise zones in small towns (*Zhonghua gongshang shibao* 9/30/94). They are generally concentrated in more developed areas of the interior, including the suburbs of big and medium-sized cities and well-situated small towns. Some of the demonstration zones also fall under the rubric of State Spark Technology-intensive Zones sponsored by the State Science and Technology Commission (*Zhongguo xiangzhen qiye bao* 10/13/94). The number of demonstration zones approved by the Ministry of Agriculture reached a total of 124 in spring 1995 (Jiang Xia 1995).

The Cooperation and Demonstration Project is designed to generate a big wave, in externalities such as information about the feasibility of certain kinds of projects, with a small amount of money. The Ministry of Agriculture has had little choice. When it asked the Ministry of Finance and local financial departments to contribute 5 million yuan each in special training funds in its plan for the Cooperation and Demonstration Project in February 1994, the Finance Ministry replied that under the present fiscal system such funds should be provided by local governments and instructed local governments to "properly arrange [for the funds] in light of local conditions." The State Science and Technology Commission likewise believed that local governments should be the main source of funds for the project. With no central financial backing in sight, the Ministry of Agriculture dropped the original request for funds in the revised project plan that was reported to the State Council in June 1994 (*Zhonghua gongshang shibao* 9/7/94: 6).

The bureaucratic wrangling notwithstanding, some progress has been made via an innovative inter-regional exchange program. Under this program, thousands of township officials in poor regions, such as Shaanxi, received training in coastal provinces, such as Jiangsu and Shandong, beginning in 1994. The exchange program also dispatched cadres from coastal provinces to work in poor areas. Funding came from local governments and private donations in more developed areas (Cao Min 1995: 2). By spring 1995, 16 provincial units had established partnerships under the auspices of the program (*CD* 4/24/95: 1).

It appears that the initiation of the Cooperation and Demonstration Project has prompted some local governments and enterprises in the coastal region to think seriously about heading to the west or accelerating the pace for doing so. In Shandong, the Rural Enterprise Bureau of the prosperous Yantai Municipality announced that 100 Yantai-based industrial enterprises were to invest 300 million yuan in the western region in a three-year period. It was forecast that the investment would increase western tax revenue by 100 million yuan (Liu Haijie 1994: 18–19). The Shandong provincial government formulated a plan to enlist 300 backbone town and township enterprises to establish partnerships with their counterparts in interior regions (Jiang Xia 1995). Most prominently, the Zhejiang-based Wanxiang Group announced with much fanfare a "Going West Scheme" to develop interior China in April 1994. By October 1994, the group had elicited some 1,092 domestic and foreign business letters and was visited by 48 delegations, including several from interior governments, interested in cooperation. The Group had plans to invest 100 million yuan in interior regions in order to reduce production costs and gain better access to raw materials and potential markets (Plan 1994; *Zhongguo xiangzhen qiye bao* 7/18/94). Other high-profile cases have included Jiangsu's Huaxi Village, which is investing 20 million yuan in Heilongjiang and Ningxia and Guangdong's Nanshan Group, which plans to invest 200 million yuan in Guangxi (*QB* 6/17/96: 2).

While Yantai, Wanxiang, and others jumped on the bandwagon of a central policy, it should be clear that they did so not just to gain publicity – although Chinese companies have come to appreciate the value of good publicity – but to seek room for business expansion, since the interior regions are rich in raw materials and are an expanding market. Moreover, coastal entrepreneurs also hope to partake of the 10-billion-yuan special loans for rural enterprise development in interior regions. In the meantime, the interior regions benefit from the superior managerial and technical skills outside investors bring in. Between 1995 and mid-1996, over 10,000 cooperative agreements involving 30 billion yuan were signed between rural enterprises in the two regions. Under these agreements, the interior regions are expected to receive nearly 15 billion yuan through investments in 2,100 enterprises (*QB* 6/17/96: 2).

CONCLUSIONS

In spite of the adjustments in central government policies, the deficit-plagued central government has lacked the fiscal strength to bring about a major shift in the patterns of regional development. From the fiscal perspective, the restructuring of central–local relations through fiscal and tax reforms offers an important avenue for promoting interior development. Yet, while the interior regions supported and cheered the fiscal restructuring, the structure of the fiscal and taxation reforms imply that the center is not likely to see a sharp increase in its discretionary spending power soon. In consequence, the center is not likely to have much more money to redistribute to the interior regions until the fiscal reforms truly bring up the center's control over fiscal resources.

Fiscally constrained, the central government has resorted to various low-cost measures, such as calls for more overseas investment in the interior, and for rural enterprise development and inter-regional cooperation to at least partially fulfill its promise of more balanced regional development. Has implementation of the State Council decision on speeding up rural enterprise development in interior regions been successful in achieving its goals? Has it helped to narrow the coast–interior economic gap? In spite of the short duration of the program, it appears that, like the other policy measures, the policies promoting rural enterprises in interior regions have had some positive effect. Following the promulgation of the policies, growth of the rural enterprise sector in interior regions accelerated. For 1993, the gross output value of rural enterprises rose by 77.6 percent in the interior regions, compared with a 61.6 increase in the eastern region (the national figure was 66.6 percent).[15] In the first three quarters of 1994, the gross industrial output value of township and village enterprises increased by 72.6 percent in interior regions and 46.14 percent in the eastern region compared with the same period of 1993 (Liu Jiang 1994). In consequence, the interior regions' share of rural enterprise gross output value rose *vis-à-vis* that of the eastern region.

However, leaving aside the question of data reliability, the gross output value figures are a poor indicator of developmental progress.[16] The development of rural enterprises in interior regions started from a lower base and needed to grow faster just in order not to fall further behind. In fact, the rapid growth of interior rural enterprises has failed to put a dent in the per capita income gap between coast and interior in the 1990s. Similarly, even though in 1993 rural enterprise wage income as a percentage of rural net income per capita increased by 6.8 percentage points in interior regions compared with only 5.3 percentage points in the eastern region, because of the higher wage levels in the eastern region, rural households' per capita wage gap as a proportion of per capita net income gap between the eastern region and interior regions remained steady (44.6 percent in 1992 and 44.8 percent in 1993). As a result, the actual rural per capita net income gaps between the eastern region and interior regions has risen.

In conclusion, during the short period since the State Council decision on speeding up rural enterprise development in interior regions was promulgated, rural enterprise development in the interior has indeed picked up substantially, aided by various forms of government support. Unlike central government sponsored poverty-relief programs, rural enterprises in the east are not forced to march inland (Wu Guoqing 1995: 6). Many local governments and rural enterprises responded enthusiastically to the central government policies because these suited their interests. Yet partly because of its short duration and partly because it was still limited in scale, the program as a whole has not stopped the economic gap between coast and interior from widening further. While helpful, the regionally based rural development program as well as the calls for more overseas investment and inter-regional cooperation are not enough to alter the existing patterns of regional development. In any case, as the debate over the future of the special economic zones (chapter 7) indicates, the central government has no intention of promoting interior development at the expense of coastal interests.

7 The debate over special economic zones

As mentioned in earlier chapters, for interior interests, the special economic zones epitomized the center's preferential treatment toward the coastal region and symbolized China's favor-the-rich regional development strategy. Nevertheless, by the late 1980s, central leaders had already started to urge the special economic zones to pay heed to the interests of the interior. When Vice Premier Tian Jiyun visited Shenzhen in April–May 1987, he commented that Shenzhen's experiences should not only radiate to the rest of the coastal region but also reach western China (Shenzhenshi Dang'anguan 1991: 255). Similarly, in late 1987 the senior statesman Bo Yibo called on Shenzhen and other special economic zones to help the interior through capital investment, technical transfer, information exchanges, and personnel training. Bo commented that the interior should be made to feel that it benefitted from the zones.

With the ascendance of Li Peng and Yao Yilin – the latter was a persistent critic of the special economic zones in the 1980s – and the imposition of economic austerity in 1988, the special economic zones were apprehensive about their future. During the annual session of the National People's Congress in spring 1989, then Shenzhen Mayor Li Hao argued against the view that Shenzhen was fattened through state investments and that it only made money out of the interior. He enumerated Shenzhen's growing financial contributions to the country, including 800 million yuan in fiscal revenue handed over to the center and to Guangdong province. Moreover, banks in Shenzhen remitted more than 1.09 billion yuan in profits and taxes and customs revenue amounted to over 7.2 billion yuan. One-third of the enterprises in Shenzhen had interior links. Interior areas also received nearly 4 billion yuan in labor remittances, and enterprises based on lateral linkages earned 2 billion yuan in net profits (Shenzhenshi Dang'anguan 1991: 338).[1]

The Tiananmen crackdown spread more political jitters through the southeastern coastal areas. Shenzhen, in particular, launched a major "diplomatic" offensive to cement relations with interior provinces and promote its image as reformer with a conscience. At the end of August 1989, Mayor Li Hao led an 11-person delegation and visited Heilongjiang and Jilin provinces to discuss economic cooperation. Deputy Mayor Zhou Xiwu paid a 20-day visit to Yunnan and Sichuan and negotiated various industrial and commercial ventures. Deputy Mayor Zhang Hongyi spent half a month in Xinjiang and Gansu and agreed to a variety of cooperative projects (Shenzhenshi Dang'anguan 1991: 346–47).

Shenzhen and other zones' fear of political backlashes from hardliners proved to be short-lived. Instead, as has been discussed in chapter 3, the 1990s have seen the rapid extension of various preferential policies to the rest of the country.[2] Political jitters were soon replaced by concerns about growing competition from Shanghai, Tianjin, and other areas. Unbeknownst to the special economic zones, however, a new storm was brewing over their status as a debate arose over the direction of China's regional development policy for the Ninth Five-Year Plan period (1996–2000) and beyond.

THE INTERIOR PROVINCES DEMAND THEIR OWN SPECIAL ECONOMIC ZONES

Ironically, the immediate cause of the debate over the status of the special economic zones was a demand for more such zones by interior interests. Recall that the central government had promised in earlier economic plans to gradually shift its regional development focus to the interior, and interior regions had steadily requested preferential policies of their own. As the Yunnan economist Liu Long reasoned, once the border areas were offered preferential policies, capital and human talent would flow into the underdeveloped ethnic minority areas and other problems would be easily resolved (Liu Long 1991: 23). Later, Liu and others argued that the central government and more developed areas should not only bring capital and technology to underdeveloped areas but should do more to compensate for past policy decisions. Because the rising regional disparities are partly caused by preferential policy treatment for the coastal region, it behooves the central government to offer underdeveloped, especially ethnic, areas policies that are even more preferential than those enjoyed by the coastal special economic zones so that the underdeveloped areas may start to catch up with the coast (Liu Long 1993: 11).

After more than a decade of waiting for the center to modify its pro-coast policies, interior interests stepped up their demand for regional policy change in anticipation of the drafting of the Ninth Five-Year Plan (1996–2000). Since previous five-year plans had indicated that the geographic focus of China's development would gradually shift to the interior by the 1990s, interior interests in essence called the central government's bluff by arguing that "it's time to extend the policy [for the coastal region's success] to the less developed areas" (Cheung Lai-kuen 1996).[3] In the words of Shanxi Governor Sun Wensheng: "The central government has repeatedly identified the east–west divide as one of the main problems facing national development, now we are giving it an opportunity to act" (Hewitt 1995).

In spring 1994 a proposal gained favor among some, especially older, CCP leaders. The proposal called for establishing special economic zones in western

China, particularly in the old revolutionary base areas of the northwest that still suffered from abject poverty nearly half a century after the Communist Party had assumed power. The proposal won substantial support from NPC delegates as well as retired revolutionary leaders (Chen Ko 1994). There was a further rise in the number of local demands for preferential policies, tax exemptions, and special economic zones during the National People's Congress session in spring 1995 and during meetings in Beidaihe in August 1995 (*RMRBO* 12/30/95: 1; Lam 1995f).[4]

The demand for special economic zones in the interior won preliminary support from senior members of the State Council Office of Special Economic Zones. According to Liu Fuyuan, a deputy director of that office who was a staunch advocate of regional rather than industrial policies, it was time to consider having a number of special economic zones in the central region, such as Hunan, Hubei, Anhui, and Henan, as new growth centers integrating into the national economy even though, as mentioned a little later, members of the same office indicated that the preferential treatment for the coastal special economic zones ought to be temporary (Liu Fuyuan 1994; China Considers 1995; Hubei People's Radio, FBIS-CHI-95-164, 8/24/95, 1995: 28-29).[5] The possibility of new special economic zones appeared to add momentum to the lobbying for interior-based special economic zones. In Sichuan, supporters for the establishment of a free-trade zone in Chengdu believed that it was crucial to set up such a zone in landlocked Sichuan in order to narrow the economic gap between the southwest and the coastal region. By fall 1994, Sichuan had set up an office to prepare for the establishment of a free-trade zone and a consortium of companies also formed a joint company to the same effect in December 1994 (Guo Yongqing 1995). Nowhere was the interior drive for special economic zone status more ambitious and determined than in landlocked Shanxi. Once he became Shanxi governor in March 1994, Sun Wensheng advocated that the whole of Shanxi should be designated a special economic zone so that the province could "act as a bridge between western China and the developed coastal regions." He brought in the same experts who put together the Pudong Development Program to conduct a feasibility study of Shanxi's proposal and argued that the model of the coastal special economic zones was just as applicable to inland areas that needed a catalyst "to jump-start the process" of interior development (Hewitt 1995).

THE ARGUMENT AGAINST SPECIAL ECONOMIC ZONES

The interior demand for special economic zones elicited a range of responses. Within the government, it provoked government officials to defend the *status quo*. For instance, Sun Shangqing, the late director of the State Council Development Research Center, offered the lame argument that inland provinces should not follow the same industrial and trade practices or the same economic policies as coastal provinces and should instead concentrate on improving living standards by their own means (Crothall 1995).

More interestingly, a small number of commentators began to offer principled arguments against preferential policies in general and the special economic zones in particular. They pointed out that, while the myriad preferential policies played some positive role in promoting China's economic take-off, these policies also distorted economic incentives and produced various negative consequences. As a result, government departments and enterprises seek preferential policies and treatment, e.g., by passing themselves off as joint ventures, school-run enterprises, or collective enterprises, instead of devoting their energy to improving technology and management. This hinders China's efforts to readjust its industrial structure and improve economic efficiency. Moreover, by encouraging local authorities to offer tax reductions and exemptions, the proliferation of preferential treatment undermines the integrity of state laws and stipulations. Finally, preferential treatment for foreign investors weakens the competitiveness of domestic enterprises rather than fostering fair competition (Kan Cunduan and Pan Fengqiu 1994; Zhang Jun 1994). Seeking an early closure to the debate, President Jiang Zemin said in June 1994 that it was erroneous to think that the role and function of the special economic zones would weaken and gradually disappear with China's comprehensive opening up. While he urged the special economic zones to move labor-intensive industries inland and pay attention to narrowing the disparities between the coast and the interior, Jiang stipulated that the center had not changed its determination to develop the zones or its basic policies toward the zones. Moreover, the zones were to retain their role and functions in China's reform and opening up (*RMRB* 6/23/94: 1).

In a testimony to the progress of liberalization in China, critics of the preferential policies continued their crusade in spite of President Jiang Zemin's June 1994 statement. Especially vocal in the attack on preferential policies and special economic zones was Hu Angang, a researcher at the Chinese Academy of Sciences, who had earlier argued that the proliferation of development zones served to undermine the fiscal strength of the state because they invariably offered tax reductions or exemptions (Wang Shaoguang and Hu Angang 1993a, 1993b). In 1994 and onwards, Hu argued that rising regional inequality had become a source of social and political instability, warning that "the deep differences between the North and South more than 100 years ago led to the Civil War" in the United States. While he could not find quotes from Deng Xiaoping to support his arguments, Hu nevertheless concluded that "If Deng Xiaoping knew the disparities were as big as they are, he would be more militant than I am in trying to eliminate [the rising regional disparities]" (quoted in Tyler 1995). Accordingly, Hu openly called for ending the privileges enjoyed by special economic zones and for spreading wealth to poor interior provinces in order to preserve social stability and encourage fair competition between the special economic zones and other areas (Hsu Ching-hui 1995). For Hu, the success of China's tax reforms and move to a national market meant that the "special economic zones should no longer possess a 'special status,' that is, no longer be 'special' in terms of preferential policies." In an environment of fair competition, no localities should receive "extra economic privileges that are not prescribed by the existing laws and system" (Hu Angang 1995).[6]

It was a testimony to the popularity of the criticisms of preferential treatment that attacks on the special economic zones intensified in 1995. Delegates to the National People's Congress, particularly those from interior regions, reportedly showered the central government with grievances about the special economic zones' special privileges and called for readjustment in spring 1995 (Zhong Liqiong 1996). Indeed, even members of the State Council's Office for Special Economic Zones seemed to see the writing on the wall and conceded to the general argument against the continuation of the special economic zones. Zhao Yundong, a deputy director of that office, reportedly wrote: "All privileged policies in the special economic zones are of a temporary nature which cannot be continued in the long-term." Elaborating on a statement by Vice Premier Li Lanqing that the special economic zones should adopt international standards rather than rely on preferential policies, Zhao stated that "the special economic zones will in the future switch from relying on tax breaks and profit incentives to relying on highly efficient administration, a solid investment environment and a complete market system." In the words of Zhang Yu, a researcher at that office, "once the market economy is fully established through the country, the historical duty of the special economic zones in the reform and opening will have been completed and the 'specialness' of the special economic zones should draw to an end," though Zhang argued against an immediate end to the preferential policies (quoted in Gilley 1995).

SHENZHEN FIGHTS BACK

Caught in the political crossfire are the special economic zones such as Shenzhen and Zhuhai that have benefitted from fiscal and tax privileges and expanded local autonomy since the early 1980s. Because of the preferential treatment and proximity to overseas markets such as Hong Kong, the special economic zones have achieved phenomenal economic successes. With just 0.35 percent of China's territory and only 0.8 percent of the total population, they attracted about a fifth of actual foreign investment over 1985–94.[7] The zones also accounted for 14 percent of China's exports in 1994 (*RMRBO* 9/28/95: 2; Gilley 1995). By 1995, Shenzhen's gross value of industrial output had reached 79.8 billion yuan and its foreign trade stood at US$39.1 billion. Actual foreign investment in Shenzhen alone was US$1.65 billion (Xinhua 1/10/96, FBIS-CHI-96–013 1/19/96: 50).

In many ways, the special economic zones, including Shenzhen, Zhuhai, Shantou, Xiamen, and Hainan, have become victims of their own success. In spite of the tax holidays and import privileges, they face slower growth prospects owing to high land and labor costs and infrastructural bottlenecks while other areas have also adopted some liberal investment policies and now compete for the same investment.[8] Shenzhen's pains of adjustment were also compounded by overambitious expansion plans, the central government's tight credit policy, as well as bureaucratic inefficiencies (*WSJ* 12/29/95: 1; "Shenzhen Reports" 1995).[9] In the first half of 1995, Shenzhen experienced a 30 percent drop in the number of newly-registered companies and a rise in the volume of business terminations ("Shenzhen Reports" 1995). Zhuhai also lost important personnel and businesses to neighboring areas in Guangdong.

In this context, it was a shock to the special economic zones to hear the argument that they had fulfilled their historic mission and that their privileges should be terminated. Officials in Shenzhen and other special economic zones perceived the shifting sentiments and worked hard to lobby for retaining existing privileges. In 1994–95, Shenzhen officials made significant contributions to "help-the-poor" causes. The city had an economic development fund which provided investments to old revolutionary base areas such as Jinggangshan of Jiangxi, Yan'an of Shaanxi, Hong'an of Hubei, as well as the three gorges area and an ethnic region in Sichuan (*RMRBO* 1/22/96: 4). Local leaders spent substantial sums of money and time wining and dining central leaders on inspection trips in order to curry favor with Beijing (Lam 1995g).

Shenzhen officials and various scholars had realized that Shenzhen was facing greater challenges ahead before the calls for the abolition of preferential treatment.[10] Some argued that Shenzhen should be built into China's economic growth pole (Sang Baichuan 1994) while others, such as Professor Peng Lixun, Director of the Shenzhen Social Sciences Research Center, called for making Shenzhen into a world city or metropolitan city of the Pearl River Delta. There were also calls for making Shenzhen into a free trade port and upgrading Shenzhen into a city under the direct jurisdiction of the central government (like Beijing or Shanghai) (Li Maosheng and Bo Dongxiu 1995).

Most remarkably, Shenzhen and the other special economic zones launched a spectacular media counteroffensive against those who called for an end to the special economic zones, particularly Hu Angang, who they feared had gained favor with central leaders. Various essays by Shenzhen-based writers indirectly criticized Hu for improperly attributing the rising regional disparities to the preferential policies for special economic zones. They argued that zone critics "were exaggerating the domestic regional disparities in order to weaken the openness of China's southeastern coastal areas" (Tang Jie 1995; Tan Gang 1995; see also Zhou Wenzhang 1995). One author even went as far as to suggest that the development of the special economic zones was conducive to narrowing the disparities between coast and interior because the zones were investing in the rest of the country (Guo Can 1995). A lengthy article in the *Shenzhen tequ bao* on September 6, 1995 charged that Hu's argument was contrary to Deng Xiaoping's theories and asserted that a relatively large disparity in development for a short term was no cause for alarm. It called Hu's viewpoint "present-day egalitarianism that is damaging to the nation and the people" and "a fallacious argument sowing unnecessary discontent" (Zhong Liqiong 1996).

Shenzhen's leading fighter in the media war was none other than Party Secretary Li Youwei. As on many political issues in China, Li Youwei first linked the special economic zones with the imprimatur of Deng Xiaoping. He stated that it was Deng Xiaoping who proposed that some areas should develop first and that China could then achieve common prosperity by asking these areas to help the poor areas. But Deng was quoted as having said that those areas that developed first would not be asked to make sacrifices for other areas before the end of the century: "It is not time to make demands on you yet. At least we will not do so before the end of the century. When the time comes, you will have to contribute more to the state. Then we can support the development of the western regions and achieve common prosperity" (quote in Li Youwei 1995a: 35).

Moreover, Li Youwei pointed out that the state already depended on revenue from the coastal region. He also asserted that the state was investing more in the interior regions, especially the western region, than in the coastal areas. Li concluded, "the more you want to develop the western areas, the more you must support development in the coastal areas. When the coastal areas are developed, western China will also develop swiftly." Thus Li brushed aside criticism that the special economic zones represented rent-seeking special interests and countered that such criticism "not only amounts to mudslinging at the builders of special economic zones, but is in fact making false charges at the central leaders" such as Deng Xiaoping and Jiang Zemin (Li Youwei 1995a; see also 1995b, 1995c). Writing as if Shenzhen were making sacrifices for the country, Li Youwei declared:

Shenzhen belongs to the whole country. Shenzhen must wholeheartedly act in accordance with the spirit of the instructions of the Central Committee and Comrade Xiaoping, continue to grasp the opportune moment to deepen reforms and open wider to the outside world, and make more contributions to the country. This is our unshirkable responsibility; it is also our consistent stand. When the economy of Shenzhen becomes even stronger, our contributions will be even greater.

(Li Youwei 1995a)

Later on in 1995, Li Youwei would further elaborate on this theme and argue that "we work neither for ourselves nor for the small team of Shenzhen, but for China to be a 'championship team' in the world, and for socialism in its contest with capitalism" (Wang Zhenzhi and Wang Chien 1995).

Finally, the most substantial allies for the special zones are the overseas investors that benefitted from preferential treatment. Part of the *raison d'être* for establishing the special economic zones was to attract overseas capital, especially from ethnic Chinese who lived overseas, to facilitate China's reunification with Hong Kong, Macao, and eventually Taiwan. Thus Li Youwei emphasized that in addition to the role of pioneer reformer, Shenzhen also carried the historical mission of integrating with Hong Kong (and in the case of Zhuhai, Macao) in order to facilitate the latter's return to Chinese sovereignty (Li Youwei 1995a).

Joining Li Youwei in arguing the special economic zones' case was a curious mixture of luminaries, including the liberal economist Yu Guangyuan and Yuan Mu, the former government spokesman during the 1989 crackdown. Yu Guangyuan argued in spring 1995 that the regional disparities had been given undue prominence and suggested that the booming special economic zones had not been bad for the growth of inland areas and had in fact served as an impetus to the nation's overall economic growth. He concluded that China should not sacrifice the further expansion of special economic zones for the sake of balanced regional development (Haikou 1995; Gan Yuanzhi 1995). Yuan Mu (1994), writing as the Director of the State Council's Research Office in mid-1994, was more blunt, saying that "it is groundless and wrong to say that the special economic zones' position and role will weaken comparatively and then gradually disappear because China has opened up comprehensively." While he conceded that some of the policies first adopted by the special economic zones had spread to the rest of the country and urged the special economic zones to help promote economic development in the interior regions, Yuan nevertheless argued that the special economic zones "should have some 'special' characteristics and keep certain preferential policies" (Yuan Mu 1994). By 1995, a member of the research staff at the State Council Office for Special Economic Zones would characterize those who called for an immediate end to special economic zones' privileges as having "leftist thinking" and pointed out that the preferential policies for Brazil's Manaus free-trade zone would be phased out over an 18-year period beginning in 1995 (Gilley 1995).

By fall 1995, it appears that an official line on the special economic zones was forming. Official publications such as the *People's Daily* praised Shenzhen for laying a solid foundation for the new edifice of socialism, by emphasizing real action rather than empty talk, and for contributing to China's cultural development and urban civilization. Shenzhen was also said to have played a powerful role in setting an example for and bringing along the inland provinces (Lei Yulan 1995; Wang Chu 1995). The State Council's Development Research Center reminded its audience that President Jiang Zemin had emphasized in 1994 that Shenzhen, Zhuhai, and Xiamen had an important political role to play in integrating Hong Kong and Macao with the Mainland and, in the case of Xiamen, as a go-between between Taiwan and the Mainland (Tatlow 1995; Chung Wen 1994). As one of the official reports pointedly concluded: "Shenzhen's special historical mission and special role are far from over" (Wang Chu 1995).

THE CENTER'S DECISION

The center's resolution of the debate over the future of the special economic zones was to seek to please both sides. Toward the end of 1995, Hu Ping, director of the State Council Office for Special Economic Zones, confirmed that the center would not allow the interior to set up special economic zones or approve new state-level economic and technological development zones. Yet, as a concession, it also decided to open more interior cities to foreign investors as "open cities," thereby extending the trend toward greater geographic liberalization in the hope of encouraging more overseas investment in interior regions. In mid-1996, interior provinces were also given the same authority to approve investment projects as the coastal provinces and special economic zones (i.e., 30 million yuan per project).

In the meantime, the center also decided to allow the special economic zones, plus Pudong and the Suzhou–Singapore Industrial Park, to continue to offer low tax rates of 15 percent (compared to the national level of 30 percent) and low tariff rates for capital goods imports to overseas investors within a grace period before these privileges are phased out in 2000.[11] According to Hu Ping, the special economic zones have to face up to China's new economic situation and must prepare to compete with their Mainland counterparts and international rivals on a level playing ground rather than depend on policy preferences. China's application to become a member of the World Trade Organization was cited as leaving little room for regional preferences within China (Hu Ping 1995). However, Hu Ping dismissed the argument that "the special economic zones are no longer special" as fundamentally groundless. He stated that the basic policy on special economic zones would not change, and the zones certainly would not be eliminated (Zhong Liqiong 1996). In essence, as Li Youwei had requested, the special economic zones were allowed to keep the essential preferential policies (including low tax and tariff rates) until the end of the century, thereby allowing the zones more time to upgrade to more skill-based industries.[12]

The central government also reaffirmed its commitment to the special economic zones by allowing them to maintain a higher growth rate (15 percent per annum) than national average during the Ninth Five-Year Plan period (1996–2000) (C. Kung 1996a). Moreover, the special economic zones were also given the mandate to continue to experiment with certain reforms, including national treatment for foreign firms and liberalization in services (such as banking, insurance, and free-trade zones) (Hu Ping 1995).[13] In consequence, these zones will probably be able to acquire first-mover advantages and thus become preeminent players in these areas. The central government has promised that if foreign-funded financial institutions are allowed to use the Chinese currency (*renminbi*) in their business dealings, Pudong will be the first place to conduct selected experiments. Shenzhen and Zhuhai will also be allowed to adopt certain unspecified measures that are similar to those in Hong Kong and Macao so as to strengthen economic links with them (*CD* 12/19/95: 4).

Finally, the central government decided, with the approval of the National People's Congress, to grant law-making powers to the Shantou and Zhuhai special economic zones in Guangdong in early 1996. Following this decision, all five special economic zones acquired province-level legislative power that allows them to enact local laws and regulations.[14] This suggests that the central government is determined to ensure the continued vitality of the special economic zones (C. Kung 1996b).

THE POLITICS OF SPECIAL ECONOMIC ZONE POLICY

The final resolution of the debate over special economic zone policy indicates that the center implicitly adopted the principled objections to the special economic zones and will phase out preferential fiscal and tax policies over a period of time. In this respect, these principled objections to preferential policies served the central government's cause to bolster central authority. While there are no accurate estimates of the impact of zonal preferential policies on fiscal revenue, the phasing out of various preferential tax and tariff treatments will probably bring the government billions of yuan in extra revenue.

The center's decision also underscored, again, the difficulties the interior regions have had in securing an institutional mechanism for speeding up interior development. The center was not prepared to let inland provinces set up their own special economic zones partly because of the potential losses in central revenue, as a significant number of provinces would have legitimate claims to such a zone should the center decide to let one area go ahead, but ultimately because of the interior regions' political weakness in Chinese politics. This is a somewhat ironic outcome as some of the critics of preferential policies, such as Hu Angang, have been strong advocates of central government intervention in promoting interior development.

On the other side of the same coin, the policy outcome of the debate over special economic zone policy illuminates the way in which China's central leaders have bent backwards to please coastal interests, which now also include Hong Kong and Macao. Did the policy outcome indicate the growing importance of the special economic zones? Even though the importance of the special economic zones has risen significantly in the Chinese economy, especially in generating exports, I believe a "Yes" answer to this question would be misguided. Indeed, in his defense of the special economic zones, Shenzhen Party Secretary Li Youwei was careful to mention that the state depended on fiscal revenue from the coastal areas, but not specifically the special economic zones. Shenzhen and other zones got their reprieve because they have powerful company. As a Chinese saying goes, "the fox borrows the tiger's power by walking in the latter's company (*hu jia hu wei*)."

One such company is Shanghai, which saw the Pudong New Area enjoy the same treatment as the special economic zones in spite of the official moratorium on the approval of new special economic zones.[15] During his southern tour in 1992, Deng regretted not having made Shanghai a special economic zone in the early 1980s and asked the central authorities to make up for lost time by giving Shanghai favorable policies, which President Jiang Zemin duly provided with the support of other central leaders.[16] Invoking the words of Deng Xiaoping,

Jiang has wanted to restore Shanghai as the nation's financial center and make it the pacesetter for the development of the Yangtze River Valley region. Nevertheless, the promotion of a large number of Shanghai officials to central party and government positions in the 1990s has led to the accusation that Jiang is building up a Shanghai faction within the center. Since there is already much grumbling that Jiang is giving many favors to his Shanghai base, scrapping the special privileges for other special economic zones while favoring Pudong would have provided striking evidence of regional favoritism by Jiang Zemin, who has reportedly sought to deflect the criticism.[17] In consequence, all the special economic zones were allowed to keep more privileges than would have been the case had Pudong not been on the list.[18] Only by preserving preferences for the special economic zones could those granted to Pudong be justified (Kung 1996a).

Another powerful company for Shenzhen is its neighbor Hong Kong, whose return to Chinese sovereignty in 1997 marks a milestone in China's drive for national reunification. In frequent visits to the special economic zones, Chinese leaders have again and again stressed the important role being played by the zones in promoting national unification. In June 1994, for instance, Jiang Zemin toured Shenzhen, Zhuhai, and Xiamen. He stated during the tour that Shenzhen and Zhuhai should continue to make more contributions to the long-term prosperity of Hong Kong and Macao and asked Fujian to strengthen the province's economic and trade ties with Taiwan in order to promote the reunification of China. In the meantime, he refuted the view that the role and functions of the special economic zones could weaken, or even gradually disappear, following China's comprehensive opening up (Chung Wen 1994).

The central leadership's decision on special economic zone policy is thus an effort to balance various interests. On the one hand, the granting of a grace period will allow the special economic zones and Pudong to further consolidate their already formidable economic position in China and make them more competitive in the international economy. In Shenzhen, Mayor Li Zibin declared that the city was determined to sharpen its competitive edge by adjusting its economic structure, upgrading the economic efficiency of state-owned enterprises, and setting up efficient social insurance, finance, investment, and foreign trade systems (*CD* 4/11/96: 5). For Shanghai's Pudong, the State Council formulated a set of five-year functional policies to help the city adopt international practices and open up its foreign trade markets to the rest of China (Chu Chia-chien 1995). In contrast, Shantou decided to compensate for the reduction of centrally granted preferential treatment by offering overseas investors greater access to the domestic market and discounted electricity, water, and land prices (*SCMPIW*, 4/27/96: B3).

On the other hand, by promising to end the preferential policies for special economic zones within a specified time period, the decision disarmed critics of such preferential policies. It also removed a major thorn in inter-regional relations as well as relations between the central government and interior regions, although interior interests probably felt that they had been cheated out of the chance to establish their own special economic zones. Moreover, the center will capture much additional revenue by gradually reducing the degree of preferential treatment it grants the special economic zones.

President Jiang Zemin appears to have played a direct role in crafting the central decision on special economic zone policy. Before the formal decision on special economic zone policy was announced, he made high-profile tours of both the special economic zones and a number of interior provinces, in every case accompanied by civilian and military leaders from the locality, to demonstrate that he cared for everyone. While in Shantou in late December 1995, for example, Jiang pointed out that the special economic zones must adapt to new circumstances but nevertheless reassured the zones that there would be three "no changes" with regard to the central government's special economic zone policy: The party's determination to develop special economic zones would not change; the basic policies toward special economic zones would not change; and the historical status and functions of special economic zones in China's reform, opening up and modernization would not change (Jiang Zemin 1995a).[19]

Leaders in the special economic zones were jubilant that the zones had been given a new lease of life. Shenzhen Party Secretary Li Youwei believed that the Central Committee decision on special economic zone policy concluded years of controversy over the nature, role and future of the special economic zones (Wang Zhenzhi and Wang Chien 1995). A commentary in the *Shenzhen Special Economic Zone Tribune* (*Shenzhen tequ bao*) was more pointed than Li Youwei. It reminded readers that some people had seen the special zones as special interests impeding the progress of China's reform and opening up and declared that "all this criticism and doubt have become bankrupt" (*Shenzhen Tequ Bao Commentator* 1995).

Yet President Jiang Zemin was also careful to placate interior sentiments. While delivering his assurances on special economic zone policy, Jiang also urged the zones to stick to the goal of common prosperity and encouraged those who got rich first to help those who had not been as successful as themselves (Jiang Zemin 1995a). During the spring 1996 session of the National People's Congress, Jiang Zemin specifically called on Hainan and other special economic zones to help other areas to develop (*SCMPIW* 3/16/96: 7). The zones did not need much urging, however, and saw such expenditure as political insurance that helped create a hospitable political environment. Once the center made its decision on special economic zone policy, Shenzhen gladly reported that it had just allocated an additional 90 million yuan to the Shenzhen Economic Development Fund. The fund would concentrate its anti-poverty efforts on four poor counties in Guangdong and selected areas in Sichuan and Guizhou (*RMRBO* 1/22/96: 4).

In fact, President Jiang's effort to please both the special economic zones and the interior was blatantly evident in that he sandwiched his visit to poverty-stricken Shaanxi and Gansu between visits to the special economic zones. While in Shaanxi and Gansu, Jiang emphasized the strategic importance of developing the western region and called for speeding up the pace of development of the western region through local efforts, state assistance, and help from other relatively prosperous areas. He argued that China's revitalization would not occur without the full revitalization of the western region and China's modernization would not fully succeed without the modernization of the western region (*RMRBO* 12/27/95: 1). During the annual session of the National People's Congress in spring 1996, Jiang talked further about "the sense of mission" for "our generation" to develop the western region (*CD* 3/7/96: 1).

Left out of Jiang's morale-boosting talks to interior interests was the assumption that Jiang and his senior colleagues would not sacrifice China's overall growth, driven by the coast, to bring up the interior, especially the western region. As Jiang put it during one of his visits to Guangdong: It would not be possible or desirable to seek absolute equality. For a very long period to come, Hong Kong will remain Hong Kong, Shenzhen Shenzhen, and the interior the interior. Their differences will remain. The talk of "common prosperity" should not be mistaken for egalitarianism. In any era, Jiang maintained, even in the remote future, differences will exist for various reasons (Chen Xitian 1995).[20]

CONCLUSION

The rare public skirmish over China's special economic zone policy again demonstrated the political salience of regional issues in the contemporary Chinese political economy. On the surface, it appears that the forces that were against the special economic zones and preferential treatment for the zones won because the preferential treatment will be gradually phased out over the next few years. Symbolically, the eventual adoption of uniform rules throughout the country represented the triumph of the idea of fair competition over the territorial particularism of the Dengist era and thus seems to be a more balanced approach to regional issues in China. Such a stance may appear to be neutral, as a number of Chinese regional economists have argued (Yang Kaizhong 1993: 4).

In reality, however, the final resolution of the debate over China's special economic zone policies and preferential policies in general represented far less than a victory for interior interests. For the special economic zones in particular and the coastal region in general have been given a very strong headstart in the competition and will also be given a grace period to ease the pains of adjustment.[21] By promising to end preferential policies for the special economic zones, the central government has merely removed a symbol of favoritism toward the coast, which in any case has substantially enhanced its dominance in the Chinese economy (and politics). In spite of the central leaders' strong rhetoric for helping the interior regions to develop, the central policies have, in reality, legitimated the existence of substantial disparities and failed to address the issue of how to deal with the historical legacy of a pro-coast regional development strategy throughout the reform era. Interior leaders whose provinces have little to start with and who have all along hoped to have their own special economic zones to compensate for past difficulties in attracting overseas investment cannot but feel that they have been offered a hollow victory and lament that the interior regions do not have enough political clout within Chinese politics. Some opinion makers, including the economist Zhong Pengrong, have continued to argue the case for special economic zones in the western regions (*Nanfang zhoumo*, 3/21/97: 4).

The central government is the true winner in this debate. Not only did it remove a major thorn in inter-regional relations and will it in time increase its revenue base, but it has demonstrated that it retains the prerogative to determine who receives preferential treatment and who does not. By playing different music to the ears of different regions, President Jiang Zemin had another chance to balance different interests without giving much. By offering a reprieve for the special economic zones, Jiang was far less radical than the policy advocates and thus appears generous toward the special economic zones. In the meantime, he also demonstrated that he cared about the issues and his high-profile visits to the interior and the promises of more funding showed again that he was a compassionate leader. In fact, the central government will probably have a net revenue gain and yet still have managed to please both sides.

8 Regional dominance and regional change

Regional planning . . . could serve as midwife to a spatial pattern in the ordering of activities that would in any event occur; it could not change that pattern. Any dramatic departure from familiar forms would require a very different kind of politics.

(Friedmann and Weaver 1979: 172)

Politics has dominated regional development in China. While the Mao era favored the interior, the backlash against Maoist policies led the Dengist leadership to give preferential treatment to the more prosperous coast. The move from one extreme to another has in turn prompted interior interests to cry "foul" and demand remedial action from the central government. The politicization of regional development thus begets more political involvement by central policy makers.

In this final chapter, I shall begin with a summary look back at the crosscurrents of regional policy reorientation. Then I would like to offer some comments on the replication of regional development patterns and the vicious circle faced by underdeveloped areas. Finally, I discuss a number of areas in which interior interests might be able to improve their situation.

THE POLITICAL ECONOMY OF REGIONAL POLICY REORIENTATION

In one of the most important books on regional planning, Friedmann and Weaver offered the quote on the potential and limitations of regional planning that appears at the beginning of this chapter. Friedmann probably had China in mind when he wrote about the need for a different kind of politics to enable regional planning to have a dramatic impact on patterns of regional change. In the Chinese case, that "very different kind of politics" occurred in the form of the third-front program and the predominance of politics over economics. Given the paucity of knowledge about China at the time of their writing, Friedmann and his coauthor could not have known just how grossly inefficient regional development under Mao had been. Indeed, much of the dramatic rise in interior investment was not due to regional planning at all but to political and military considerations.

It is worth noting that the end of the Mao era marked the return of normal regional planning as China, under Deng, formally incorporated regional development objectives into economic plans. What is truly remarkable about the Deng era, however, has been the intensity of the backlash against the Maoist regional development strategy and the dramatic shift to a regional development strategy that favors the coastal region. As a recent report from the State Planning Commission (1996) indicated, the basic premise of China's development strategy has been to "give first consideration to narrowing the gap between [China] and the well-developed countries." With the introduction of myriad reforms, including economic decentralization and market-based transactions, this strategy has been a clear success in generating rapid growth. But it has also contributed to the rapid rise in disparities between coastal and interior regions.

Yet, as Albert Hirschman would have predicted, the Dengist unbalanced development strategy has generated a strong reaction from interior interests and their sympathizers. In a process that bears much resemblance to the evolution of regional planning objectives in the United States from the 1950s to the end of the 1960s (Friedmann and Weaver 1979: 7), the Chinese discourse on regional development has become increasingly uneasy about the single-minded pursuit of national growth as the interior regions lagged further and further behind the coastal region. Interior interests have actively sought to change the prevailing regional development strategy by emulating coastal experiences, by insisting on local development, and by lobbying central leaders and influencing public opinion.[1]

There has been some organized expression of regional interests through various regional cooperation conferences, such as the the North China Joint Conference of Governors, Mayors, and Chairmen; the South–Central Region Joint Conference for Economic and Technological Cooperation (Guangdong, Hubei, Hunan, Henan, and Guangxi), and the Southwest Economic Coordination Conference. A number of major central government institutions have also consistently argued for more government attention to interior regions. The advisory Chinese People's Political Consultative Conference (Yang Rudai, the former Political Bureau member from Sichuan, is a CPPCC vice chairman) has been a major institution calling for narrowing coast–interior disparities through government assistance to interior regions (*CD* 3/9/96: 2; *RMRBO* 6/19/96: 1). Another example is the State Commission for Restructuring the Economy, which recently suggested that if China establishes a third stock exchange it should be based in the hinterland (particuarly the midwest) to help it boost its economy (*CD* 5/25/96: 3). For the most part, however, the lobbying for regional policy change has taken place informally through delegate speeches to the National People's Congress, participation in central economic and financial work conferences, individual meetings with central leaders, and advocacy in academic and popular publications. In spite of a lack of transparency in Chinese policy making, there has nevertheless been a lively policy debate over the direction of China's regional development strategy.

For all such lobbying and advocacy for interior interests, however, it would be far-fetched to claim that they were strong enough to bring about a major policy change. All the reforms notwithstanding, there is as yet no institutionalized process by which popular and local interests are represented and enacted. Chinese politics remains authoritarian and the whims of central leaders still carry great weight. But, as mentioned earlier, none of the current members of the Political Bureau hails from the interior. The institutions that have consistently championed interior interests, such as the CPPCC, are at best secondary institutions that can advise but not execute.

Ultimately, for interior demands to be translated into regional policy change, they must win the sympathy of central leaders. This may occur in two ways. Central leaders may change their views and become sympathetic to interior demands. Alternatively, leaders who promoted the coastal development policy, such as Zhao Ziyang, may be removed and leadership change may bring into power those who favor a more balanced regional policy. The modifications in regional development policy since the late 1980s reflected both types of mechanisms but especially the ascendance of new leaders, such as Li Peng and Jiang Zemin. While Zhao as Deng's protégé promoted coastal development as far as he could, Jiang Zemin and Li Peng have had to get ready for the post-Deng era following the crisis of Tiananmen and the collapse of communism in the Soviet Union and Eastern Europe. In this context, interior interests couched their demands in terms of the specter of social and ethnic instability and persuaded the central leaders to take seriously the widening regional gap between coast and interior.[2] (In the meantime, the regional policy reorientation served to broaden the regional base of support for the current leaders.)

In contrast to the drastic shifts in regional policy under Mao and Deng, the current reorientation is more an adjustment than a radical departure from past practice. This is because Jiang Zemin and Li Peng face very different political and economic circumstances. First, they lack the stature and authority of the founding generation of leaders and can ill afford to alienate major political forces unless absolutely necessary. Given the preponderance of coastal interests within the top leadership and the central government's dependence on the coastal region for revenue, even though Jiang has shown concern about the political implications of relative economic deprivation of the interior for China's socio-political stability, he is not expected to push for drastic changes in regional policy that severely affect the coastal region. As the last four chapters suggest, apart from central government pledges to channel a larger proportion of the central government projects into the interior, the center has given the special economic zones an adjustment period and emphasized that coastal provinces should help their interior partners through voluntary cooperation. In the words of Ye Qing, a vice minister of the State Planning Commission, "We should never try to narrow the inter-regional gap by putting a check on coastal areas' development" (Yang Tsu-kun and Lin Ping-hua 1995: 30).

Second, the Chinese economy had by the mid-1990s largely made the transition from plan to market and, in contrast to the command economy of the Mao era, the central government now directly commands only a small proportion of total economic resources and has been under much fiscal pressure and plagued by persistent budget deficits. These fiscal constraints have made it difficult for the central government to increase investment in the interior substantially, a point recognized by interior interests. As one Guizhou official noted: "I don't expect a lot from the central government, because they don't have a lot of money" (quoted in P. Tyler 1995). In the meantime, the center cannot dictate the investment decisions by local governments and investors and must seek to win their cooperation by offering various incentives.

In conclusion, while the regional policy adjustments will help placate interior discontents and moderate the rise in regional disparities, they are not designed to fundamentally reshape the regional patterns of economic activities in China. Indeed, Chinese leaders have taken care not to overpromise, conceding that even with the policy changes the state will not be able to eradicate coast–interior inequalities for a long time to come (*RMRBO* 3/8/95: 1; 3/9/95: 4; *CD* 3/11/95: 2). Chinese economists project that the coast–interior gap will show a slower increase in the next few years but that gap will not start to decrease until a time in the next century when the coastal region's economy will have reached a more mature stage.[3]

INCREASING RETURNS AND THE REPLICATION OF REGIONAL PATTERNS

In seeking to redress the balance in regional economic growth, the Chinese government must contend with the long shadow cast by history over the location of production. As is well known, the center of China's economy has been moving toward the southeastern coast for centuries. Seen from this perspective, the Maoist era appears to be an aberration from an enduring trend. In any case, China's regional economic configurations have largely reverted back to the pre-Mao patterns by the 1990s. Because of the role of increasing returns in regional growth (Arthur 1994; Krugman 1995; Myrdal 1957) and the factors affecting regional policy change analyzed earlier, it is highly likely that the current patterns of regional development will persist long into the future.

Regional production hierarchies

In one of the more provocative essays on international political economy, Bernard and Ravenhill (1995) suggest that in international production the various Asian countries are settling into different positions along the "food chain" of international production. While it is debatable how fixed these positions are in the hierarchy of production networks, it does appear that a similar process of production diffusion appears to be taking hold within China.

The emergence of such a process may look like a vindication of the conventional wisdom of regional development in that the more developed provinces are transferring more labor-intensive production to less developed areas and integrating factories in outlying areas into a national and even international network of production relations. Local authorities in less developed areas have eagerly sought investments from Shanghai, Shenzhen, and other coastal areas by offering various forms of incentives, including access to credit and the local market, tax privileges, and the offer of entering into cooperative agreements with more developed provinces and cities.

There is no denying that such inter-regional economic ties are beneficial to both parties. Companies in cities such as Shanghai and Shenzhen are burdened by high labor and land costs and relocation of some of their production to outlying areas make these companies viable and competitive in the marketplace. Between early 1992 and March 1995, Shanghai alone set up 1,917 enterprises in other parts of China with total investment of 6.4 billion yuan (Shanghai 1996). These investments have taken various forms, ranging from subsidiaries to joint ventures with local enterprises. For the investment recipient areas, these investments generated local employment and revenue and contributed to the upgrading of the industrial structure.

While it is possible, as some interior economists suggested, that some enterprises in the interior, such as Erdos Cashmere in Inner Mongolia, may jump ahead of their coastal competitors, overall the intermeshing of economic ties across regions indicates no fundamental restructuring of the patterns of regional development. Whereas in the command economy the interior regions were tied to the manufacturing centers through the central planning apparatus, under market conditions the linkages are negotiated and legitimated through voluntary exchanges and, at best, facilitated by government bureaucrats. Through these exchanges, however, the manufacturing centers are extending their reach and taking over the driver's seat in the Chinese economy.[4]

One may argue that the choices faced by China's underdeveloped areas *vis-à-vis* enterprises from the economic centers are similar to what China and many "emerging" economies have faced *vis-à-vis* powerful multinational corporations. In the latter case, China has done quite well in recent years. It is well known that China has been able to use its market potential to gain leverage over potential multinational investors, such as General Motors and Motorola. These investors have had to promise technology transfers by meeting certain local content requirements and other conditions; otherwise, they may find themselves shut out of the Chinese market and lose global market share to competitors who are more willing to capitulate to Chinese demands. By analogy, the less developed areas in China may seek the same sort of leverage over companies from metropolitian centers, such as Shanghai or Shenzhen.

The analogy is flawed, however, because local governments in China's less developed areas can no longer close off their markets to outsiders from other parts of the country as had frequently occurred in the 1980s. In consequence, these local governments have relatively little leverage over investors from the coast and must, in fact, compete with each other for such outside investment. Not infrequently enterprises in these areas have already been severely weakened by mounting domestic competition and local governments saddled with subsidies to these enterprises have little choice but to bring in outside help in the form of equity investment and management expertise; sometimes they let these enterprises become subsidiaries or group members in enterprise groups centered in the manufacturing centers.

Shanghai No. 2 Wool Textile Co., for instance, took advantage of the downturn in the textile industry to acquire ten-plus enterprises to reinforce its superiority in product innovation and management (Yuan Enzheng 1994). Similarly the Beijing-based Caihong Group leased a moribund textile factory in Ningxia and turned it around by improving management and marketing. Caihong made substantial profits out of the deal and founded a linen textile group and revived six linen factories that were in difficulty (Wu Guoqing 1995: 5).

Such deals obviously benefit both sides, but there is little doubt that coastal manufacturing centers have held the upper hand. Moreover, the ties are not confined to old-line industries, such as textiles, but have also become prevalent in the new pillar industries as identified by the central government. In fact, by requiring minimum scale and other requirements, the central government's industrial policies have offered strong incentives for smaller interior manufacturers to link up with bigger manufacturers. In the automotive industry, for instance, Shanghai now has 66 automotive components manufacturers outside the city with an annual output of 3.6 billion yuan. Shanghai Bell Telephone equipment has invested 126 million yuan in 28 enterprises in eight other provinces. In 1995, Shanghai signed 43 industrial structural adjustment projects with other provinces averaging 10 million yuan in investment per project (*QB* 4/27/96: 10). For its part, the Shanghai municipal government has decided to focus on six pillar industries in the future. These industries are the automotive industry, telecommunications equipment, power-generating equipment, petrochemicals, steel, and consumer electronics. The city is also making strenuous efforts to break into bio-technology, aerospace, and new materials. While production is farmed out to other parts of the country through acquisitions, equity investments, and new investments, particularly in declining industries such as textiles, the city has nevertheless avowed to remain the center for information, product design, and finance (Yuan Enzheng 1994).

As a brand new city, Shenzhen has faced fewer pains of adjustment than Shanghai because it did not have much of a traditional industrial base. Nevertheless, faced with growing competition from both domestic and foreign firms, the Shenzhen municipal government made it a strategic task in the early 1990s to help Shenzhen-based companies develop and open up markets in other parts of China. While Shenzhen companies set up sales outlets and invested throughout the country, the municipal government itself facilitated these ties by signing cooperative agreements with other local governments and holding trade fairs. As is the case in Shanghai, various Shenzhen companies now only design and manufacture the high value-added core of their products in Shenzhen and do assembly in subsidiaries close to the sales destination. These efforts are believed to have helped increase the market share of Shenzhen companies. In a variety of products, ranging from computer diskettes, LCD displays, television sets, cassette recorders, wrist watches, bicycles, and audio-visual equipment, Shenzhen companies now account for more than half of the domestic market (Wei Jinkui 1995).

In short, the replication of the economic relations discussed here will imply the continued predominance of the coastal region, even though some cities in the interior, such as Wuhan, Chongqing, and Xi'an, may become significant players as well. By granting the special economic zones and Pudong the mandate to experiment with new reforms, including national treatment for foreign firms and liberalization in services such as banking, insurance, and free-trade zones, these special zones will likely acquire first-mover advantages and thus reinforce their leadership positions in the Chinese economy. As Ke Jian (1995) recognized, China's step-by-step liberalization across space has served to strengthen the dominant position of the coastal region in technology, capital, and human resources, which have in turn allowed these areas to reap "high profits" from such a position and maintain their interests in China's politicial economy.

REGIONAL DISPARITIES AND THE TRAP OF BACKWARDNESS

The replication of the patterns of regional development extends beyond the economy into areas such as education and elite mobility, reinforcing the perpetuation of existing regional patterns. In fact, a survey conducted by the Institute of Sociology of the Chinese Academy of Social Sciences reveals that from 1978 to 1993 the top seven high achievers in socio-economic development were all located along the coast while the seven laggards were all located in the western region. Moreover, the gap widened further between 1989 and 1993, with the ratio of the general indices of social development rising from 2.4 in 1989 to 2.6 in 1993 (Coastal 1994). I also mentioned that none of the current Political Bureau members represents the interior regions. A recent study of Chinese provincial leaders also finds that provincial leaders of more populous and richer provinces are more likely to be promoted than those in less populous and less developed ones (Bo 1996). In other words, as on the board of directors of corporations, economically more powerful provinces that contribute more to the central treasury also receive more voting power which makes it unlikely that the center will sacrifice coastal interests in favor of the interior except in the most unusual circumstances. In a sense, the less developed areas in China are caught in a vicious circle of backwardness.

Nowhere demonstrates this vicious circle, as well as the central government's potential remedial role, more clearly than the area of basic education.[5] As in the economy, the defining trend in Chinese education since the 1980s has been the decentralization of resources as well as responsibilities from central to local governments. The Chinese government's Decision on Reforming the Educational System (May 27, 1985) entrusted the responsibility for basic education and the realization of nine-year compulsory education to local authorities, particularly county, city, and township governments. Thus the spread of basic education has hinged upon funding from local revenue and the mobilization of non-governmental resources (Li Peng 1986). While properous coastal localities have ample funds to upgrade their educational facilities, a high percentage of inland areas have found it difficult to raise enough funding just for basic operations such as paying teachers' salaries (Xu Jialu 1994). Using data for 1993, for instance, we find a strong positive correlation between the regional economic development level and the level of community contributions and donations as well as between the regional economic development level and the level of per capita educational spending.[6] Thus, the widening economic disparities are expected to translate into growing disparities in the level of educational expenditure.

Even though less developed areas spend less on education in per capita terms, a 1991 survey of 371 counties found that local governments in these areas have in fact had to allocate a higher percentage of government expenditure to education than is the case in high income areas (Guojia Jiaowei 1991: 62–63). This is because more than 80 percent of the budgeted educational expenditure is for faculty and staff salaries that are fixed by centrally determined salary scales (Guojia Jiaowei 1994: 36). Yet student families in less developed areas also share a higher percentage of the educational expenditure through payment of tuition and miscellaneous fees than in more developed areas. In 1993, for example, tuition and miscellaneous fees as a percentage of educational expenditure were 15.76 percent in Anhui, 14.44 percent in Hubei, and 14.01 percent in Hebei, compared to only 0.61 percent in Shanghai and 1.20 percent in Beijing.

The widening regional disparities in educational expenditure have important consequences for educational performance across regions. We find that the rate of primary school graduates entering junior secondary schools (PRP) has a strong, or moderately strong, positive relationship to per capita gross domestic product and educational expenditure.[7] While primary school graduates in more developed provinces almost certainly enroll in secondary schools, those in poorer areas are much less likely to do so.

As mentioned earlier, in underdeveloped areas in China, both student families and local governments have to allocate a higher percentage of their resources to education even though both have less money per capita than their counterparts in more developed areas. This economic factor is the major explanation for both the lower enrollment rate in secondary schools and the higher primary school drop-out rate in economically underdeveloped areas.[8] Chinese studies have found that a majority of the students dropping out of primary school came from families that could not afford tuituion and miscellaneous fees (Yue Xikuan 1991: 7–9). Not surprisingly, all but one of the provinces that had high primary school drop-out rates were in the western region of the interior, including Tibet, Guizhou, Yunnan, Qinghai, Gansu, and Ningxia. Given the importance of education to the formation of human capital and economic development (Becker 1993), one easily sees a trap of backwardness for China's underdeveloped areas. Underdevelopment makes for poor human capital formation which in turn makes it difficult for these areas to attain economic development and political influence. This cycle is further exacerbated by the out-migration of talented personnel as well as the flight of capital from the interior to coastal provinces. Indeed, Chinese researchers have often referred to the so-called "Matthew effect" in discussing the persistence of poverty in parts of China: "For everyone who has will be given more, and he will have an abundance. Whoever does not have, even what he has will be taken from him" (*The Holy Bible*, Matthew xxv: 29).

Two major initiatives launched in recent years – one by the central government, the other by a government-sponsored foundation that depends on private donations – suggest that efforts are being made to tackle the very significant regional disparities in education. The former is an effort by the State Education Commission to increase spending aimed at universalizing nine-year compulsory education by 2010. For the 1996–98 period, government funds earmarked for this purpose reportedly will reach one billion yuan per year (*CD* 1/24/96). In the latter case, the China Youth Foundation in fall 1989 launched Project Hope to raise private funds for education. The funds are used to help build and supply primary schools in poor rural areas and return poor drop-out students to school. By the end of 1995, Project Hope had received 692 million yuan in donations and expended 396 million yuan to put 1.25 million drop-out students back in school and build 2,074 Hope primary schools (*RMRBO* 1/26/96: 12; see also Yue Xikuan 1991). Overall, however, although these initiatives are good for the provision of basic education in impoverished areas they are unlikely to alter the patterns of regional educational disparities. While most coastal provinces can already provide at least nine years of compulsory education to students, it will take several years more for children in the poorest provinces to receive just nine years of basic education as prescribed in China's law on compulsory education.[9]

POLITICS THE INTERIOR INTERESTS MAY PLAY

With so many factors stacked against the rise of the interior regions, it is no wonder that interior interests have turned to the rhetoric of crisis in recent years in order to capture the attention of central leaders. But it will be a long time before the interior regions break out of the vicious circle. While increased central government investment in infrastructure (broadly defined to include both roads and education) and basic industries will help improve the interior's ability to pull itself up by its own bootstraps, there is as yet no guarantee that the central effort will be sustained.

There are signs that interior interests have recognized the political obstacles they face in accelerating interior development. In a fascinating essay on why Jiangxi province lagged behind many other provinces in economic development in modern history, Zhao Shugui and Wang Shuzi (1988: 108) concluded that the province's relative backwardness partly resulted from the lack of major industrial enteprises or economic growth centers under its own control.[10] They then attributed the lack of local control to the absence of political advocacy for Jiangxi in national politics. Jiangxi did not have someone like Zuo Zongtang or Li Hongzhang, two of the foremost viceroys of the Qing Dynasty, to speak for it and provincial governors in Jiangxi had short tenures and failed to exercise long-term economic leadership.

Chinese writers have often used discussions of the past to comment on the present. There is little doubt that Zhao and Wang's historical argument is also intended as a comment on Jiangxi's relatively slow development under communist rule. Some of the policy issues are spelt out by Fan Chengshi (1991: 27), who pointed out that Jiangxi has lost out during both the Maoist and the Dengist eras. While Jiangxi was considered to be too close to the coast to benefit from the third-front investment program under Mao (whose hometown Hunan was nevertheless included), it has also lost out as an interior province under Deng.[11] As the discussions in earlier chapters indicate, many other interior provinces have also felt neglected and exploited.

Had China been a representative democracy, then the task would have been far easier for interior interests, with more than half of the total population, to secure some sort of political umbrella for interior development. Instead, the authoritarian regime dominated by coastal interests has so far dictated preferential treatment for the richer coastal region since Mao's death.

Even in the absence of a fully-fledged democracy, however, the Chinese political system has become more pluralistic over the past two decades; the lively debate over regional policy was just one example of the trend toward open discussion. Apart from village and district level elections, there also appears to be greater acceptance of some measure of representation for different interests and this is likely to open up some opportunities for interior regions. In this connection, it will not be far-fetched to argue that the interior regions should have at least one member, and perhaps two, on the powerful CCP Political Bureau, as was the case in the early 1980s. Indeed, following the ouster of Chen Xitong, Beijing Party Secretary and Political Bureau member, a majority of the central committee members reportedly favored promoting an interior leader to fill the seat vacated by Chen. The reason this has not happened is believed to be due to disagreement over the candidate (Lam 1995d).

Another major opportunity for increasing interior representation in Chinese politics lies in the National People's Congress, which has in recent years steadily increased its legislative clout and control over government activities. The current membership on the NPC is heavily biased in favor of urban and thus coastal interests. However, this will likely change and become more representative of the general population in future in accordance with the revised Election Law of the National People's Congress and Local People's Congresses and the Organic Law of the Local People's Congresses and People's Government. One report suggests that the number of deputies from rural areas to the National People's Congress will rise from the current 760-odd members to more than 1,090 in 1997, while the number of deputies from urban areas will be reduced from 1,500-odd members to about 1,260 (*CD* 5/20/95: 1; *RMRB* 3/7/97: 2). It is likely that the interior regions, which have a higher proportion of rural population than the coastal regions, will benefit from this reform. A rise in the number of interior representatives is likely to increase the number of interior representatives serving on the increasingly influential specialized comittees on legislative affairs, finance and economic affairs, law, and so on and thus help promote the interests of the interior. There have also been proposals for including representatives from all 30 provincial units on the NPC standing committee and financial committee and for the establishment of a special oversight committee in the NPC to oversee fiscal transfer payments (*SCMPIW* 1/11/96: B2; Wang Fang 1995: 44). Developments toward greater interior representation, advocacy, and supervision will be crucial in making sure that part of the projected increase in central revenue will be channelled toward interior development when the revenue increase materializes.

The interior interests will also do well to fine-tune their argument for interior development. They should scrupulously avoid appearing as if they are engaged in a zero-sum struggle for scarce resources. Instead, their strongest argument is to demand the equality of opportunity for development to which fairness and equity have entitled them. In concrete terms, improvement in that opportunity entails improvement in the interior's access to markets, so that their natural resources will not go to waste, as well as access to education so that precious human resources will realize their potential. Thus, rather than seeking specific factories, they should emphasize their need for schools, roads, airports, and telecommunications networks. When given the same chance, children from the poorest areas will do just as well as those from the coast.

In fact, one could make a strong case that the central government made a big mistake in decentralizing educational financing as far as the poorest communities are concerned. When it comes to educational access, the 1980s were a disaster for children in poor communities. As one interviewee lamented to me, it is a national disgrace for a socialist government in one of the fastest-growing economies to rely on private donations for Project Hope to assist students dropping out of primary school. In my own view, the least the Chinese government could have done was to offer a matching grant to the project.

CONCLUSION

The dominance of coastal interests in Chinese politics is unlikely to be significantly altered without fundamentally transforming the mechanisms of governance. The continuance of the coastal oligarchy will in turn make it unlikely for fundamental changes in the patterns of regional development to occur. Nevertheless, the political transition from the rule of revolutionary founders to the cohort of Jiang Zemin provides interior interests with more political opportunities. In contrast to Mao and Deng, Jiang Zemin is compelled to be more even-handed in his effort to balance reform, development, and stability. The debate on regional development policy thus reflected China's transition beyond the politics of strong-man rule. While the pinnacle of the ruling oligarchy is entirely composed of elites from the coastal region, it still has a strong interest in promoting a semblance of balance in regional development. The specter of social and ethnic instability has made this objective even more desirable.

Moreover, as China has become more open, the discourse of regional disparities has gained a life of its own, leading some economists such as Yu Guangyuan to charge that the issue of regional disparities has been blown out of proportion. While most unequal treatment of the regions has been removed, entrepreneurial political interests from local leaders to academic policy advisers have focused on the persistence of regional disparities as a major political issue. Even though the coast–interior disparities would have existed in any case even if there had been no regional preferential policies, it can now be argued that these disparities have been accentuated by such regional policies and the legacy of these policies will have to be counteracted over a long period to come. The politics of regional disparities thus lives on. For better or worse, the issue of regional inequality will remain highly visible on China's political agenda for a long time to come.

Appendix I Reform and intra-provincial inequality in China

A preliminary study[1]

INTRODUCTION

The release of abundant statistical data from reformist China has made possible an outpouring of studies on China's regional disparities (Denny 1991; Lyons 1991; Tsui 1991; Veeck 1991; Walker 1989; D. Yang 1990). While these studies have contributed to our understanding of the patterns of regional changes across provinces and big regions (such as coast versus interior), little has been published on disparities at sub-provincial levels.[2] In light of the enormous size of each of China's provinces, trends of regional inequality at the provincial and macro-regional levels can at best provide us with an incomplete view of the patterns of regional change in contemporary China (Cannon 1990: 33).

Making use of a county-level data series on the rural economy, this study represents a preliminary effort at filling the above lacuna in the literature on the political economy of regional change in China. The *raison d'être* of this study is to look at the impact of post-Mao reforms on patterns of regional disparities at sub-provincial levels. Since it is generally recognized that the reforms have been more far-reaching in the rural rather than the urban economy throughout the 1980s, the use of the rural economic data series serves to more fully reflect the impact of reforms on regional disparities *within* China's provinces than would data for both urban and rural areas.

The rest of this chapter is divided into three sections. Section I discusses the nature of the data used. Section II describes and analyzes the patterns and determinants of inter-county economic disparities within each of China's provinces during the 1985–90 period. It is found that intra-provincial inequality increased significantly in most Chinese provinces over this period. Section III focuses on the variations in patterns of intra-provincial inequality and patterns of fiscal subsidies in an attempt to uncover the policy implications of recent changes. Through an examination of individual cases, it is suggested that in the long run the process of economic diffusion will help alleviate the trend toward increasing intra-provincial disparities. In the short run, however, it is difficult to overcome the trend toward greater inequality among less developed areas, though government efforts at poverty reduction may have moderated that trend in provinces such as Gansu.

I THE DATA

The main source of data for this study is the *Summary Rural Economic Statistics of China's Counties* (*Zhongguo fenxian nongcun jingji tongji gaiyao*), a series compiled by the Bureau and later the General Team on Rural Society and Economy of the State Statistical Bureau on the basis of the Card File System on rural society and economy of counties (cities). Due to the nature (and limits) of the original data, this study will use the county-level per capita rural gross social product as the basic unit of measurement. As a measurement of economic activity, the gross social product is less meaningful than measures of value-added, but the latter are not systematically available at the present.

By definition, the rural gross social product (*nongcun shehui zong chanzhi*) is the sum value of all rural outputs of agriculture, industry, construction, transport and communications, and commerce (including catering and material supply).[3] It includes the output values of rural households and various cooperative economic organizations (including all types of rural enterprises), regardless of the provenance of their outputs such as agriculture, industry, construction, transportation, commerce, and catering. This value also includes the agricultural output value of state farms but excludes the non-agricultural output values of state farms as well as other state enterprises, even when they are located in the countryside. However, when an enterprise is a joint venture between a rural cooperative enterprise and a state enterprise, and if the venture depends on the rural organization for labor, capital, land, and facilities such as housing, its output is included in the rural gross social product (*Zhongguo fenxian nongcun jingji tongji gaiyao* 1989: 4).[4] Moreover, rural areas under the jurisdiction of cities are also included and treated as separate units, just as counties are, since the population in these areas is officially designated "rural"; and throughout this study, we shall only speak of counties or county-level data even though some of the data pertain to the rural gross social product of cities. The data series used in this study permits us to derive the per capita rural gross social product for each county for the 1985–90 period, allowing for comparisons across time. As a piece of exploratory research, this study will deal with the years of 1985 and 1990 only. Finally, the unweighted coefficient of variation in per capita rural gross social product will be used as the basic measure of intra-provincial (inter-county) inequality.[5]

Since Hainan did not become a separate province until 1988, I have decided to include it in the data on Guangdong for 1990 to facilitate temporal comparison. In fact, in separate calculations, it is found that the subtraction or addition of Hainan does not affect the measure of inequality for Guangdong. The data for Tibet are very incomplete for 1990 (the number of observations or county-level units drops from 72 to 58) and are therefore non-comparable with 1985 for our purpose. Hence Tibet is excluded from the aggregate data set and statistical analysis.

II RESULTS

1 Summary statistics

The county-level per capita rural gross social product data are summarized in Table A.1. Included in the table are summary statistics for 26 provincial units (including four autonomous regions), covering 1985 and 1990 respectively. In the table, "St. dev." stands for standard deviation, "C.v." is the coefficient of variation of the county-level per capita rural gross social product calculated on a provincial basis. "No. of obs." stands for the number of observations or the number of counties included in each calculation. Please note the usually small changes in the number of observations from 1985 to 1990, mostly arising from administrative changes.

From Table A.1 and the accompanying Figure A.1, using the coefficient of variation for per capita rural gross social product as the inequality index, we find overall intra-provincial (inter-county) inequality increased significantly between 1985 and 1990 in most provinces. The average provincial coefficient of variation rose from 0.486 in 1985 to 0.677 in 1990, an increase of 39.3 percent over the period. If all Chinese county-level units are put together in one data sample, the increase in the coefficient of variation is even greater, rising from 0.869 in 1985 to 1.325 in 1990, or by 52.4 percent. This contrasts with earlier findings with respect to *inter*-provincial inequality, where no increase in inequality was reported (Denny 1991; Lyons 1991: 476).[6] In other words, while *inter*-provincial inequality has shown little change, *intra*-provincial inequality calculated on the basis of county-level data has increased substantially for the period under observation.

The overall figures on inter-provincial inequality masks the diversity of provincial trajectories, however. Of the 28 provincial units covered here, 19 (68 percent) saw relative inequality within each province jump by double-digit percentages. In contrast, measurements of inequality for eight other provinces either decreased (Jiangsu, Guangdong, Zhejiang, Shanghai, Liaoning, Guangxi, and Qinghai) or just increased slightly (Gansu). As will be discussed later, these variations in the temporal changes of intra-provincial inequality have important implications for public policy.

2 Determinants of intra-provincial disparities in China

Earlier theoretical and empirical work on regional disparities across countries, especially the seminal article by Williamson (1965), extended the Kuznets thesis to suggest that regional economic disparities and the level of national economic development are linked together in the form of an inverted U-shaped curve. Moreover, Williamson also found that regional disparities are positively related to country size; the larger the geographic size of the national unit, the greater will be the degree of regional inequality.

Table A.1 County-level per capita rural gross social product: summary statistics for 1985 and 1990

Province	No. of obs.	Median	Mean	St. dev.	C.v.	No. of obs.	Median	Mean	St. dev.	C.v.
		1985					1990			
Jilin	47	943.47	984.04	230.57	0.234	47	2212.29	2438.19	866.95	0.356
Tianjin	5	1297.19	1448.28	371.78	0.257	5	4476.00	5224.27	2021.79	0.387
Beijing	9	2009.05	2039.84	574.18	0.281	9	6678.96	7224.08	3524.83	0.488
Guizhou	82	337.30	352.25	100.79	0.286	82	620.43	690.13	246.69	0.357
Shanghai	10	4465.21	4228.22	1340.15	0.317	10	9698.51	10091.30	2731.64	0.271
Anhui	82	665.17	712.97	234.94	0.330	81	1400.38	1583.61	693.99	0.438
Jiangxi	98	602.52	628.32	220.94	0.352	90	1312.38	1464.30	642.55	0.439
Yunnan	126	389.99	439.26	167.46	0.381	125	771.64	907.23	552.86	0.609
Sichuan	193	502.38	563.08	218.37	0.388	194	948.65	1213.51	1079.27	0.889
Fujian	68	688.31	759.23	296.86	0.391	69	1712.21	2020.26	1060.81	0.525
Hunan	104	572.43	620.49	249.21	0.402	103	1140.69	1317.71	726.51	0.551
Henan	127	583.73	644.84	260.27	0.404	129	1420.27	1734.00	944.95	0.545
Shaanxi	97	431.28	491.67	206.40	0.420	97	975.86	1105.82	527.30	0.477
Hubei	79	784.91	806.76	340.23	0.422	79	1603.03	1772.24	1115.38	0.629
Hebei	149	711.81	801.76	338.41	0.422	149	1671.50	1910.93	1009.87	0.528
Shanxi	106	597.60	683.55	297.75	0.436	105	1220.15	1417.51	779.19	0.550
Heilongjiang	80	789.98	911.37	411.23	0.451	79	2358.50	3125.06	2070.11	0.662
Ningxia	19	567.68	535.97	264.99	0.494	20	1375.88	1409.99	1028.60	0.730
Guangxi	87	452.79	467.82	233.92	0.500	89	934.33	993.08	488.16	0.492
Shandong	112	872.02	1002.45	523.56	0.522	110	2317.44	2818.05	1953.46	0.693
Xinjiang	83	727.15	788.33	464.62	0.589	85	1704.26	2078.31	2523.63	1.214
Qinghai	39	633.40	766.91	461.41	0.602	40	1006.19	1392.04	829.16	0.596
Inn. Mongolia	86	672.93	871.35	536.18	0.615	87	1518.04	3685.92	9632.44	2.613
Liaoning	57	1023.98	1182.30	755.85	0.639	58	2558.40	3097.70	1933.98	0.624
Zhejiang	77	999.52	1341.12	865.15	0.645	77	2540.29	3143.83	1982.42	0.631
Gansu	79	349.82	504.36	394.98	0.783	79	938.02	1138.40	915.46	0.804
Jiangsu	75	1321.47	2056.69	1896.24	0.922	75	2930.92	4599.98	3873.87	0.842
Guangdong	109	718.33	1098.99	1235.25	1.124	113	1904.12	2743.53	2798.86	1.020

Source: *Zhongguo fenxian nongcun jingji tongji gaiyao* 1989–93.

We tested the effect of the two variables identified by Williamson, level of economic development (measured in terms of the mean of the county-level per capita rural gross social product in a province) and geographic size (in 1,000 km^2), as well as an additional variable – the size of a province's rural population – on intra-provincial inequality for Chinese provinces for 1985 and 1990 respectively.[7] The regression results are presented in Tables A.2.

For 1985, only one of the models showed anything of statistical significance. In Model 1a, it is shown that, removing the three centrally administered municipalities (Beijing, Shanghai, and Tianjin), then the level of economic

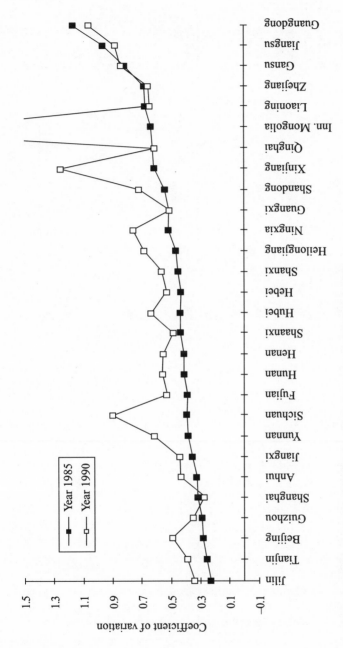

Figure A.1 Intra-provincial disparities in China's provinces, 1985 and 1990

Source: Zhongguo fenxian nongcun jingji tongji gaiyao 1989–93.

Table A.2 Regression coefficients for models explaining intra-provincial inequality

1985

Independent variables	Model 1	Model 1[a]	Model 2	Model 2[a]
1 Mean county-level per capita rural gross social product	0.0000337 [0.0000556]	0.0003342** [0.0000984]	0.0003132[b] [0.0001732]	0.0001514 [0.0003942]
2 (1)-squared			−6.63E-08 [0.0000000391]	8.20E-08 [0.0000000171]
3 Geographic size	0.0001523 [0.0001117]	0.0000962 [0.0000964]	0.0001569 [0.0001076]	0.0001046 [0.0000998]
4 Rural population size	0.0020979 [0.001925]	−0.0001255 [0.0017594]	0.002016 [0.0018544]	−0.0001549 [0.0017937]
R-squared (adjusted)	−0.0181	0.2778	0.0559	0.2503

1990

Independent variables	Model 1	Model 1[a]	Model 2	Model 2[a]
1 Mean county-level per capita rural gross social product	0.0000363 [0.0000324]	0.0001778** [0.000062]	0.0002262* [0.0000952]	−0.000042 [0.0002827]
2 (1)-squared			−2.02E-08* [0.00000000961]	4.50E-08 [0.0000000564]
3 Geographic size	0.0008736*** [0.0001728]	0.000764*** [0.0001678]	0.0008237*** [0.0001634]	0.000775*** [0.0001698]
4 Rural population size	0.0029829 [0.0028807]	0.0010985 [0.0028303]	0.0023673 [0.0027107]	0.0010575 [0.0028566]
R-squared (adjusted)	0.4554	0.5576	0.5234	0.5498

Figures in brackets are the standard errors.

* Significant p < 0.05   ** Significant p < 0.01   *** Significant p < 0.001   a Excludes the municipalities of Beijing, Shanghai, and Tianjin.   b p = 0.084.

Source: Zhongguo fenxian nongcun jingji tongji gaiyao 1989–93.

development was positively related to the level of intra-provincial disparities. In other words, excepting the three central cities, the more developed a province was, the greater the inequality among the counties in that province.

In contrast to 1985, in 1990, the geographic size of a provincial unit emerged as the most important determinant of intra-provincial inequality in China's provinces in all the models. As in 1985, the size of the rural population in a province had no statistically significant effect on intra-provincial inequality. When the data set includes the three centrally administered cities, a linear model (Model 1) showed no statistically meaningful relationship between the level of economic development and the degree of intra-provincial disparities; in contrast, a quadratic relationship (Model 2) was statistically confirmed. Removing the three cities from the sample, we then obtain a linear (Model 1a) but no quadratic (Model 2a) relationship between these two variables. This indicates that in 1990, based on cross-sectional data on China's provinces, the relationship between the level of economic development and the magnitude of intra-provincial disparities was in the form of an inverted U-shaped curve, increasing at lower levels of economic development but declining for provinces that have the highest economic levels.

In the ideal world of economics there is no prima facie reason why increasing geographical size should lead to increases in regional disparities. In reality, however, increasing geographical size could cause such disparities to increase through a variety of mechanisms – which is probably why Williamson did not spell out the logical linkages between these two variables. Greater geographic size may increase transport costs and undermine market integration and economic diffusion, making regional economic disparities persist. It also usually means more geographic diversity (in terms of mountains, deserts, and so forth) and thus regional economic diversity and disparities. What is interesting in the present study is that geographic size had no effect on intra-provincial inequality as late as 1985, when a series of rural reforms had already led to the abandonment of collective farming, but became very important in 1990.

I can provide no conclusive explanation as to why this has been the case. My speculation is that a command economy, with a greater degree of economic centralization at both central and provincial levels than in a more decentralized economic system, was able to mitigate and indeed suppress an important factor behind the incidence of regional inequality (Lardy 1978). By 1990, however, geographic size had emerged as the dominant factor explaining the pattern of intra-provincial disparities. This lends support to the thesis that the reforms, characterized by fiscal decentralization and the decline of centralized control over resources, have permitted environmental conditions to play a greater role in determining patterns of intra-provincial economic inequalities (Naughton 1987; Wong 1991; D. Yang 1990). Similarly, reforms have also permitted the Kuznets–Williamson relationship between the level of economic development and the magnitude of regional disparities (the U-shaped curve) to come into play as far as intra-provincial inequality is concerned.

Table A.3 Regression coefficients for models explaining percentage changes in intra-provincial inequality, 1985-90

Independent variables	Model 1	Model 1a (robust regression)	Model 2
1 Mean county-level per capita rural gross social product (1985)	−0.0000107 [0.0001322]	−0.0000625 [0.00006]	
2 Coefficient of variation for 1985	−0.8561252 [0.4970568]	−0.7792137** [0.2257608]	
3 Geographic size	0.0011744*** [0.0002791]	0.0005128*** [0.0001268]	0.001078*** [0.0002695]
R-squared (adjusted)	0.3809	0.4759	0.3572

Figures in brackets are the standard errors.

* Significant p < 0.05
** Significant p < 0.01
*** Significant p < 0.001

Source: Zhongguo fenxian nongcun jingii tongii gaiyao 1989–93.

Finally, we tested the effect of a number of variables on the percentage changes in intra-provincial inequality between 1985 and 1990 (Table A.3). As can be expected from the above discussions, geographic size was again the leading factor, explaining 35.7 percent of the variations in the dependent variable (Model 2). Interestingly, the initial level of development had no impact on the changes in intra-provincial disparities. The effect of the initial level of intra-provincial inequality was significant when we used a robust regression process (Model 1a). In this case, the relationship was a negative one; in other words, the greater the initial inequality, the smaller the increase in inequality over the 1985–90 period. This suggests that there has been a tendency toward convergence in the magnitude of intra-provincial disparities between 1985 and 1990.

III INTRA-PROVINCIAL DISPARITIES AND PUBLIC POLICY

In commenting on the diverse temporal patterns of changing intra-provincial inequalities, we suggested that the variations had implications for public policy. I discuss these implications in this section.

1 Budgetary subsidies and intra-provincial disparities

I begin with a tentative look at the relationship between fiscal transfers through China's unitary budgetary system and factors affecting intra-provincial disparities (Denny 1991: 194–97). The views here are tentative because the inter-provincial fiscal transfers are undertaken through provincial administrations and *not* specifically targeted at rural areas, although the province-wide data appear to represent the patterns of fiscal aid to rural areas as well; Chinese sources regularly give the per capita amount of revenues and expenditures for each province.

Table A.4 presents the statistical results for 1985 and 1990.[8] For both years, it is found that the amount of fiscal subsidies calculated on a per capita basis was negatively related to the level of economic development; in other words, rich provinces subsidized poorer ones. The same is true with regard to the size of rural population; provinces that had a smaller population base received more subsidies on a per capita basis.

The amount of fiscal subsidies is also positively related to the percentage of counties in a province that are classified as ethnic (autonomous) counties. This measure of ethnicity is correlated with geographic size ($r = 0.608$ in 1985; $r = 0.593$ in 1990) as China's ethnic minorities tend to reside in such large border provinces as Xinjiang, Yunnan, Inner Mongolia, and Tibet. These areas receive more subsidies from the unitary budgetary system for a variety of reasons; two major factors are their relatively lower level of economic development and the center's concern about social stability in its more volatile regions.

Given our knowledge about the flow of fiscal subsidies and the determinants of intra-provincial disparities, can we say anything definite about the effect of

Table A.4 Regression coefficients for models explaining fiscal subsidies

Independent variables	1985			1990		
	Model 1	Model 2	Model 3	Model 1	Model 2	Model 3
1 Mean county-level per capita rural gross social product	-0.000352* [0.000148]	-0.0005032** [0.0001558]	-0.0003501* [0.000145]	-0.0001123*** [0.0000183]	-0.0001227*** [0.0000159]	-0.0001133*** [0.0000171]
2 % of counties classified as ethnic autonomous counties	1.493945*** [0.3053048]		1.118647** [0.3557977]	0.2798182** [0.1000262]		0.1526032 [0.1116805]
3 Geographic size		0.001174*** [0.000313]	0.0005892 [0.0003288]		0.000282** [0.0000849]	0.000208* [0.0000994]
4 Rural population size	-0.0119311* [0.0051896]	-0.0183929** [0.0053948]	-0.0126777* [0.0051762]	-0.0026896 [0.0016382]	-0.0037873* [0.0014152]	-0.0028917 [0.001537]
R-squared (adjusted)	0.6884	0.6075	0.7078	0.7377	0.7617	0.77

Figures in brackets are the standard errors.

* Significant p < 0.05
** Significant p < 0.01
*** Significant p < 0.001

Source: Zhongguo fenxian nongcun jingji tongji gaiyao 1989–93.

the fiscal transfers on the patterns of intra-provincial disparities? Unfortunately, no. Using fiscal subsidy as the independent variable, we tested the relationship between fiscal subsidy and the indices of intra-provincial disparities as well as changes in the latter variable and found no statistically significant relationship (even when adjusted for other factors shown in Table A.4).

This does not mean that the present pattern of budgetary subsidies is not relevant to intra-provincial disparities. The flow of subsidies to ethnic areas, if used more or less evenly within the province, is likely to help temper the tendency toward greater intra-provincial inequality in these areas. Nevertheless, the subsidization of poorer provinces may not necessarily reduce intra-provincial inequality since the Williamson thesis suggests that inequality tends to increase in the early stages of economic development. Even assuming that the transfers are conducive to economic growth, however, such transfers may help reduce intra-provincial inequality only in the long run. On balance, the fiscal subsidies allocated through the unitary budget will not help alleviate the growing intra-provincial disparities in the short and intermediate term and in any case are not designed for this purpose.

2 The role of provincial governments

Yet one might still wonder whether the government can do anything to alleviate widening intra-provincial disparities under market-oriented reforms. Our tentative (and pessimistic) answer is that local governments, especially provincial governments, may be able to play a significant role in facilitating the alleviation of intra-provincial disparities only when the economy is more developed.

Yet we must begin with the admission that this answer raises questions about leadership, administrative capacity, and organizational performance, all of which are exceedingly difficult to measure and answer with confidence. In the case of China, a rigorous comparative assessment of the performance of local leaders and administrative organizations has yet to be started. For this reason, the following discussion will rely more on anecdotal evidence derived from the author's broad readings than systematic findings required by social science; it is offered in the hope that future field surveys may address the issues raised here.

The Williamson hypothesis, confirmed in the case of China's intra-provincial disparities as of 1990 (Table A.2), predicts that as an area becomes more economically developed, its degree of regional inequality will stabilize and then decline. This may be accounted for by two complementary processes: economic diffusion (or trickle-down, spread effect) and government intervention. In the initial stages of development, resources (capital and labor) tend to move to growth centers and from rural to urban areas. As an economy has reached a more mature stage, however, the countervailing effect of economic diffusion starts to play a more important role. By economic diffusion, we mean the migration of capital from economic core areas to the periphery, often in search of lower costs for land and labor. Until very recently, there were severe constraints on both rural-to-urban migration and inter-provincial labor mobility in China, which probably also helped drive up labor costs faster in more developed areas than would have been the case had such constraints been fewer, thus providing greater incentives for low-tech manufacturers and assembly plants to move inland to reduce costs.

The other important factor besides diffusion is government intervention. Whether financially or administratively, governments in more developed areas are likely to be more capable of dealing with issues such as regional inequality than their counterparts in less developed areas, where the overriding concern is usually not of inequality within but of catching up with others, especially one's neighbors. Intuitively, a fast-growing pie is less painful to divide than one that is fixed in size.

Figure A.2 presents a graphic depiction, derived from Table A.1, of the patterns of change in the provincial indices of intra-provincial inequality, plotted against the background of the initial level of development for the province in 1985. It permits us to discern details that are obscured by the statistical equations presented earlier when we were discussing the determinants of intra-provincial inequality. From the figure, it can be seen that a fairly large percentage of the more economically developed provinces saw decreases or just slight increases in intra-provincial inequality over the 1985–90 period. Evidence of both diffusion and government intervention can be found in these areas, probably contributing to the equalization of intra-provincial economic levels. The following account will focus on Guangdong. Using the coefficient of variation of county-level per capita national income for 1980–90, it is found that while intra-provincial disparities in Guangdong increased over the 1980–85 period they dropped back in the latter part of the 1980s, albeit still at a higher level than in the early 1980s.[9]

We shall not belabor the point of diffusion or spread effects in Guangdong; there are almost daily accounts of how businesses looking for new investment options will spread out from core cities such as Shenzhen, where labor costs have risen significantly in recent years, to inland areas (K. Chen 1993; Zhu Xinhong, Zhan Weihong, and Guo Wanda 1993). Instead, our attention will be on the elusive role of the provincial government. There is no doubt that the provincial government in Guangdong is heavily concerned about and involved in addressing the issue of intra-provincial inequality. The central focus of its program is on helping economically underdeveloped areas – 47 mountainous counties, mostly in northern Guangdong. The province relied mainly on budgetary assistance in the mid-1980s, but has since combined budgetary assistance with other types of more active development assistance, including preferential policies such as tax concessions, infrastructural development, and administrative guidance (Zhang Pingli 1992; Yukawa 1992; Ma Encheng 1991: 229). The Guangzhou–Meizhou–Shantou railway, which runs 500 kilometers across Guangdong and was opened in late 1995, was intended to help eliminate poverty in Guangdong's inland areas. A major component of administrative

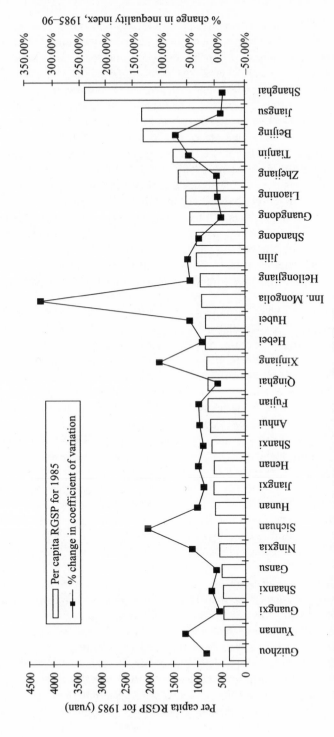

Figure A.2 Development level and changes in intra-provincial inequality, 1985–90

Source: Zhongguo fenxian nongcun jingji tongji gaiyao 1989–93.

guidance has been a one-to-one assistance program started in late 1990, in which more prosperous localities were paired up with less developed ones.[10] Facilitated by the Provincial Economic Cooperation Office, the program helped eight poverty-stricken cities and counties to forge cooperative ties with seven prosperous coastal cities in 1991. For instance, Shenzhen was paired with the mountainous Meixian prefecture. Shenzhen facilitated the relocation of labor-intensive enterprises to Meixian to take advantage of the raw materials available there. By late 1995, the county-to-county cooperation had resulted in 520 cooperation projects involving 800 million yuan and 250,000 jobs for farmers in underdeveloped areas (Guangdong 1995). In 1996, Shenzhen used 60 million yuan from its cooperation and development fund to assist four counties that were particularly poor (*QB* 6/12/96: 20). In Qingyuan, which has a heavy concentration of poor localities, China's first economic development zone for alleviating poverty was launched in early 1992. Among its special features, poor counties or towns are allowed to retain all the profits and taxes if they operate enterprises in the zone. And the employees will be recruited mainly from the poor areas. The zone has since attracted a number of international investments (Xinhua 1992b, 1992c).

When the usual types of development assistance prove of very limited effect owing to extremely unfavorable natural conditions in the target county, the province has in recent years resorted to the resettlement of inhabitants to more prosperous areas in order to fulfill the provincial goal of eradicating poverty. Such relocations not only allow the migrants to leave their infertile land behind but also open up new employment opportunities. In Liannan county, 2,000 rural households living in limestone areas were relocated within the province and successfully shook off poverty (Guangdong People's Radio 1992). In Qingxin County, at least 10,000 local residents have been resettled. Some of the migrants have found farming work in richer areas where most farmers have turned to industrial or commercial trade; others have found employment in the poverty-relief experimental zones set up by local governments. It appears that such relocations have encountered some resistance from communities receiving the migrant population, but the provincial government has justified the move as necessary for the overall prosperity of the province and it is reported that new measures will be developed and imposed to help ease the pains of resettlement (Li Zhuoyan 1993: 3).

The Guangdong experience shows the role of the government's visible hand in counteracting intra-provincial disparities. Although the measurement of cause and effect is difficult, the official effort appears to have contributed to the alleviation of such disparities. Such government involvement can also be found in other areas such as Jiangsu and Shandong. In Jiangsu province, the provincial effort to deal with intra-provincial inequality has focused on the north–south contrast (*subei* vs. *sunan*), with northern Jiangsu being less economically developed than its smaller southern counterpart.[11] The provincial government has developed programs to accelerate infrastructural construction in the north, provide low-interest loans for the less developed northern part to start agricultural and processing industries, and encourage cooperation between more advanced southern enterprises and their northern counterparts. Selected personnel from the north will receive training in the south and the provincial government will dispatch technical personnel to poor areas to offer assistance (Xinhua 1992d). The Jiangsu provincial government has stipulated that rural enterprises from the more prosperous Sunan (southern Jiangsu) will enjoy the same preferential treatment as foreign enterprises if they invest in northern Jiangsu (Wang Zenong 1994).

Like Jiangsu, the provincial government in neighboring Shandong has pledged more support in terms of funds, technology, manpower, and special policy for rural enterprises located in the northwestern part of the province and the Yimeng mountains (Liu Peifang 1994: 13). Since the mid-1980s, the province has organized cooperation and mutual support between units in Qingdao, Yantai, and other cities in the eastern coast and those in Linyi, Liaocheng, Binzhou, and other prefectures and cities in the west, launching over 100 projects in 1993 alone (Li Chunting 1995). In the meantime, Zhejiang province has worked out concrete measures to help poverty-stricken counties develop their economies through aid and technical assistance (Xinhua 1992e). As in Guangdong, both Zhejiang and Jiangsu have seen their indices of intra-provincial disparities decrease; yet it is presently not possible to trace the causal linkages between official action and the reduction in intra-provincial disparities because the official programs were launched only recently and we have little information on how they have been implemented.

In contrast to more developed provinces, prospects for the alleviation of intra-provincial disparities in the poor provinces are far more daunting because of the fact that such disparities tend to increase in the early stages of economic development. As Thomas Lyons points out in an important study on Fujian, despite heavy investment in social overhead capital in 17 poverty counties in Fujian, both the absolute and relative gaps between them and the rest of Fujian had increased over the 1980 to 1990 period (Lyons 1992). This does not mean that the inverted-U trend admits no exceptions, however. Gansu appears to be such an exception.

Of all the provinces, Gansu had one of the highest concentrations of rural poor and an incidence of poverty that was much above the national average (40 percent in 1982 compared with the national average of 13 percent) (World Bank 1988: ix). Since 1983, Gansu has been the target of China's most comprehensive poverty-reduction programs. The Three-Xi region – where 75 percent of the total farming population lived below the level of basic subsistence in the early 1980s – of Gansu–Ningxia is centered in Gansu and has received much attention not only from the central government but also from international aid agencies such as the World Bank. In 1989, for example, the special Three-Xi grant supported 20 counties in Gansu, the provincial government supported another 12, and the center another nine as poor counties, covering more than half of all the counties in the province (Ahmad and Yan Wang 1991: 252). As a result of such fiscal support, government expenditures per capita on social services and other items are higher in Gansu than in some richer provinces, such as Jiangsu, and total government expenditure has also increased more rapidly in the province than in the country as a whole. With the support, the province has been able to launch a massive resettlement program for inhabitants of the Three-Xi region. By the end of 1990, 320,000 of the projected 450,000 people had been resettled. The settlement program has been declared "outstanding" for raising the living standards of the target population (Zhang Shusheng 1991). By 1990, the number of poverty-stricken households living below subsistence in the Three-Xi region had dropped to 10 percent from the original 75 percent of the total farming population (Tian Jiyun 1992). Thus we think that the major anti-poverty program in Gansu that has been undertaken by an alliance of the localities concerned, the central government, and international organizations such as the World Bank may have contributed to the relatively less rapid increase in intra-provincial inequality within the province for the period under study. Yet even in Gansu, we think as the economy grows after the conclusion of the anti-poverty program, it will probably also fall prey to the normal pattern.

CONCLUSION

The patterns of intra-provincial inequality in China saw significant changes between 1985 and 1990. In most provinces, intra-provincial economic disparities increased significantly over the period. Moreover, the magnitude of intra-provincial inequality suggests that it is incomplete to focus our attention on regional inequalities across provinces and between the coast and the interior. A similar criticism may also be made of China's national, and most regional, leaders, who appear to be more preoccupied with the development gap between coast and interior and between their own province and others than with development gaps within the provinces.[12] It is hoped that the present study may contribute to reshaping the terms of the debate regarding regional inequality in China.

Whereas intra-provincial inequality increased overall, other trends can also be discerned. A number of more developed coastal provinces saw decreases in intra-provincial inequality. As Guangdong, Jiangsu, and Zhejiang are in the forefront of economic growth, the prognosis is encouraging, as these areas are looked upon as models for other areas. This suggests that as an area becomes more developed economically, it is likely to pay more attention to combatting the incidence of poverty, such as aid to poverty-stricken counties, thereby alleviating intra-provincial inequality (see Yu Honghui and Yan Xiaohong 1995: 4). The evidence does seem to indicate that growth can be combined with more regional (inter-county) equity within provinces and that significant government involvement can have a salutary effect in promoting factor mobility into less developed areas.

Table A.5 Summary statistics for variables contained in Tables A.2–4

Number of observations: 28	1985			1990		
	Mean	Standard deviation	Median	Mean	Standard deviation	Median
Mean county-level per capita rural gross social product (yuan)	990.44	763.86	777.62	2583.61	2078.27	1841.59
Coefficient of variation (c.v.)	0.486	0.202	0.422	0.677	0.432	0.574
Geographic size (1,000 square kilometers)	296.034	370.525	171.525	296.034	370.525	171.525
% change in c.v. between 1985 and 1990				42.48%	64.71%	32.85%
Rural population size (millions)	29.75	21.66	25.36	31.71	23.20	26.70
Fiscal subsidy as % of provincial revenue	38.04%	91.30%	18.31%	10.89%	32.08%	13.74%
% of counties classified as ethnic autonomous counties	26.46%	37.53%	6.22%	28.07%	37.62%	6.42%

Source: Zhongguo fenxian nongcun jingji tongji gaiyao 1989–93.

Nevertheless, one must caution that whether other areas can replicate the experiences of Guangdong and Zhejiang remains to be seen and ought to be further monitored. With regard to China's poor provinces, the prospects for alleviating intra-provincial disparities are expected to worsen in the intermediate future and even if central subsidies to poor areas were allocated with the alleviation of intra-provincial disparities in mind, they would probably only have a temporary effect. For the long run, the promotion of growth is the best medicine for promoting more even regional economic development patterns within the less developed provinces.

Notes

CHAPTER 1: ANALYTICAL PERSPECTIVES

1 See especially Denny (1991); Lyons (1991); Tsui (1991); and more recently Chen and Fleisher 1996. In contrast, earlier works by Paine (1976, 1981) and Lardy (1978, 1980) paid more attention to government policy partly because these authors had relatively little data to work with.

2 For analysis of the great administrative region, see Solinger (1977). There is media speculation that China may decide to set up six regional administrative bureaux in 1996 or 1997 that will partially resurrect the great administrative regions. The six regions according to this classification will probably be: central southern China, east China, the north, northeast, northwest, and southwest (*SCMPIW* 6/29/96: 7).

3 Of the provincial level units, four (Beijing, Shanghai, Tianjin, Chongqing) are centrally administered municipalities and five (Guangxi, Inner Mongolia, Ningxia, Tibet, Xinjiang) are designated ethnic autonomous regions. In addition, Hong Kong will become part of China in mid-1997 as a Special Administration Region. For the sake of convenience, I will use "province" or "provincial unit" to denote all provincial level units rather than write, as in most Chinese writings, "provinces, municipalities, and autonomous regions."

4 For studies that alert to or deal with this issue, see Cannon (1990: 33), Lyons (1992), and D. Yang (1995b).

5 The regional classification of provinces has evolved over time. When the terms were between east versus interior rather than coast versus interior, Guangxi was often assigned to the western region owing to its relative poverty. Moreover, some have argued that Sichuan and Shaanxi belong to the central region, not the western region (Liu Zaixing 1993: 101; for other views, see Hu Xiyin 1991). This study adopts the most widely used coast–interior regionalization scheme as used in China's Seventh Five-Year Plan. An exception will be the case study on rural enterprise policy in chapter 6, which makes a small adjustment to the prevailing regionalization to accommodate available data.

6 An incomplete list of major industrial cities in the coastal region would include Beijing, Tianjin, Shanghai, Dalian, Anshan, Fushun, Shenyang, Qingdao, Jinan, Nanjing, Hangzhou, Fuzhou, Guangzhou and Shenzhen. Hong Kong, which will revert to Chinese sovereignty in mid-1997, is obviously part of the coastal region but is currently excluded from Chinese statistics.

7 In making this statement, I am aware that not every coastal province has gained equally; nor has every interior province lagged behind either.

8 Friedmann (1988: 103) would consider Myrdal's assertion a mere first step and go on to call for a fundamentally restructured political community where there is continuous

progress toward the bases of social power (including knowledge, skills, social and political organization, health care, information, social networks, and financial means) among households and a public sphere for discourse over development objectives.

CHAPTER 2: FROM MAO TO DENG: REGIONAL DEVELOPMENT POLICIES AND PRACTICES

1 As in the case of Maoist development strategy, the phrase "Dengist development strategy" is used as a shorthand. As I argue elsewhere (D. Yang 1996a), Deng's role in launching the reforms has been overestimated by the conventional literature. As will be discussed in the rest of this book, while Deng's influence on regional development policy appears great, it may simply reflect other, more structural, political forces that are driving China's political economy.

2 For a useful delineation of the positions discussed here and their respective advocates, see Yan Kaizhong (1989: 26).

3 While the First Five-Year Plan covers the 1953–57 period, the decision on the plan was not officially approved until July 1955.

4 The two measures for China and the US are not exactly the same but in practice they are roughly comparable when measuring relative changes over time.

5 Provinces whose percentage of the national average changed by a mere 1 percent are counted as "even." Hence, Shanxi and Sichuan, both interior provinces, are not counted as losers. Nevertheless, even if they were counted as such, a larger proportion of the coastal provinces still suffered decline.

6 Mao Zedong (1974: 67) was clearly aware of the productivity differential between the coastal and interior industries when he wrote: "The technical level of coastal industry is high, the quality of its products good, its costs low, and it produces many new products."

7 An excellent analysis of the Maoist self-reliance policy is found in Riskin (1987: chapter 9). See also Yang (1996a: chapter 4).

8 Throughout his career, Chen stressed the importance of balance. Chen also had reservations about the special economic zones. For studies of Chen Yun, see Bachman (1985) and Ye Yonglie (1995).

9 It appears that Hu Yaobang, Zhao Ziyang's predecessor as Party General Secretary, was more concerned about interior development and may have had a moderating effect on Zhao before 1987, when Hu was forced to resign.

10 The metaphor of the three regions being three steps on a ladder partly corresponds to the altitude-shifts in Chinese geography (Lu Dadao *et al.* 1990: 14–15).

11 The principle of comparative advantage holds the seemingly innocuous notion that each country (or region within a country) will specialize in the production and export of those goods it can produce at relatively low cost. In recent years, however, economists have recognized that a country's comparative advantage is not static and may be changed through human action. As will be discussed in chapter 5, some provinces in China have sought to jump-start their development.

12 For a summary and critique of the liberal economic theory of development, see Gilpin (1987), especially chapter 7.

13 Owing to space limitation, I will not try to compare in detail the three regions with the widely used six political-administrative regions (northeast, north, east, central south, southwest, northwest). It suffices to say that, while the division of the country into six regions was mainly based on political, military, and administrative considerations, the three-region scheme is almost entirely based on administrative divisions (1949–80); see Suzanne Paine (1981: 193–94).

14 To be more exact, the four zones were first called special export zones and were

renamed special economic zones in May 1980. For the various local interests that were involved in the creation of the special zones, see Song Renqiong (1992: 2–3); Crane (1990: 26–31); Liu Zhigeng (1991: 4–5).

15 Deng (1993: 84) stated that he did two things in 1984. One was the opening of the 14 coastal cities. The other was to decide on using the formula of "one country, two systems" to facilitate the recovery of Hong Kong.

16 The existence of insurance and housing as a commodity has enabled workers and staff members to cease their dependence on their work units and thus provide the conditions for a genuine labor market.

17 Lardy (1994) provides an excellent survey.

18 If the value of agricultural output (i.e. figuring in the rapid growth of rural industries as well as agriculture) is included in calculating regional shares, the trend identified here is even more robust (D. Yang 1990: 251). Incidentally, on the basis of trends in the early 1980s, I forecast earlier (*Ibid*.: 250) that the coastal share of national GVIO would increase between 0.1 and 0.4 percentage points per year. I was far too conservative!

19 It is worth noting that spatial references often vary in different locations and thus are prone to cause terminological confusion. For Hong Kong, for example, Guangdong is already the "interior." While officially China demarcates south and north by the Yangtze River, for residents of Guangdong, those areas that are north of their native province belong to the "north."

20 Even under market conditions, government policy would still have an impact on patterns of regional development. I do not mean to deny this in the text.

CHAPTER 3: THE DYNAMICS AND PROGRESSION OF COMPETITIVE LIBERALIZATION

1 In fact, several waves of decentralization in the fiscal and administrative system have occurred since the Great Leap Forward to stimulate local enthusiasm and initiative. For general discussions, see Schurmann (1968), Donnithorne (1981), Zuo Chuntai and Song Xinzhong (1988), Oksenberg and Tong (1991), Shirk (1993), D. Yang (1994).

2 It must be pointed out that local cadres may have mixed motives for pursuing certain policies, including economic growth. Local cadres may want to win promotions, but as local resources have expanded officials in prosperous areas have few incentives to move to the center and become functionaries.

3 I elaborate on this theme in D. Yang (1993). Howell (1993) points to the spiral nature of China's Open Policy.

4 For contemporary criticisms of the special economic zones, see Chan, Chen, and Chin (1986: 95–98); and Crane (1990: 35–40).

5 Shortly after Hu's visit, joint ventures that were previously required to export all output were given permission to sell some products within China. Other changes followed.

6 It should be pointed out here that the opening of special zones in other parts of the country would not lead to terminations of the earlier cooperative arrangements for two reasons. First, the four SEZs still had more liberal business environments. Second, most cooperative ventures were likely to have become used to doing business in the zones and it was costly to relocate. For a useful discussion of the many advantages Shenzhen possessed as an extension of Hong Kong, see Vogel (1989: 148–49).

7 The zone was formally called *gaige kaifang guodu shiyan qu* (transitional and experimental zone for reform and opening up). The two counties were Binzhou and Lingling. Both have since been upgraded to city status.

8 Central leaders including Li Peng, Zhu Rongji, Qiao Shi, Tian Jiyun visited the SEZs in 1991 to allay their fears.

9 For discussion of other probable reasons behind Deng's move, see Tony Saich (1993). For background analysis as well as chronology surrounding Deng's southern tour, see Directorate of Intelligence (1992). A number of Chinese books include detailed reports on Deng's southern tour and its ramifications; see, for example, Yuan Shang and Han Zhu (1992).

10 For a compilation of local preferential policies, see Renmin ribao guonei zhengzhi bu (1993).

11 Note, however, that the *People's Daily* reported a different set of figures, saying that the number of development zones was reduced from 1,006 to 249 in four months (*RMRBO* 8/17/93: 1).

12 For Chinese discussions of the political advantages of emphasizing reforms in some areas first, see Yang Zhongwei, Chen Kaiguo, and Pei Changhong (1988); and Jiang Qinghai (1995).

13 In fact, the Ministry of Construction began to implement a new set of regulations to control development zones on July 1, 1995. Under these regulations, new development zones must get approval from urban planning departments to ensure that they conform to the City Planning Act (Yang Yingshi 1995).

14 The present game can also be modeled as a game between the CG and a province with incomplete information where the province cannot be sure if liberalization will be met with punishment from the center. The introduction of uncertainty makes the game more complicated but the basic dynamic remains unchanged.

CHAPTER 4: RESOURCES, REGIONAL CLEAVAGES, AND MARKET INTEGRATION

1 Obviously the phenomenon described here is not confined to relations between regions but also occurs within regions.

2 For a regional breakdown of mineral and raw materials deposits, see Yang Jianrong and Yao Xiaobo (1993: 4).

3 Until the late 1980s, most output was purchased by the state and market demand was therefore not an issue.

4 Interview with Chen Yizi, Princeton, N.J., 1991.

5 In the early 1980s Chinese reformers sought to rationalize the price system but could not carry it through owing to bureaucratic resistance and technical difficulties (Naughton 1995: 129–30).

6 Hu's profit-sharing proposal called for raw materials processors to receive the profits arising from their superior technical level and for raw materials exporters to receive the profits that the exporters might have derived from processing the raw materials locally. The proposal stood no chance of actual implementation because of the enormous difficulties in calculating the profits due to each potential beneficiary.

7 It should be pointed out that such feelings could also be found in parts of the coastal region. For example, until it became a separate province, Hainan Island saw itself as being shortchanged and that it was not adequately compensated for the high-quality iron ore, rubber, and salt that it produced and exported. Outside financial help was niggardly, "enough to create economic dependence on the outside without contributing to island development" (Vogel 1989: 289).

8 On the fiscal linkages between the local economy and local governments, see Byrd and Gelb (1990: 358–87). While the focus of Byrd and Gelb is on rural industries, their argument is also applicable to other types of local industries.

9 Needless to say, the cleavage discussed here can also be found within regions.

10 For an impressionistic overview of regional cleavages, see Dick Wilson (1996).
11 The wool textile industry accounted for 20 percent of provincial revenue in Qinghai, over 10 percent in Xinjiang, and over 8 percent in Gansu and Inner Mongolia.
12 The share produced by the interior = 100 − coastal share.
13 The later reversal of the trends identified here is discussed later in this chapter.
14 See, for instance, the data in Yang Kaizhong (1993: 190–92).
15 For data covering the 1989–91 period, see *Zhongguo hengxiang jingji nianjian* (Yearbook of Chinese horizontal economy). For a case study of regional cooperation in southwest China, see Zheng Yongnian (1995: chapter 6).
16 This section draws on D. Yang (1996b: 445–48); and Yang and Wei (1996a).
17 See, for example, "State Council Regulations on Lateral Economic Ties," Xinhua, March 23, 1986, translated in FBIS-China, April 1, 1986, p. K1.
18 See the collection of essays by Chinese writers on local protectionism in *Chinese Economic Studies*, vol. 26, no. 5 (Fall 1993).
19 For the distinction between two different types of decentralization (firm versus local government), see Schurmann (1968: 175–78 and 196–99).
20 For an interesting discussion of the difference size makes, see J. Lewis (1991).
21 In personal interviews with municipal planning officials, a palpable sense of competition comes through. Planning officials often stressed to me that their planned projects should not be revealed publicly for fear that other localities might use such information to get ahead of them.

CHAPTER 5: THE POLITICS OF REGIONAL POLICY REORIENTATION

1 The "tunnel effect" is put forward by Albert Hirschman (1978). He used the analogy of a driver in a jammed tunnel. If the driver sees the other line moving, he will feel his situation has improved too. Apparently, he cannot wait forever. That waiting period of quiescence, Hirschman points out, is determined by many factors. We cannot determine in advance when the period is going to end with the driver resorting to some sort of action.
2 Chen Huai (1994: 3) reports that the disparities between the eastern, central, and western regions will unavoidably grow in the medium and long term according to various forecasts made by the State Council Development Research Center.
3 Of course, this is not to deny that interior provinces have grown quite rapidly as well since the reforms.
4 The following discussion makes no attempt at an exhaustive survey of the vast body of relevant Chinese literature. Besides such major publications as *Jingji yanjiu* (Economic research), *Renmin ribao* (People's daily), *Jingji ribao* (Economic daily), *Kexue guanli yanjiu* (Research in scientific management), *Jingji dili* (Economic geography), *Jingji tizhi gaige* (Economic structural reform), many of the writings on the debate are found in the regionally based publications such as *Neimenggu jingji yanjiu* (Inner Mongolia economic research), *Jingji, shehui* (Economy and society, Inner Mongolia), *Jingji wenti tansuo* (Explorations in economic issues, Yunnan), and *Kexue, jingji, shehui* (Science, economy, and society, Gansu).
5 While they called for readjusting the national regional development strategy, there is a certain irony that economists in underdeveloped provinces, such as Qinghai and Yunnan, drew on regional science to argue that their individual provinces should focus on certain more developed areas within each province to make the best use of existing economic circumstances and better promote provincial economic development (Zhu Xianmin 1993). Their top priority was for their provinces to make a leap in economic development to catch up with the more developed areas of the country just as Zhao Ziyang and other national leaders emphasized the development of the coastal region

so that China could catch up with other countries. For all of them, balanced development within each geographic unit had to take a back seat to the goal of catching up with others.

6 During his southern tour of 1992, however, Deng indicated that China was still in an era when some areas had to grow faster than others and that it was not yet time to give equal emphasis to common prosperity. Deng in effect made use of what Albert Hirschman (1978) had termed the "tunnel effect."

7 Hu was the more moderate of the two and called for the development of the great southwest in 1984.

8 By this time, Zhao had lost control of the economic agenda.

9 For a Chinese critique of the Yangtze River Valley Development Strategy centered around Shanghai, see Wen Qiangzhou (1994). Wen is based in Wuhan.

10 It is not certain whether Deng said everything contained in the transcript of his tour talks and to what extent the transcript was edited by his daughter.

11 Note, however, that this is not a survey based on a representative sample but a survey of cadres who have a vested interest in nationality affairs and happened to be attending study sessions in Beijing.

12 For a useful critique of the development panacea for ethnic issues, see Alan Liu (1996: 212–17).

13 It should be pointed out that central aid and even economic growth does not necessarily lead to ethnic harmony. In resource-rich Xinjiang, for example, the Uighurs have complained of economic apartheid and powerlessness as they believe the benefits of economic growth are going largely to the immigrant Chinese population and that the profits of agricultural and mineral exploitation are going to state enterprises that remit their profits to Beijing. In consequence, instead of growth reducing racial tension, one visitor suggests that ethnic tension has increased as the economy prospers. While ethnic youths become demoralized by the lack of opportunities, the regime takes precautions against minority groups accused of threatening the unity of the motherland (C. Tyler 1996).

14 Xinhua 11/17/95, FBIS-CHI-95–223 11/20/95: 29. See also the comment by Vice Premier Zou Jiahua in "Inland Areas Must Expand Economies," *CD*, 8/30/95: 2; and Zhang Haoruo (1996).

15 For the 1995 budget, central subsidy to local finances amounted to 244.96 billion yuan (43 percent of national revenue). Of the subsidy, 189.4 billion will be tax refunds calculated on the basis of the 1993 revenue base and 37.9 billion will be pure subsidies (Liu Zhongli 1995).

16 In 1996, the central government allocated 3.01 billion yuan in funds for aiding underdeveloped areas, up from 2.75 billion in 1995 (*QB* 4/20/96: 4).

17 Japan announced at the end of 1994 that it would shift the focus of its soft government loan program in China from coastal infrastructural development to other areas so as to help China reduce the gap between interior and coast (Dawkins 1994: 4).

CHAPTER 6: THE DILEMMAS OF REGIONAL POLICY REALIGNMENT

1 In a number of areas such as currency and price reforms, the economic conditions for reform were excellent but Chinese leaders were clearly afraid of major moves and later regretted the missed opportunities or delays. At the time, the official and black market currency exchange rates were converging and inflation was falling, partly owing to the austerity program and partly owing to the impact of the military crackdown on consumer expectations.

2 In tandem with the changes in civilian leaders, there has also been a series of reshuffles in the People's Liberation Army.

3 All references to the Plenum decision shall be to "Decision of the CPC Central Committee on Issues Concerning the Establishment of a Socialist Market Economic Structure" (November 14, 1993), *China Daily* (Supplement), November 17, 1993.

4 According to the Plenum decision (Art. 18) and the Ministry of Finance, the major taxes and responsibilities shall be allocated as follows: the central government is responsible for funding national defense, diplomacy, armed police, key state projects, the national deficit, and governmental administrative departments; other expenditures shall be the responsibility of local governments. Central revenue will come from tariffs, a consumption tax collected by customs, value-added taxes, and (nationally based) business taxes. Taxes collected by local governments include business tax, income tax of local enterprises, and a personal income tax. Taxes shared by both central and local governments include the value-added tax (3:1), securities trading tax (1:1), and natural resources tax (TBA). In other words, the center will rely on indirect taxes, leaving the politically hazardous and administratively cumbersome personal income tax to local authorities. Moreover, it appears that some extra-budgetary revenue is likely to be redefined as budgetary revenue for local authorities.

5 It might be objected that a federal-style economic system is unlikely in the absence of a formal legal system. In reality, such a federal system may evolve into shape historically without taking on the formal trappings. The constitution of a nation depends more on what the nation does than on what it proclaims; some countries have done well without a written constitution. For a recent argument to the same effect, see Montinola, Qian, and Weingast (1995).

6 Some key provisions of the tax reforms will probably be renegotiated. For example, personal income tax revenue is currently assigned to local governments in what I believe to be an act of subversion. Because this revenue stream is growing extremely fast, the center will very likely seek to capture at least part of it in the future.

7 In fact, the stipulation that the local revenue base for the future will be based on the 1993 revenue figures prompted local governments to collect as much revenue as possible in 1993, in some places even collecting part of the 1994 revenue to count as 1993 revenue. This delays the time when the center will benefit from the fiscal restructuring. Moreover, because the rapidly growing personal income tax has been assigned to local governments, there is the possibility that the fiscal restructuring may not meet the center's objectives.

8 This case study is based on Yang and Wei (1996b).

9 Participants in the studies and document drafting came from the Ministry of Agriculture, the State Planning Commission, the State Commission on Nationality Affairs, the People's Bank of China, the State Industry and Commerce Bureau, the State Taxation Bureau, and the Agricultural Bank of China. The papers presented at the symposium are collected in State Council Office of Research (1993).

10 The Department of Rural Enterprises at the Ministry of Agriculture classifies Chinese provinces into the following regions: the east or coastal region includes Beijing, Tianjin, Hebei, Liaoning, Shanghai, Jiangsu, Zhejiang, Fujian, Shandong, and Guangdong; the central region includes Shanxi, Inner Mongolia, Jilin, Heilongjiang, Anhui, Jiangxi, Henan, Hubei, Hunan, Sichuan, and Shaanxi; Guizhou, Yunnan, Tibet, Gansu, Qinghai, Ningxia, Xinjiang, Guangxi, and Hainan belong to the western region. This regional classification scheme thus differs slightly from the conventional scheme as adopted in this volume. For analytical convenience we follow the MoA classification in this case study since it is used in the formulation and evaluation of the program discussed here.

11 While the transient population has contributed to these problems, it should also be pointed out that these problems would still exist in the absence of the transient population. On the political economy of the urban transients phenomenon, see

Solinger (1995). Most transient workers have tended to originate from Sichuan, Jiangxi, Hunan, Hubei, Henan and Anhui provinces. In 1993, these provinces were estimated to have accounted for more than one-third of the total number of migrant workers (Zhu Ze 1993).

12 Authors' interviews; *RMRB* 3/24/95: 2.

13 In 1990, 1,036 (60 percent of the region's total) counties in the central region and 813 (47 percent of the region's total) in the western region received fiscal subsidies (Ministry of Finance 1993: 1).

14 Among 66 demonstration zones, seven are in Sichuan; five each in Henan, Hubei, Jiangxi, Anhui, Heilongjiang, Shaanxi and Gansu respectively; four each in Hunan and Inner Mongolia; three each in Guangxi and Xinjiang; two each in Yunnan, Guizhou, Ningxia and Qinghai; and one each in Jilin and Shanxi.

15 Calculated in current prices based on data from Ministry of Agriculture Bureau of Rural Enterprises (1994).

16 In late 1994 the State Statistical Bureau requested local governments to recheck their 1993 figures on rural enterprise output. It was believed that there was substantial exaggeration of output figures at the local level. We have not yet seen the revised figures.

CHAPTER 7: THE DEBATE OVER SPECIAL ECONOMIC ZONES

1 The financial flow was not all going into the interior, however. By the end of 1990, there were 3,945 *neilian* enterprises registered in Shenzhen (about one-third of the total). These enterprises had agreements to invest a total of 9.5 billion yuan in Shenzhen and actual investment reached 4.5 billion yuan (Liu Zhigeng 1991: 203).

2 See Guowuyuan teq"u bangongshi (1993: 184); details on each zone may be found in Wang Sanmin, Xu Fan, and Huang Deli (1993).

3 Or, as Hu Ping, head of the State Council Office for Special Economic Zones, was quoted as saying: "Provinces and autonomous regions in the landlocked middle and western part of China are desperate for their turn to develop" (Macartney 1995b).

4 Usually the suggestions and demands are referred to the relevant government departments for response or action.

5 In an interview with *Jingji ribao* reporters in July 1995, Hu Ping, director of the State Council Office of Special Economic Zones, formally announced that the central government had no plans for designating special economic zones in the interior (*JJRB* 7/19/95: 1).

6 Ironically, Hu Ping, director of the State Council Office for Special Economic Zones, seemed to be in agreement with Hu Angang at the start of the debate. In an interview published in November 1994, Hu Ping agreed that the differentiation between "special" and "nonspecial" zones had been reduced or basically levelled up. He thought that the fact that the special economic zones were no longer special was a good thing because it indicated that the experiments in the zones had become widely adopted (Ma Ling 1994). For a critique of Hu Angang's justification of his argument by invoking international practices, see Yin Yan (1996), who reports on an article published in *STB* by Wang Zhenzhong of the Institute of Economics of the Chinese Academy of Social Sciences.

7 The figure peaked at 28 percent in 1989 and fell to 18 percent in 1994.

8 As of 1995, investor privileges at the special economic zones (Shenzhen, Zhuhai, Xiamen, Shantou, and Hainan) include the following: 15 percent income tax rate, as opposed to 33 percent for most other areas of China; tax holidays for companies during their first two years of profitability, 50 percent tax exemptions for third and fourth years; tax exemption on reinvested profits; exemptions from import duties on

production equipment and materials; wide-ranging autonomy in setting other economic policies (Smith 1995).

9 For Hainan's difficulties, see Tan Chieh-hua (1995).

10 While I have focused on Shenzhen in this chapter, other special economic zones are also involved in this debate through both local and national publications. See, for example, the essay by Xiamen Party Secretary Shi Zhaobin (1994). Shi rebutted the argument that China would not be able to have special economic zones once it joined GATT and pointed out that many countries belonging to GATT had various special development zones.

11 In addition, the controversial Yangpu Economic Development Zone in Hainan was also given free-trade zone status in spring 1995. The leadership pledged that Yangpu would enjoy all preferential policies with the exception of passenger car imports (Jiang Shijie 1996).

12 In the words of one Guangdong official: "We are not opposed to central and western areas speeding up their growth, but the central authorities should let the coast continue with its existing policies" (quoted in Lam 1995a).

13 Shenzhen is the only city in China that has been granted the power to decide interest rates. When the People's Bank of China trimmed interest rates on loans by an average of 0.75 percent and those on deposits by 0.98 percent on May 1, 1996, Shenzhen followed suit with cuts of 1.12 and 0.83 percentage points respectively.

14 Hainan acquired the same power in 1988 by virtue of its provincial status while Shenzhen and Xiamen were given such power in 1992 and 1994 respectively.

15 Skeptics have suggested that bureaucratic rent-seeking and competition have made Pudong less attractive than it appears in the official media (Sender 1994).

16 In addition to Deng, Pudong also enjoyed the endorsement of Chen Yun (Ye Yonglie 1995: 288–89). For changes in Pudong, see the journal *Pudong kaifa* (Pudong development).

17 Jiang reportedly criticized Shanghai's leaders for going beyond their authority in extending favorable treatment to foreign enterprises, retailing, and banking, and for the premature announcement of several autonomous powers given to them by Beijing (Lam 1995c; see also Lien Ho Pao Reporters 1995).

18 It has been reported that the central leadership originally planned to give Pudong a very generous revenue arrangement but shelved the plan amid China's tax and fiscal reforms (Chu Chia-chien 1995).

19 During his tour of Shenzhen, Jiang discussed Shenzhen's role in helping China's recovery of sovereignty over Hong Kong and maintaining Hong Kong's prosperity and stability. He said: "In reality, you have been playing this role to a great extent over the last dozen years and more. Imagine if Shenzhen were still a little backward border town while Hong Kong enjoyed a high economic profile, this would be a striking contrast, and it would not have been good for Hong Kong's smooth transition and for maintaining its prosperity and stability after China has resumed sovereignty over it" (Chen Xitian 1995).

20 For similar reports on Premier Li Peng, see Lim (1996) and *RMRBO* (4/5/96: 1 and 3).

21 Indeed, as Yu Xianpei and Guo Shiping point out, following more than a decade of rapid growth, Shenzhen already possesses substantial economic strength and can do quite well even without tax and fiscal privileges (Yu Xianpei and Guo Shiping 1994).

CHAPTER 8: REGIONAL DOMINANCE AND REGIONAL CHANGE

1 Historically, provinces have been more influential in the CCP (through the Central Committee) than in the government. But the Central Committee tends to be packed by central leaders. Currently, none of the Political Bureau members comes from the interior. See Shirk (1993: Chapter 6). Central leaders including Jiang Zemin and Li Peng have become more sympathetic toward the poor through their extensive travels across the country.

2 I do not deny that many officials are also driven by a sense of fairness and equity. It should also be pointed out that economically redistribution does not necessarily discourage economic growth. A recent study has in fact found a positive relationship between government transfers (including spending on unemployment insurance, education, and pensions) and economic growth (Benabou 1996).

3 "Efforts To Bridge Economic Gap Detailed," Xinhua in English, August 27, 1995; FBIS-CHI August 28, 1995, 36–37.

4 The inter-regional ties are not limited to manufacturing and have increasingly spread to the service sector.

5 The rest of this subsection draws heavily on Wei and Yang (1997).

6 For regional economic development level, the indicators used include per capita gross domestic product (PGDP) and per capita rural household net income (PNI). The indicators for regional educational expenditure include per capita educational expenditure, budgeted educational expenditure per capita, and primary education expenditure per pupil.

7 For 1991, the correlation coefficient between PRP and gross domestic product per capita (logged) was 0.7583. PRP instead of primary school enrollment rate is used here because enrollment of school-age children (aged 7–11) in primary schools is nearly universal with the exception of a few underdeveloped provinces such as Tibet (52.35 percent), Qinghai (83.89 percent), Guizhou (93.78), and Sichuan (94.54 percent).

8 A social explanation is also needed, however, because most students (about 70 percent) dropping out of school tend to be girls.

9 For details of the government goals, see Cui Ning (1996).

10 Jiangxi's major coal mine in the early twentieth century was operated by outsiders.

11 With about 3.3 percent of the total population, Jiangxi garnered only 1.8 percent of the state capital construction investment over 1949–80, but even this figure fell steadily and hovered around 1.5 percent over 1986–89.

APPENDIX 1: REFORM AND INTRA-PROVINCIAL INEQUALITY IN CHINA: A PRELIMINARY STUDY

1 Originally written in 1993, this is an exploratory study of the patterns of intra-provincial disparities in China. It is preliminary because it focuses on a relatively short time period and uses only a small number of indicators. I have included it here in the hope that others may find the theme worthwhile to pursue further. A partial Chinese translation of the study appeared as D. Yang (1995b). C. Fan (1995) deals with changes in a number of provinces.

2 Exceptions to this trend include the volume edited by Gregory Veeck, *The Uneven Landscape*, which includes several studies of individual provinces and recent works by Cindy Fan. Professor William Skinner is widely known to have been compiling and examining county-level data.

3 On the problems of defining what is "rural" in China, see Martin (1992).

4 In contrast to the present study, both Tsui and Lyons use net material product (NMP),

a value-added measure, in their studies of inter-provincial disparities cited above. The NMP is clearly a superior yardstick compared with gross social product, which admits to some double counting, especially in the industrial sector, although the trends for both measures are similar. The Chinese government has not released data based on NMP for the rural sectors.

5 According to Lyons (1991: 475), "If regions themselves are the units of interest, use of unweighted coefficients may be more appropriate." Denny (1991) also uses unweighted coefficients.

6 Lyons examined the relative dispersion of aggregate output for Chinese provinces over the 1978–87 period. It must be kept in mind that inequality measurement is sensitive to the time periods used as well.

7 Additional sources of data are from *Zhongguo nongye nianjian* (1986: 150; 1991: 270, 273).

8 Additional data are from World Bank (1990b: 147); Ministry of Finance (1992: 336–37); *ZGTJNJ* (1986: 1, 64; 1991: 3, 66).

9 Bo (1993: Table 24). The data used here are from Guangdong Provincial Statistical Bureau (1991).

10 Similar programs can also be found in other provinces.

11 For background and an exploration of the socio-ethnic ramifications of the north–south contrast in Jiangsu, see Honig (1992).

12 See, for example, *Beijing Review* (1992); Kung Shuangyin (1992); People's Daily Commentator (1992); Xinhua (1992a); Li Anding and Xie Shiqiu (1992); Chen Yanhua (1992); Liu Haimin (1992); He Ping (1992). It should be pointed out, however, that in China, as in other East Asian nations such as Japan and South Korea, such "gap consciousness" or crisis mentality has served as a powerful ideological force for economic development.

Works cited

Agnew, John. (1987) *The United States and the World Economy*, Cambridge: Cambridge University Press.

Ahmad, Ehtisham and Yan Wang. (1991) "Inequality and Poverty in China: Institutional Change and Public Policy, 1978 to 1988," *World Bank Economic Review*, vol. 5, no. 2.

Anhui Shengwei Zhengyanshi (Office of Policy Research at the Anhui Provincial CCP Committee). (1993) "Zhuahao siyou, tiaozheng jiegou, cujin wosheng xiangzhen qiye gaosu gaoxiao fazhan" (Grasp rationalization, adjust structure and promote the rapid and efficient development of rural enterprises in our province), *Anhui shengqing shengli* (Anhui: provincial situation and strength), nos 2–3: 10–13.

Arthur, Brian. (1994) *Increasing Returns and Path Dependence in the Economy*, Ann Arbor: University of Michigan Press.

Bachman, David. (1985) *Chen Yun and the Chinese Political System*, Berkeley: University of California, Berkeley Center for Chinese Studies.

——. (1989) "The Ministry of Finance and Chinese Politics," *Pacific Affairs*, vol. 62, no. 2 (Summer): 167–87.

——. (1990) "Planning and Politics in Mainland China Since the Massacre," *Issues and Studies*, vol. 26, no. 8: 43–66.

Baum, Richard. (1992) "The Paralysis of Power: Chinese Politics Since Tiananmen," pp. 7–36 in William Joseph (ed.) *China Briefing 1991*, Boulder, Colorado: Westview Press.

——. (1994) *Burying Mao: Chinese Politics in the Age of Deng Xiaoping*, Princeton: Princeton University Press.

Becker, Gary S. (1993) *Human Capital*, Chicago: University of Chicago Press.

Beijing Review. (1992) "Zou Jiahua Discusses Regional Economies," *Beijing Review*, no. 31, August 3–9: 14–18.

Benabou, Roland. (1996) "Inequality and Growth," *NBER Macroeconomic Annual*, forthcoming.

Bernard, Mitchell and John Ravenhill. (1995) "Beyond Product Cycles and Flying Geese: Regionalization, Hierarchy, and the Industrialization of East Asia," *World Politics*, vol. 47, no. 2: 171–209.

Bernstein, Thomas. (1984) "Stalinism, Famine, and Chinese Peasants," *Theory and Society*, vol. 13, no. 3 (May).

Bhagwati, Jagdish. (1987) "Outward Orientation," in Vittorio Corbo, Morris Goldstein, and Mohsin Khan (eds) *Growth-Oriented Adjustment Programs*, Washington, D.C.: IMF/The World Bank.

Bo, Zhiyue. (1993) "Redistribution and Economic Growth in Guangdong," qualifying paper, Department of Political Science, University of Chicago, May 1993.

——. (1996) "Economic Performance and Political Mobility: Chinese Provincial Leaders," *Journal of Contemporary China*, vol. 5, no. 12 (July): 135–54.

Bogdanor, Vernon (ed.) (1991) *The Blackwell Encyclopaedia of Political Science*, Oxford: Blackwell.

Brauchli, Marcus. (1993) "China's Hinterland Seeks Coast's Progress," Dow Jones Newswire, November 3.

Burns, John P. (ed.). (1989) *The Chinese Communist Party's Nomenklatura System*, Armonk, N.Y.: M.E. Sharpe.

Byrd, William, and Alan Gelb. (1990) "Why Industrialize? The Incentives for Rural Community Governments," in William Byrd and Lin Qingsong (eds) *China's Rural Industry: Structure, Development, and Reform*, New York: Oxford University Press: 358–87.

Cannon, Terry. (1990) "Regions: Spatial Inequality and Regional Policy," in Terry Cannon and Alan Jenkins (eds) *The Geography of Contemporary China: The Impact of Deng Xiaoping's Reforms*, London: Routledge.

Cao Min. (1995) "Exchanges Aim to Narrow Wealth Gap," *CD*, February 11: 2.

CBR. (1986) "Overview of Investment Incentives," *China Business Review*, vol. 13 (May–June): 20–23.

Chan, Thomas, E.K.Y. Chen, and Steve Chin. (1986) "China's Special Economic Zones: Ideology, Policy and Practice," in Jao and Leung (eds): 87–104.

Chang Mu. (1991) "A New Economic Operational System Will Be Established in 10 Years with the Aim of Seeking the Unity of the Nucleus and Ensuring the Stability of the General Situation," *Ching Pao,* Hong Kong, no. 163, February 10: 22–25; FBIS-CHI-91–040, February 28: 38–39.

Che Guocheng. (1995) "Guanyu suoxiao dongxi bu jingji fazhan chaju de sikao" (Thoughts on reducing the economic disparities between east and west), *Jingji tizhi gaige* (Reformation of economic system), no. 4: 78–83.

Chen Chien-ping. (1993) "Inside Story of Drafting Third Plenary Session's Decision," *Wen Wei Po*, November 24: 2, FBIS-CHI-93–228, November 30: 21–22.

Chen Guojun. (1995) "Xinjiang Greets Important Turning Point in Economic Construction", *Liaowang*, no. 40 (October 2): 30–32; FBIS-CHI-95–229, November 29: 86–91.

Chen Huai. (1994) "Jiushi niandai zhongguo diqu jingji fazhan de jiben zhanlue" (The basic strategy for China's regional economic development in the 1990s), *Jingji lilun yu jingji guanli* (Economic theory and economic management), no. 2: 1–6.

Chen, Jian and Belton Fleisher. (1996) "Regional Income Inequality and Economic Growth in China," *Journal of Comparative Economics*, vol. 22: 141–64.

Chen Jiaze. (1987) "Tidu tuiyi he fazhan ji – zengzhang dian lilun yanjiu" (A study of the theories of ladder-step diffusion and growth poles – points), *JJYJ*, no. 3: 33–39.

Chen, Kathy. (1992) "In Some Provinces, Beijing's Go-Slow Directives Spawn Innovative Strategies for More Growth," *AWSJW*, July 19: 2.

——. (1993) "China's Hunan Province Hopes to Match Neighbors," *AWSJW*, June 14: 1.

Chen, Kathy and Julia Leung. (1993) "China Endorses Swift Market Reform, Signals Privatization," Dow Jones Newswire, November 15.

Chen Ko. (1994) "Will There be Special Economic Zones Set Up in the Northwest?" *Tang tai* (Contemporary), no. 43, October 15: 57–59; FBIS-CHI-95–007, January 11: 66–69.

Chen Minzhi (ed.). (1985) *Shanghai jingji fazhan zhanlue yanjiu* (A study of Shanghai's Economic Development Strategy), Shanghai: Shanghai renmin chubanshe.

Chen Xitian. (1995) "While Meeting with Shenzhen's Responsible Comrades, Jiang Zemin Stresses that Shenzhen Must Increase Its Strong Points to Scale New Heights", *STB*, December 14: 1; FBIS-CHI-95–243, December 19: 49–50.

Chen Yanhua. (1992) "Commentary Views Interior–Coastal Economic Gap," ZXS, April 1; FBIS-CHI-92–070, October 4: 26–27.

Chen Yuan. (1991) "Woguo jingji de shenceng wenti he xuanze (gangyao)" (The deep problems and choices of our country's economy), *JJYJ*, no. 4: 18–26.

Chen Yun. (1981) "Jingji jianshe de jige zhongyao fangzhen" (Several important principles in economic construction), in Chen Yun 1986: 275–77.

——. (1982) "Jiaqiang he gaijin jihua jingji gongzuo" (Strengthen and improve economic planning work), in Chen Yun 1986: 278–80.

——. (1986) *Chen Yun Wenxuan (1956–1985)* (Selected writings of Chen Yun), Beijing: Renmin chubanshe.

Cheng, Chu-yuan. (1982) *China's Economic Development: Growth and Structural Change*, Boulder, Colorado: Westview Press: 435.

Cheng, Elizabeth. (1989) "Beggar Thy Neighbor," *FEER*, January 12: 46.

——. (1991a) "Power to the Center," *FEER*, January 24: 34–35.

——. (1991b) "Shifting the Trade Balance," *FEER*, August 8: 35.

Cheng Mu. (1992) "Neilu shengfen yaoqiu zhonggong junheng jingji fazhan" (Inland provinces ask the central government to balance economic development), *Zhonggong wenti ziliao zhoukan* (Weekly on Chinese Communist affairs and documents), no. 516, April 27.

Cheng Shan. (1994) "Yi dongxi hezuo duikang dongxi chaju" (Make use of east–west cooperation to narrow the east–west gap), *Zhongguo xiangzhen qiye* (China rural enterprises) no. 11: 1–3.

Cheung Lai-kuen. (1989) "Ministry to Impose Tough Export Controls," *Hong Kong Standard*, September 21: 1 and 3, in *FBIS-CHI*, September 29: 49.

——. (1996) "Income Chasm Still Yawns Wide," *SCMP*, February 8: 6.

China Considers. (1995) "China Considers Opening Up New Special Economic Zones in Central Region," *Ching chi tao pao*, July 24: 16; FBIS-CHI-95–164, August 24: 47.

Chinese Economic Studies. (1993), vol. 26, no. 5, Fall.

Choi, Jang Jip. (1993) "Political Cleavages in South Korea," in Hagen Koo (ed.) *State and Society in Contemporary Korea*, Ithaca: Cornell University Press: 13–50.

Chu Chia-chien. (1995) "Backdrop of the Introduction of New Policies for Pudong," *Wen Wei Po*, September 19: A2; FBIS-CHI-95–203, October 20: 36–37.

Chung Wen. (1994) "New Instructions by Jiang Zemin during his Southern Trip," *Kuang Chiao Ching*, August 16: 58–62; FBIS-CHI-94–161, August 19: 12–14.

Circular 1991. "Circular of the State Council on Breaking Interregional Marketing Blockade to Further Vitalize Commodity Circulation," *Zhonghua Renmin Gongheguo guowuyuan gongbao* (Gazette of the State Council of the People's Republic of China), No. 26, January 28: 956–58.

Coastal. (1994) "Coastal Areas Lead Economic, Social Development," Xinhua, December 13; FBIS-CHI-94–240, December 14: 24–25.

Cong Jin. (1989) *Quzhe fazhan de suiyue* (The years of tortuous development), Henan: Henan renmin chubanshe: 468.

Crane, George T. (1990) *The Political Economy of China's Special Economic Zones*, Armonk, N.Y.: M.E. Sharpe.

Crothall, Geoffrey. (1995) "State To Unify Tax Rates Within 2 Years," *SCMP*, November 1: B5.

Cui Ning. (1996) "State Launches Education Drive," *CD*, May 8: 1.

Cumberland, J.H. (1971) *Regional Development Experiences and Prospects in the United States of America*, The Hague and Paris: Mouton.

Dawkins, William. (1994) "Tokyo to Lend China Y580bn," *Financial Times*, December 23: 4.

Decision. (1993) "Decision of the CPC Central Committee on Issues Concerning the Establishment of a Socialist Market Economic Structure (November 14, 1993)," *CD* (Supplement), November 17.

Delfs, Robert. (1991) "Saying No to Peking," *FEER*, April 4: 21–22.

Deng Xiaoping. (1992) "Deng Xiaoping tongzhi zai Wuchang, Shenzhen, Zhuhai, Shanghai dengdi de tanhua yaodian" (Major points of comrade Deng Xiaoping's talks in Wuchang, Shenzhen, Zhuhai, and Shanghai), in Lu Keng, *Deng Xiaoping zuihou de jihui* (Deng Xiaoping's last chance), Hong Kong: Pai Shing Cultural Enterprise Ltd: 201–215.

———. (1993) *Deng Xiaoping wenxuan* (Selected works of Deng Xiaoping), Beijing: Renmin chubanshe, vol. 3.

Denny, David L. (1991) "Provincial Economic Differences Diminished in the Decade of Reform," in Joint Economic Committee, *China's Economic Dilemmas in the 1990s: The Problems of Reforms, Modernization, and Interdependence*, Washington, D.C.: Government Printing Office, April: 186–208.

Deputies. (1995) "Deputies Urge Efforts to Improve Financial Macro-Control," Xinhua, March 14; FBIS-CHI-95–050, March 15: 24.

Ding Xing. (1985) "Gongye buju yu jiage zhengce qianlun" (Industrial location and price policies: a preliminary discussion), *JJWTTS*, no. 7: 6–9.

Directorate of Intelligence, the Central Intelligence Agency. (1992) "The Chinese Economy in 1991 and 1992: Pressure to Revisit Reform Mounts," paper submitted to the Subcommittee on Technology and National Security of the Joint Economic Committee, Congress of the United States, August.

Dittmer, Lowell. (1990) "China in 1989," *Asian Survey*, vol. 30, no. 1, January: 25–41.

Dong Fan. (1993) "Guanyu diqu jian shoulu chaju biandong fenxi de jidian bulun" (A few supplementary comments on analyzing changes in inter-regional income disparities), *Jiangxi shehui kexue* (Jiangxi social sciences), no. 3: 10–15.

Dong Fan and Cheng Yaoping. (1990) "Xibu kaifa mianlin de wuzhong tiaozhan" (Five challenges facing the development of the western region), *JJWTTS*, no. 1: 36–38.

Dong Fureng. (1988) "Development Theory and Problems of Socialist Developing Economies," in Gustav Ranis and T. Paul Schultz (eds) *The State of Development Economics: Progress and Perspectives*, Oxford and New York: Basil Blackwell: 228–59.

Donnithorne, Audrey. (1981) "Center–Provincial Economic Relations in China," *Contemporary China Papers*, no. 16, Canberra: Contemporary China Center, Australian National University.

Du Shiguo. (1993) "Xiangzhen qiye: jiyu yu tiaozhan tong zai" (Rural enterprises: opportunity and challenge coexist), *Henan ribao* (Henan daily), February 7.

The Economist. (1993a) "China: Money to Burn," *The Economist*, February 6: 42.

———. (1993b) "China – Can the Center Hold?" *The Economist*, November 6: 32.

———. (1996) "China's Feuding Regions," *The Economist*, April 20: 27–28.

Efforts. (1994) "Efforts To Eliminate 'Abject Poverty' Increase," Xinhua, July 26; FBIS-CHI-94–143, July 26: 25–26.

Eggertsson, Thrainn. (1990) *Economic Behavior and Institutions,* Cambridge: Cambridge University Press: 40–45.

Encarnation, Dennis. (1992) *Rivals Beyond Trade: America Versus Japan in Global Competition*, Ithaca: Cornell University Press.

Fairbank, John King. (1992) *China: A New History*, Cambridge, Mass.: Harvard University Press.

Fan, C. Cindy. (1995) "Of Belts and Ladders: State Policy and Uneven Regional Development in Post-Mao China," *Annals of the Association of American Geographers*, vol. 85, no. 3: 421–49.

Fan Chengshi. (1991) "Dui Jiangxi sheng jingji fazhan de huigu he fansi" (A look back at and reflections on the economic development of Jiangxi province), *JXSHKX*, no. 6: 25–30, 37.

Fang Weizhong (ed.). (1984) *Zhonghua renmin gongheguo jingji dashiji (1949–1980)* (Chronicle of major economic events in the People's Republic of China 1949–1980), Beijing: Zhongguo shehui kexue chubanshe.

Feng Bin. (1985) "Bu fada diqu jingji fazhan wenti tantao" (An inquiry into the economic development of underdeveloped areas), *JJWTTS*, no. 5: 13–16.

Fields, Gary S. and T. Paul Schultz. (1980) "Regional Inequality and Other Sources of Income Variation in Columbia," *Economic Development and Cultural Change*, vol. 28, no. 3: 447–67.

Friedmann, John. (1972) "A Generalized Theory of Polarized Development," in Niles Hansen (ed.) *Growth Centers in Regional Economic Development*, New York: The Free Press.

——. (1988) *Life Space and Economic Space: Essays in Third World Planning*, New Brunswick, N.J.: Transaction Books.

Friedmann, John and Clyde Weaver. (1979) *Territory and Function: The Evolution of Regional Planning*, Berkeley: University of California Press.

Fujian. (1990) Waixiangxing jingji yanjiu ketizu, "Dui Fujian sheng fazhan waixiangxing jingji de zhiyue yinsu ji duice de ruogan kanfa" (Various opinions on the constraints on developing an outward-oriented economy in Fujian and the countermeasures), *ZGJJWT*, no. 1: 54–65.

Gan Yuanzhi. (1995) "Zhongguo jingji tequ hai you xi ma?" (Do China's special economic zones still have a future?), *Xin shiji* (New century), no. 6: 12–16.

Gao Shangquan. (1988) "The key to implementing the strategy of economic development for coastal areas lies in deepening reform," *Qiushi* (Seek Truth), no. 6, September 16: 16–20; FBIS-CHI-88–189, September 22: 53–55.

Gilley, Bruce. (1995) "Senior Official: 'Imminent' End to SEZ Privileges," *Eastern Express*, June 10: 6.

Gilpin, Robert G. Jr (1987) *The Political Economy of International Relations*, Princeton: Princeton University Press.

Gladney, Dru C. (1994) "Ethnic Identity in China: The New Politics of Difference," in William Joseph (ed.), *China Briefing, 1994*, Boulder, Colorado: Westview Press, 171–92.

Glain, Steve. (1995) "South Korean Governor Clashes With Seoul to Bring Investment to Agrarian Province", *AWSJW*, December 25: 1, 13.

Goldstein, Avery. (1991) *From Bandwagon to Balance-of-Power Politics*, Stanford: Stanford University Press.

Goldstein, Carl. (1993) "Full Speed Ahead: Guangdong Party Congress Ignores Calls to Slow Growth," *FEER*, June 3: 21.

Gong Yu. (1989) "Jingji bu fada diqu yao duo yanjiu yidian ruan zhanlue" (Economically underdeveloped areas should conduct more research of soft strategies), *Qinghai shehui kexue* (Qinghai social sciences), no. 6: 13–19.

Goode, Richard. (1990) "Obstacles to Tax Reform in Developing Countries," in Richard Bird and Oliver Oldman (eds) *Taxation in Developing Countries*, fourth edn, Baltimore: Johns Hopkins University Press.

Goodman, David S.G. and Gerald Segal (eds). (1994) *China Deconstructs: Politics, Trade and Regionalism*, London and New York: Routledge.

"Government Measures To Combat Tax Evasion", ZXS, 20 November 1995; FBIS-CHI-95–224, November 21: 32–33.

Granick, David. (1990) *Chinese State Enterprises: A Regional Property Rights Analysis*, Chicago: University of Chicago Press.

Guangdong. (1995) "Guangdong Antipoverty Projects Examined," Xinhua, November 17; FBIS-CHI-95–223, November 20: 82–83.

Guangdong jingji. (1986) *Guangdong jingji fazhan zhanlue yanjiu* (A study of Guangdong's economic development strategy), Guangzhou: Guangdong renmin chubanshe.

Guangdong People's Radio. (1992) "Guangdong's Xie Fei Inspects Poor Mountain Areas," Guangdong People's Radio, July 15; FBIS-CHI-92–144, July 27: 45–46.

Guangdong Provincial Statistical Bureau. (1991) *Guangdong sheng xian [qu] guomin jingji tongji ziliao, 1980–90* (County [district] economic statistical data for Guangdong province), Guangdong: Guangdong Provincial Statistical Bureau, December.

Guo Can. (1995) "Dui tequ renshi de jidian sikao" (Several thoughts on the special economic zones), *STB*, April 19: 10.

Guo Fansheng and Wang Wei. (1988) *Pinkun yu fazhan* (Poverty and development), Hangzhou: Zhejiang renmin chubanshe: 55–86.

Guo Kesha and Li Haijian. (1995) "Zhongguo duiwai kaifang diqu chayi yanjiu" (A study of regional variations in China's opening to the outside), *Zhongguo gongye jingji* (China's industrial economy), no. 8: 61–68.

Guo Yongqing. (1995) "Jiakuai jianshe xinan baoshuiqu de biyaoxing he kexingxing yanjiu" (On the necessity and feasibility of building free trade zones in the southwest), *Changzhang jingli ribao* (Managers' daily), June 8: 6; June 15: 6.

Guojia Jiaowei. (1990–94) Guojia Jiaoyu Weiyuanhui Caiwusi. *Zhongguo jiaoyu jingfei niandu fazhan baogao* (Annual report on educational finance in China), Beijing: Gaodeng jiaoyu chubanshe, 1991–95.

Guowuyuan tequ bangongshi. (1993) *Zhongguo dui wai kaifang diqu touzi huanjing he zhengce* (China's open areas and open policies), Kunming: Yunnan renmin chubanshe.

Haikou. (1995) "Haikou Hosts Symposium on Development of SEZs," Xinhua, April 21; FBIS-CHI-95–078, April 24: 40.

Harding, Harry. (1987) *China's Second Revolution: Reform After Mao*, Washington, D.C.: The Brookings Institution.

He Bochuan. (1990) *Shan'ao shang de Zhongguo: wenti, kunjing, tongku de xuanze* (China on the edge: problems, dilemmas, and painful choices), rev. edition, Hong Kong: Joint Publishing.

He Pin. (1993) "Difang zhuhou longhu dou" (Local dukes fight each other), *ZGSBZK*, November 7: 21–23.

He Ping. (1992) "More on Li Peng Remarks on Inner Mongolia Economy," Xinhua Domestic Service in Chinese, March 24; FBIS-CHI-92–058, March 25: 11.

He Ping. (1995) "Characteristics of Ethnic Issue in the New Period," *Xinjiang ribao*, May 26: 8; FBIS-CHI-95–174, September 8: 46–47.

He Xin. (1990) "Analysis of the Current Student Protests and Forecasts Concerning the Situation," *Australian Journal of Chinese Affairs*, no. 23: 64–76.

He Zhiqiang. (1991) "Yunnan jingji fazhan ruogan wenti de sikao" (Thoughts on various issues in Yunnan's economic development), *JJWTTS*, no. 2: 3–10.

Hewitt, Giles. (1995) "Shanxi Plans SEZ To Link Coast, Hinterland," AFP in English, June 6; FBIS-CHI-95–109, June 7: 80–81.

Hirschman, Albert. (1958) *The Strategy of Economic Development*, New Haven: Yale University Press.

——. (1978) "The Changing Tolerance for Income Inequality in the Course of Economic Development," in S.P. Singh (ed.) *Underdevelopment to Developing Economies*, Bombay: Oxford University Press: 519–43.

——. (1986) "A Dissenter's Confession: *The Strategy of Economic Development* Revisited," in Hirschman, *Rival Views of Market Society and Other Recent Essays*, New York: Viking.

The Holy Bible, New International Version. (1984) New Jersey: International Bible Society.

Honig, Emily. (1992) *Creating Chinese Ethnicity: Subei People in Shanghai, 1850–1980*, New Haven: Yale University Press.

Howell, Jude. (1993) *China Opens Its Doors: The Politics of Economic Transition*, Boulder, Colorado: Lynne Rienner.

Hsu Ching-hui. (1995) "Hu Angang Expresses View That 'Special Economic Zones Should Not Be Special'," *Ming pao*, August 21: C1; FBIS-CHI-95–164, August 24: 47–48.

Hu Angang. (1994) "It Has Become an Urgent Matter to Solve the Widening Gap Between Minority Nationality Regions and Coastal Developed Regions," *Lien ho pao*, November 7: 7; FBIS-CHI-94–229, November 29: 59–61.

——. (1995) "Why I Am for 'No Preferential Treatment for Special Economic Zones'," *Ming Pao*, August 23: C6; FBIS-CHI-95–188, September 28: 36–40.

Hu Ping. (1995) "Hu Ping on Developing Special Economic Zones," ZXS, September 11; FBIS-CHI-95–176, September 12: 17.

Hu Tongyuan. (1982) "Guanyu fahui diqu youshi lilun yu fangfa de yixie wenti" (Several issues concerning the theory and practice of realizing a region's potential), *JJWTTS*, no. 5: 25–29.

Hu Xiyin. (1991) "Woguo quyu fazhan chayi de dingliang fenxi yu sanda jingji didai huafen" (A quantitative analysis of China's regional development differentials and the classification of three major economic belts), *JJWTTS*, no. 2: 15–18.

Hu Xuwei. (1989) "Zhongguo quy kaifa de jige zhuyao wenti" (Some major issues in China's regional development), in Leung Chi-keung, Jim Chi-yung, and Zuo Dakang (eds) *Resources, Environment and Regional Development*, Hong Kong: University of Hong Kong Center for Asian Studies Papers and Monographs no. 85: 263–71.

Hua Hua. (1996) "Economic Gap To Be Narrowed," *CD*, March 22: 4.

Huang Ming. (1991) "Yetan caizheng 'dangao' zai zhongyang yu difang zhijian de zuo yu qe" (Another discussion of the making and cutting of the fiscal 'cake' between center and localities), *JJWTTS*, no. 4: 10–13.

Huang Qifan. (1992) "Shanghai Pudong xinqu touzi kaifa de zhengce tedian" (Characteristics of the investment and development policies for Shanghai Pudong New Area), in Shanghai Shehui Kexue Xuehui Lianhehui (ed.) *Pudong kaifa yu changjiang liuyu xietiao fazhan yanjiu* (Studies on the development of Pudong and the Yangtze river valley), Beijing: Zhongguo guangbo dianshi chubanshe: 31–36.

Huang, Yasheng. (1996) *Inflation and Investment Controls in China: The Political Economy of Central–Local Relations During the Reform Era*, New York: Cambridge University Press.

Huntington, Samuel. (1991) *The Third Wave: Democratization in the Late Twentieth Century*, Norman: University of Oklahoma Press.

Inside China Mainland. (1988) "Zhao Ziyang Discusses the Outward Oriented Strategy for Economic Development," vol. 10, no. 5.

Jacobs, Bruce and Lijian Hong. (1994) "Shanghai and the Lower Yangzi Valley," in Goodman and Segal (eds): 224–52.

Jao, Y.C. and C.K. Leung (eds). (1986) *China's Special Economic Zones: Policies, Problems and Prospects*, New York: Oxford University Press.

Jiang Baoqi, Zhang Shengwang, and Ji Bing. (1988) "Guofang gongye zhanlue tiaozheng he tizhi gaige de jige wenti" (Several problems concerning the strategic readjustment and system reform of the defense industry), *JJYJ*, no. 12.

Jiang Hai. (1994) "Chaju de yinhuan" (The hidden dangers of disparities), *Xinjiang shehui jingji* (Xinjiang society and economy), no. 5: 39–41.

Jiang Qinghai. (1990) "Lun 'zhuhou jingji'" (On feudatory economies), *JJWTTS*, no. 5: 10–14.

——. (1995) "Jingji tizhi gaige de quyu xing toushi" (A regional perspective on economic system reforms), *Jingji tizhi gaige* (Economic system reforms), no. 3: 49–56.

Jiang Shijie. (1996) "Yangpu, xianzai zenyang le" (How is Yangpu now?), *RMRBO*, January 6: 2.

Jiang Xia. (1995) "Demonstration Project of Cooperation among Town and Township Enterprises in the Western and Eastern Parts Will Get Into Gear," *RMRB*, April 25: 1; FBIS-CHI-95–086, May 4: 45–46.

Jiang Zemin. (1995a) "Jiang Zemin Tours Guangdong; Cites SEZ Policy", Xinhua, December 31; FBIS-CHI-96–001, January 2, 1996: 41.

——. (1995b) "Zhengque chuli shehui zhuyi xiandaihua jianshe zhong de ruogan zhongda guanxi" (On correctly handling several major relationships in socialist modernization and construction), *Xinhua yuebao* (New China monthly), no. 11: 7–11.

Kan Cunduan and Pan Fengqiu. (1994) "Negative Effect of 'Preferential Policies' Should Not Be Overlooked," *Fazhi ribao (Legal daily)*, September 20: 7; FBIS-CHI-94–217, November 9: 44–45.

Ke Jian. (1995) "Kaifang de tidu lilun" (The theory of step-by-step opening up), *Chengshi gaige yu fazhan* (Urban reform and development), no. 9: 10–11.

Kleinberg, Robert. (1990) *China's "Opening" to the Outside World: The Experiment with Foreign Capitalism*, Boulder, Colorado: Westview Press.

Kristof, Nicholas D. (1990) "In China, Too, Centrifugal Forces Are Growing Stronger," *The New York Times*, August 26, section 4: 2.

Krugman, Paul. (1991a) *Geography and Trade*, Leuven, Belgium: Leuven University Press; Cambridge, Mass.: The MIT Press.

——. (1991b) "Increasing Returns and Economic Geography," *Journal of Political Economy*, vol. 99: 183–99.

——. (1993) "On the Number and Location of Cities," *European Economic Review*, vol. 37: 293–98.

——. (1995) *Development, Geography, and Economic Theory*, Cambridge, Mass.: The MIT Press.

Kung, Cécile. (1996a) "Privileges for Special Economic Zones Maintained," *Hong Kong Standard* (via WWW), February 21.

——. (1996b) "SEZs To Be Given Role in Lawmaking," *Hong Kong Standard* (via WWW), February 28.

Kung Shuangyin. (1992) "Interior Provinces Urge Central Authorities to Provide Them with More Flexible, Open Policies," *Ta Kung Pao*, March 30: 2; FBIS-CHI-92–072, April 14: 36.

Kwan, Daniel. (1993) "Zhu: Guizhou To Be Spared Austerity Drive," *SCMP*, July 21: 11; FBIS-CHI-93–138, July 21: 15.

——. (1994) "China's Central Dilemma," *SCMP*, July 30: 13.

Lam, Willy Wo-Lap. (1989) *The Era of Zhao Ziyang: Power Struggle in China, 1986–1988*, Hong Kong: A.B. Books & Stationery Ltd.

——. (1993a) "Plenum's Push for Growth Masks a Power Scramble," *SCMP*, November 20: 11.

——. (1993b) "Strange Case of the Missing Economic Czar with Nothing to Lose," *SCMP*, December 11: 6.

——. (1995a) "Coastal Provinces Said Unhappy With 5-Year Plan," *SCMPIW*, November 17: 9.

——. (1995b) "Coffers Being Drained by Tibetan Demands," *SCMPIW*, September 9: 6.

——. (1995c) "Jiang Zemin Criticized on Favoritism to Shanghai," *SCMPIW*, November 20: 10.

——. (1995d) "Leaders Reportedly Split on Politburo Vacancy," *SCMPIW*, October 4: 10.

——. (1995e) "Peasants Angry as Income Gap Widens," *SCMPIW*, February 18: 1.

——. (1995f) "Provincial Leaders Link Aid, Law, Order," *SCMPIW*, September 9: 7.

——. (1995g) "Shenzhen Needs to Keep Winning Special Favors," *SCMP*, July 1: 6.

Lang Yihuan and Li Dai. (1991) "Kaifa sanxian gongye qianli, jiasu xibu jingji fazhan" (Develop the potential of third-front industries and speed up the development of the western economy), *JJWTTS*, no. 5: 31–35.

Lardy, Nicholas. (1978) *Economic Growth and Distribution in China*, Cambridge: Cambridge University Press.

——. (1980) "Region Growth and Income Distribution in China," in Robert F. Dernberger (ed.) *China's Development Experience in Comparative Perspective*, Cambridge: Cambridge University Press: 153–90.

——. (1989) "Dilemmas in the Pattern of Resource Allocation in China, 1978–1985," in Victor Nee and David Stark (eds) *Remaking the Economic Institutions of Socialism: China and Eastern Europe*, Stanford: Stanford University Press.

——. (1994) *China in the World Economy*, Washington, D.C.: Institute of International Economics.

Lei Yulan. (1995) "On Cultural Building in Special Economic Zones," *RMRB*, September 16: 6; FBIS-CHI-95-211, November 1: 16–18.

Leung, Julia. (1993) "Minister Says Beijing, Provinces Have Reached Consensus on Adoption of Tax-Sharing System," *AWSJW*, October 25: 3.

Lewis, Arthur. (1955) *Theory of Economic Growth,* London: Allen & Unwin.

Lewis, John P. (1991). "Some Consequences of Giantism: The Case of India," *World Politics*, vol. 43, April: 367–89.

Li Anding and Xie Shiqiu. (1992) "Zou Jiahua Unveils West, Southwest Strategy," Xinhua, April 22; FBIS-CHI-92-079, April 23: 21–23.

Li Chunting. (1995) "Making Concerted Efforts to Speed Up Economic Development in Less-Developed Regions," *Qiushi* (Seek truth), no. 2, January: 6–10; FBIS-CHI-95-040, March 1: 41–46.

Li Hao. (1986) "Kuoda neiwai hezuo, tigao tequ jianshe shuiping" (Expand internal and external cooperation and raise the level of special zone construction), *RMRB*, April 30.

Li Ke, Yu Senqing, and Wang Yuqi. (1988) "Jiakuai neidi fazhan xuyao xin de silu" (New thinking is needed to speed up development of the interior), *JXSHKX*, no. 3: 1–4.

Li Maosheng and Bo Dongxiu. (1995) "Lun xin jieduan Shenzhen tequ de gongneng dingwei ji qi shixian" (The functions of Shenzhen special economic zones in a new era and their realization), *Caimao jingji* (Finance and trade economics), no. 4: 58–64.

Li Peng. (1986) "Guanyu 'zhonghua renmin gongheguo yiwu jiaoyu fa (cao'an) de shuoming" (Explanation regarding the "Law of the People's Republic of China on Compulsory Education [Draft]"), *RMRB*, April 18.

——. (1991) "Guanyu guomin jingji he shehui fazhan shinian guihua he dibage wunian jihua gangyao de baogao" (Report on the outline of the ten-year program and the eighth five-year plan for national economic and social development), *Xinhua yuebao* (New China monthly), no. 4: 8–24. English translation can be found in FBIS-CHI-91-059, March 27.

——. (1992) "Jixu xia da liqi zhua nongye, zhengqu nongcun jingji geng kuai fazhan" (Continue to vigorously develop agriculture and strive for more rapid growth of the rural economy), in *Xin shiqi nongye he nongcun gongzuo zhongyao wenxian xuanbian* (Selection of important documents on agriculture and rural work in a new era), Beijing: Zhongyang wenxian chubanshe.

——. (1995) "Guanyu zhiding guomin jingji he shehui fazhan 'jiuwu' jihua he 2010 nian yuanjing mubiao jianyi de shuoming" (Explanations for drafting the suggestions on drafting the ninth five-year plan and the long-range targets to 2010 for national economic and social development), *Xinhua yuebao* (New China monthly), no. 11: 20–26.

——. (1996) "Guanyu guomin jingji he shehui fazhan 'jiuwu' jihua he 2010 nian yuanjing mubiao gangyao de baogao" (Report on the outline of the ninth five-year plan and the long-range targets to 2010 for national economic and social development), *RMRBO*, March 19: 1, 3–4.

Li Qiaonian, Qian Desan, and Huang Qiuyan. (1982) "Diqu zhijian jingji jishu xiezuo wenti chutan" (A preliminary inquiry into the issue of inter-regional economic and technical cooperation), *JJWTTS*, no. 5: 1–6.

Li Xianghua and Wu Shaohua. (1990) "Zhili zhengdun huanjing xia de Jiangxi jingji celue" (Jiangxi's economic strategy within an environment of [macroeconomic] control and adjustment), *JXSHKX*, no. 4: 43–47.

Li Yongzeng and Li Shuzhong. (1985) "Zhongguo sanxian jianshe de lishi zhuanzhe" (The historic turning-point in China's third-front construction), *Liaowang* (Outlook), no. 30, July 29: 10.

Li Youwei. (1995a) "Consciously Take the Road of Common Prosperity Illustrated by Deng Xiaoping,' *Wen Wei Po*, August 21: B2; FBIS-CHI-95–188, September 28: 35–36.

——. (1995b) "Give Play to Local Advantages and Achieve Common Prosperity," *RMRB*, June 22: 9; FBIS-CHI-95–162, August 22: 37–41.

——. (1995c) "Strengthen Regional Integration, Play Role Well as a Showpiece," *STB*, January 19: 1 and 2, FBIS-CHI-95–061, March 30: 56–58.

Li Zhengping. (1990) "Qunian difang baohu zhuyi taitou, dalu chuxian jingji geju jumian" (Local protectionism rose last year, and economic warlordism appears in the Mainland), *Dangdai* (Contemporary), September 8: 13–14.

Li Zhuoyan. (1993) "Guangdong Evacuates People From Poor Areas," *CD*, June 17: 3.

Liang Shutang. (1995) "Foreign Investment Increases in Southwest", Xinhua, August 24; FBIS-CHI-95–176, September 12: 26.

Lieberthal, Kenneth. (1992) "Introduction: The 'Fragmented Authoritarianism' Model and Its Limitations," in Kenneth Lieberthal and David Lampton (eds) *Bureaucracy, Politics, and Decision-Making in Post-Mao China*, Berkeley: University of California Press: 1–32.

——. (1995) *Governing China: From Revolution Through Reform*, New York: Norton.

Lien Ho Pao Reporters. (1995) "Jiang Zemin Went to Shanghai Last Month to Personally Reassure and Pacify Shanghai Faction," *Lien Ho Pao*, November 9: 9; FBIS-CHI-95–217, November 9: 13.

Lim, Benjamin Kang. (1996) "China Says Policy on Special Economic Zones Unchanged," Reuters, April 5.

Lin Fatang and Ling Chunxi. (1986) "Guanyu woguo jinhou de shengchanli buju wenti" (Concerning the distribution of productive forces in our country's future), in Tian Fang and Lin Fatang (eds).

Liu, Alan P.L. (1996) *Mass Politics in the People's Republic: State & Society in Contemporary China*, Boulder, Colorado: Westview Press.

Liu Fayan. (1995) "Xigaze City Enjoys Steady Economic Growth," *Xizang ribao* (Tibet daily), October 13: 1; FBIS-CHI-95–216, November 8: 45.

Liu Fuyuan. (1994) "Lun tequ yu puqu fazhan de bianzhengfa" (On the dialectics of development in special zones and ordinary areas), *Tequ jingji* (Special zone economies), no. 5: 7–8.

Liu Guoguang *et al.* (1984) *Zhongguo jingji fazhan zhanlue wenti yanjiu* (A study of the question of China's economic development strategy), Shanghai: Shanghai renmin chubanshe.

Liu Haijie. (1994) "Xijin zhanlue nai shunshi er dong" (The heading west strategy conforms to the historical trend of the times), *Zhongguo xiangzhen qiye* (China rural enterprises), no. 11: 18–19.

Liu Haimin. (1992) "Jottings on the 'Two Sessions': Rectifying Positions after Becoming Aware of Gaps," Xinhua, March 19; FBIS-CHI-92–055, March 20: 14.

Liu Jiang (ed.). (1992) *Zhongguo xibu diqu kaifa nianjian* (The China yearbook on the development of western regions), Beijing: Gaige chubanshe.

——. (1994) "Tuidong woguo xiangzhen qiye zai shang xin taijie" (Promoting China's rural enterprises to scale new heights), *Zhongguo xiangzhen qiye bao* (China rural enterprise bulletin), November 18.

Liu Jinwen, Wang Yiwu, and Zhang Xiusheng. (1985) "Shehui zhuyi jingzheng yu bufada diqu de jingji fazhan" (Socialist competition and the economic development of underdeveloped areas), *Qinghai shehui kexue* (Qinghai social sciences), no. 4: 36–41.

Liu Li. (1993) "State Must Get Basics Right to Boost Economy," *CD*, July 23: 4.

Liu Long. (1991) "Lun bianjing maoyi yu neilu bianjing tequ jianshe" (On border trade and the establishment of special zones in border areas of the interior), *JJWTTS*, no. 6: 22–24.

——. (1993) "Bianjiang minzu diqu shengchanli tiaoyao shi de fazhan zhi wo jian" (My views on development leap-frogging in ethnic border areas), *JJWTTS*, no. 8: 10–13.

Liu Luyan. (1991) "An guoji guifan banshi" (Do things according to international norms), *RMRBO*, February 12: 3.

Liu Peifang. (1994) "Shandong sheng jiada fuchi qian fada diqu xiangzhen qiye lidu" (Shandong province deepens its commitment to assisting rural enterprises in underdeveloped areas), *Zhongguo xiangzhen qiye* (China rural enterprise), no. 4: 13.

Liu Qingxuan and Zhang Jianping. (1995) "Lun yanhai fazhan jizhi xiang neidi de boji" (On the spread of coastal development mechanisms to the interior), *Qiusuo* (The search), no. 5: 34–36.

Liu Zaixing (ed.). (1993) *Zhongguo quyu jingji: shuliang fenxi yu duibi yanjiu* (China's regional economy: quantitative analyses and comparisons), Beijing: Zhongguo wujia chubanshe.

Liu Zaixing, Jiang Qinghai, and Hou Jingxin (eds). (1995) *Zhongguo shengchanli buju yanjiu* (A study of the distribution of productive forces in China), Beijing: Zhongguo wujia chubanshe.

Liu Zhigeng. (1991) *Fazhan, kaifang, gaige: Shenzhen jingji fazhan huigu yu qianzhan* (Development, opening up, and reform: A review of Shenzhen's economic development and its prospects), Shenzhen: Haitian chubanshe.

Liu Zhongli. (1995) "Guanyu 1994 nian guojia yusuan zhixing qingkuang he 1995 nian zhongyang ji difang yusuan caoan de baogao" (Report on the implementation of the 1994 state budget and the draft 1995 central and local budgets), *Jingji ribao* (Economic daily), March 21: 3–4.

Lu Dadao *et al.* (1990) *Zhongguo gongye de lilun yu shijian* (The theory and practice of China's industrial location), Beijing: Kexue chubanshe.

Lu Dongtao and Xu Yan. (1993) *Gaige lilun fengyun lu* (Storms over reform theories), Beijing: Beijing yanshan chubanshe.

Luce, Edward. (1996) "Suzhou Offers Singapore-style Gate to the Chinese Market", *FT*, January 9: 5.

Lyons, Thomas P. (1987) *Economic Integration and Planning in Maoist China*, New York: Columbia University Press.

——. (1991) "Interprovincial Disparities in China: Output and Consumption, 1952–1987," *Economic Development and Cultural Change*, vol. 39, no. 3, April: 471–506.

——. (1992) *China's War on Poverty: A Case Study of Fujian Province, 1985–1990*, USC Seminar Series, no. 7. (1992), Hong Kong: Hong Kong Institute of Asia–Pacific Studies, The Chinese University of Hong Kong.

Lyons, Thomas and Victor Nee (eds). (1994) *The Economic Transformation of South China: Reform and Development in the Post-Mao Era*, Ithaca, N.Y.: Cornell University East Asia Program.

Ma Encheng (ed.). (1991) *Zhanlue xing de tupo* (A strategic breakthrough), Guangzhou: Guangdong renmin chubanshe: 229.

Ma Ling. (1994) "How Should Special Economic Zones Become 'Special'?," *Ta kung pao*, November 29: 29; FBIS-CHI-94–240, December 24: 23–24.

Ma Zhiqiang. (1995) "Emancipate the Mind, Change Concepts, and Promote Development by Opening Up," *Gansu ribao (Gansu daily)*, September 12: 1; FBIS-CHI-95–202, October 19: 41–43.

Macartney, Jane. (1995a) "China Communist Chief Lashes Out at Graft – Again," Reuters, March 2.

——. (1995b) "China To Open Inland Cities To Foreign Investors," Reuters, October 14.

MacFarquhar, Roderick. (1983) *The Origins of the Cultural Revolution*, vol. 2: *The Great Leap Forward: 1958–1960*, New York: Columbia University Press.

Mao Zedong. (1974) "On the Ten Great Relationships," in Stuart Schram (ed). *Chairman Mao Talks to the People,* New York: Pantheon.

Martin, Michael F. (1992) "Defining China's Rural Population," *China Quarterly*, no. 130, June: 392–401.

Mathur, Ashok. (1983) "Regional Development and Income Disparities in India: A Sectoral Analysis," *Economic Development and Cultural Change*, vol. 31, no. 3, April.

Ministry of Agriculture (Bureau of Rural Enterprises). (1993) *Quanguo jiakuai fazhan zhong xi bu xiangzhen qiye jingyan jiaoliu hui wenjian huibian* (Collection of documents presented at the meeting on exchanging experiences in speeding up the development of town and township enterprises in central and western regions in China), Beijing: Ministry of Agriculture Bureau of Rural Enterprises.

——. (1994) *Zhongguo xiangzhen giye tongji zhaiyao* (China statistical digest of rural enterprises), Beijing: Ministry of Agriculture.

Ministry of Finance. (1992) *Zhongguo caizheng tongji* (China finance statistics), Beijing: Kexue chubanshe.

——. (1993) *Difang caizheng tongji ziliao 1990* (Collection of local fiscal statistics 1990), Beijing: Zhongguo tongji chubanshe.

Montinola, Gabriella, Qian Yingyi, and Barry Weingast. (1995) "Federalism, Chinese Style: The Political Basis for Economic Success in China," *World Politics*, vol. 48, no. 1: 50–81.

Mumford, Lewis. (1938) *The Culture of Cities,* New York: Harcourt, Brace.

Murphy, Kevin, A. Schleifer, and Robert Vishny. (1989) "Industrialization and the Big Push," *Journal of Political Economy*, no. 97: 1003–1026.

Myrdal, Gunnar. (1957) *Economic Theory and Under-developed Regions*, London, Gerald Duckworth.

Naughton, Barry. (1987) "The Decline of Central Control over Investment in Post-Mao China," in David Lampton (ed.) *Policy Implementation in Post-Mao China,* Berkeley: University of California Press: 51–80.

——. (1988) "The Third Front: Defense Industrialization in the Chinese Interior," *The China Quarterly*, no. 115, September: 351–86.

——. (1991) "Industrial Policy during the Cultural Revolution: Military Preparation, Decentralization, and Leaps Forward," in William Joseph, Christine Wong, and David Zweig (eds), *New Perspectives on the Cultural Revolution*, Cambridge, Mass.: Harvard University Council on East Asian Studies: 153–82.

——. (1992) "Implications of the State Monopoly over Industry and Its Relaxation," *Modern China*, vol. 18, no. 1, January: 14–41.

——. (1995) *Growing Out of the Plan: Chinese Economic Reform 1978–1993*, Cambridge: Cambridge University Press.

Ni Shidao and Wang Yang. (1989) "Luetan quyu jiage zhengce de libi" (A brief discussion of the benefits and weaknesses of regional price policies), *ZGJJWT*, no. 1: 52–53.

Nie Xinpeng. (1994) "Dongxi hezuo xuyao quan shehui zhichi" (East–West cooperation needs the support of the whole society) *Zhongguo xiangzhen qiye* (China rural enterprise), no. 7: 10–12.

Ninth Plan Suggestions. (1995) "Zhonggong zhongyang guanyu zhiding guomin jingji he shehui fazhan 'jiuwu' jihua he 2010 nian yuanjing mubiao jianyi" (CCP Central Committee suggestions on drafting the ninth five-year plan and the long-range targets to 2010 for national economic and social development), *Xinhua yuebao* (New China monthly digest), no. 11: 11–20.

Oi, Jean C. (1992) "Fiscal Reform and the Economic Foundations of Local State Corporatism in China," *World Politics*, vol. 45: 99–126.

Oksenberg, Michel and James Tong. (1991) "The Evolution of Central–Provincial Fiscal Relations in China, 1971–1984: The Formal System," *China Quarterly*, no. 125, March: 1–32.

Paine, Suzanne. (1976) "Balanced Development: Maoist Conception and Chinese Practice," *World Development*, no. 4: 277–304.

——. (1981) "Spatial Aspects of Chinese Development: Issues, Outcomes and Politics, 1949–79," *The Journal of Development Studies*, vol. 17, no. 2, January: 193–94.

Pan Danke. (1987) "Mianlin zhuanzhe de Yunnan jingji" (The Yunnan economy facing transition), *JJWTTS*, no. 2: 11–13.

Peng Yong'an and Li Hongguo. (1987) "Yunnan gongye buju zongtu de kongjian jichu he kexue shexiang" (The spatial basis and scientific plan for industrial location in Yunnan), *JJWTTS*, no. 3: 6–9.

Peng Zhigui. (1996) "Jiasu fazhan quyu fazhan caineng baozheng quanju jiankang" (Only by speeding up regional development can overall health be guaranteed), *Zhongguo gaige* (China reform), no. 1: 10–12.

People's Daily Commentator. (1992) "Speed Up Development of Township and Town Enterprises in Central, Western Regions," *RMRB*, March 30: 1; FBIS-CHI-92-064, April 2: 50–51.

Plan. (1994) "Plan Aims To Develop Central, Western Regions," in FBIS-CHI-94-220, November 15: 52.

Polanyi, Karl. (1957) *The Great Transformation*, Boston: Beacon Press.

Policy. (1995) "Policy to Support Development in Central, West[ern Regions]", ZXS, June 10; FBIS-CHI-95-112, June 12: 45.

Pred, Alan. (1966) *The Spatial Dynamics of U.S. Urban-Industrial Growth*, Cambridge, Mass.: The MIT Press.

Qi Jingfa. (1994) "Zai quanguo xiangzhen qiye zhengwu xinxi gongzuo zuotanhui shang de jianghua" (Talk at the national forum on rural enterprise political affairs information work), *Zhongguo xiangzhen qiye* (China rural enterprises), no. 10.

Qian, Yingyi and Xu Chengang. (1993) "The M-form Hierarchy and China's Economic Reform," *European Economic Review*, vol. 37, nos 2–3: 541–48.

Radio Beijing. (1991) Service to North America (in English), April 7, 1991.

Rajaram, Anand. (1992) *Reforming Prices: The Experience of China, Hungary, and Poland*, World Bank Discussion Papers no. 144, Washington, D.C.: The World Bank.

Rawski, Thomas G. (1979) *Economic Growth and Employment in China*, New York: Oxford University Press for The World Bank.

——. (1989) *Economic Growth in Prewar China*, Berkeley: University of California Press.

Renmin ribao guonei zhengzhi bu (ed.). (1993) *Dalu gedi youhui zhengce huibian* (Compendium of preferential policies of various Chinese localities), Beijing: Renmin zhongguo chubanshe. Two volumes.

Richardson, Harry, and Peter Tonwroe. (1986) "Regional Policies in Developing Countries," in P. Nijkamp (ed.) *Handbook of Regional and Urban Economics*, Amsterdam: Elsevier Science Publishers: 647–78.

Riskin, Carl. (1987) *China's Political Economy: The Quest for Development since 1949*, New York: Oxford University Press.

Roll, Charles R. Jr, and Kung-Chia Yeh. (1975) "Balance in Coastal and Inland Industrial Development," in *China: A Reassessment of the Economy*, A compendium of papers submitted to the Joint Economic Committee, United States Congress, Washington, D.C.: Government Printing Office.

de Rosario, Louise. (1988) "Asia's Fifth Dragon," *FEER*, December 8: 62.

——. (1989) "The Envy of China," *FEER*, December 8: 62.

Ruan Chongwu. (1994) "Hainan's Ruan Chongwu on Investment Environment," Hainan People's Radio, June 27; FBIS-CHI-94–127, July 1: 36–37.

Ruan Ming. (1991) *Lishi zhuanzhe dian shang de Hu Yaobang* (Hu Yaobang at a historical turning point), River Ridge, N.J.: Global Publishing.

Sai Feng and Zhu Mingchun. (1990) "Shi lun quyu chanye jiegou qutong wenti" (On the convergence of industrial structure across regions), *Zhongguo gongye jingji yanjiu* (Research in China's industrial economy), no. 4.

Saich, Tony. (1993) "Peaceful Evolution with Chinese Characteristics," in William A. Joseph (ed.) *China Briefing 1992,* Boulder, Colorado: Westview Press: 9–34.

Sang Baichuan. (1994) "Ba Shenzhen jiancheng quanguo de jingji fazhan ji" (Build Shenzhen into China's economic growth pole), *Tequ jingji* (Special zone economies), no. 12: 14–16.

Schurmann, Franz. (1968) *Ideology and Organization in Communist China*, new enlarged edition, Berkeley: University of California Press.

Sender, Henny. (1994) "Location Isn't Everything," *FEER*, June 23: 57.

The Seventh Five-Year Plan. (1986) *Zhonghua renmin gongheguo guomin jingji he shehui fazhan diqige wunian jihua (1986–1990)* (The Seventh Five-Year Plan of the People's Republic of China for Economic and Social Development [1986–1990]), Beijing: Renmin chubanshe: Chs 16, 18, 20 of Pt III.

Shang Rongguang. (1996) "Lending Them a Needed Hand", *Beijing Review*, no. 4, January 22–28: 4.

Shanghai. (1996) "Jin liangqian huzi qiye luohu wai sheng shi" (Nearly 2,000 Shanghai-based enterprises sink roots in other provinces and cities), *QB*, April 27: 12.

Shao, Qingyu. (1985) "The issues in regional planning in China," in Karlheinz Hottes, Derek R. Diamond, and Wu Chuan-chun (eds) *Regional Planning in Different Political Systems*, Stuttgart: Erdmann in K. Thienemanns Verlag: 100–108.

Shen Liren and Dai Yuanchen. (1990) "Woguo 'zhuhou jingji' de xingcheng jiqi biduan he genyuan" (The formation, adverse consequences, and roots of "duke-style economies" in our country), *JJYJ*, no. 3: 12–20.

"Shenzhen Reports 'Drastic Drop' in New Firms," ZXS, October 18, 1995; FBIS-CHI-95–202, October 19: 35.

Shenzhen Tequ Bao Commentator. (1995) "Special Economic Zones Must Be Run Better and Better," *STB*, December 15: 1; FBIS-CHI-95–243, December 19: 51–52.

Shenzhenshi Dang'anguan. (1991) *Shenzhenshi shinian dashiji* (A chronology of major events in Shenzhen, 1979–89), Shenzhen: Haitian chubanshe.

Shi Zhaobin. (1994) "Rang tequ jin yi bu 'te' qilai" (Let the special zones become more special), *Zhonghua gongshang shibao* (China industrial and commercial times), May 17: 2.

Shijie ribao (World journal), November 8, 1989: 17; February 12, 1990: 17.

Shijie xinjishu. (1986) *Shijie xinjishu geming yu Shanghai de duice* (The new world technological revolution and Shanghai's counterstrategy), Shanghai: Shanghai shehui kexueyuan chubanshe.

Shirk, Susan. (1985) "The Politics of Industrial Reform," in Elizabeth J. Perry and Christine Wong (eds) *The Political Economy of Reform in Post-Mao China*, Harvard

Contemporary China Series: 2, Cambridge, Mass.: The Council on East Asian Studies/ Harvard University: 195–221.
——. (1993) *The Political Logic of Economic Reform in China*, Berkeley: University of California Press.
——. (1994) *How China Opened Its Door: The Political Success of the PRC's Foreign Trade and Investment Reforms*, Washington, D.C.: Brookings.
The Sixth Five-Year Plan. (1983) *Zhonghua renmin gongheguo guomin jingji he shehui fazhan diliuge wunian jihua (1981–1985)* (The sixth five-year plan of the People's Republic of China for economic and social development (1981–1985)) Beijing: Renmin chubanshe: 107–111.
Skinner, William (ed.). (1977) *The City in Late Imperial China*, Stanford: Stanford Univeristy Press.
——. (1994) "Differential Development in Lingnan," in Lyons and Nee (eds): 17–54.
Smith, Craig S. (1995). "Chinese Boomtowns Emit Danger Signals," Dow Jones News, September 20.
Solinger, Dorothy. (1977) *Regional Government and Political Integration in Southwest China, 1949–1954*, Berkeley: University of California Press.
——. (1995) "China's Urban Transients in the Transition from Socialism and the Collapse of the Communist 'Urban Public Goods Regime'," *Comparative Politics*, vol. 27, no. 2, January: 127–46.
——. (1996) "Despite Decentralization: Disadvantages, Dependence and Ongoing Central Power in the Inland – The Case of Wuhan," *China Quarterly*, no. 145, March: 1–34.
Song Renqiong. (1992) "Qianyan" (Preface), in *Gaige kaifang zai Guangdong* (Reform and opening up in Guangdong), Guangdong: Guangdong gaodeng jiaoyu chubanshe: 1–5.
Song Xinzhong (ed.). (1992) *Zhongguo caizheng tizhi gaige yanjiu* (Studies on the reform of China's fiscal system), Beijing: Zhongguo caizheng jingji chubanshe.
Special Investigation Group on Rural Enterprises at the Ministry of Agriculture. (1993) "Zhong xi bu diqu jingji zhenxing de jiyu he xiwang" (The chance and hope for economic revitalization in central and western regions), *Nongcun jingji wengao* (Manuscripts on the rural economy), nos 6–7: 103–104.
State Council Development Research Center. (1992) *Zhongguo digu fazhan shuju shouce* (Handbook of regional development statistics in China 1978–1989), Beijing, Zhongguo caizheng jingji chubanshe.
State Council Office of Research (ed.). (1993) *Zhongxibu Diqu Xiangzhen Qiye Fazhan Zhanlue* (Strategies for developing rural enterprises in central and western regions), Beijing: Xinhua chubanshe.
State Planning Commission. (1989) Guojia jiwei jingji suo shengchanli buju yanjiushi. "Yanhai jingji fazhan zhanlue xia de xibu jingji" (The economy of the western region amid the coastal development strategy), *JJWTTS*, no. 1: 15–20.
——. (1996) "Basic Ideas on Regulating Regional Differences and Coordinating Regional Economic Development during the 'Ninth Five-Year Plan' Period to the Year 2010," *Guanli shijie* (Management world), no. 1, January: 167–76; FBIS-CHI-96-072, April 12: 34–45.
State Statistical Bureau. (1984–) *Zhongguo tongji nianjian* (Statistical yearbook of China), Hong Kong: Economic Information and Agency; Beijing: Zhongguo tongji chubanshe.
——. (1984) *Guanghui de sanshiwu nian: 1949–1984* (Thirty-five glorious years: 1949–1984), Beijing: Zhongguo tongji chubanshe.
——. (1990) *Quanguo gesheng zizhiqu zhixiashi lishi tongji ziliao huibian 1949–1989* (A compilation of historical statistical data of various provinces, autonomous regions, and municipalities 1949–1989), Beijing: Zhongguo tongji chubanshe.

Storper, Michael and Richard Walker. (1989) *The Capitalist Imperative: Territory, Technology, and Industrial Growth*, Oxford: Blackwell.

Strategy Group, Office of Policy Research of the Inner Mongolia Party Committee. (1984) "Xinjishu geming yu jingji bufada diqu de jiben duice" (The new technological revolution and the basic counterstrategy for economically underdeveloped areas), *Shijie jingji daobao* (World economic herald), June 18.

Sun Guoda. (1991) *Minzu gongye da qianxi* (The great migration of national industry), Beijing: Zhongguo wenshi chubanshe.

Tan Chieh-hua. (1995) "Hainan Unhappy to See Reduction in Preferential Treatment for Special Zone," *Hsin Pao*, March 9: 14; trans. FBIS-CHI-95-050, March 15: 28-29.

Tan Gang. (1995) "Tequ fazhan yu diqu chayi" (Special zone development and regional disparities), *Kaifang daobao* (Opening herald), no. 5: 3-4.

Tang Jie. (1995) "Tequ zhengce, duiwai kaifang yu diqu pingheng" (Special zone policies, opening to the outside, and regional balance), *Kaifang daobao* (Opening herald), no. 5: 1-2.

Tang Lijiu and Hu Ye. (1991) "Yanbian kaifang: Zhongguo duiwai kaifang zhanlue de xin shijiao" (Border opening: The new angle of China's strategy for opening up to the outside), *JJWTTS*, no. 2: 51-52.

Tatlow, Didi Kirsten. (1995) "Political Role Called Key to SEZ's Future," *Eastern Express*, October 26: 13.

Thornton, Emily. (1994) "Opportunity Knocks", *FEER*, December 8: 56-58.

Tian Fang and Lin Fatang (eds). (1986) *Zhongguo shengchanli de heli buju* (The rational distribution of China's productive forces), Beijing: Zhongguo caizheng jingji chubanshe.

Tian Fengshan. (1994) "Jin yi bu jiefang sixiang, zhen zhua shi gan, cujin xiang qi chixu kuaisu gaoxiao fazhan" (Further emancipate the mind, work in earnest to promote the sustained, rapid, and efficient development of rural enterprises), *Heilongjiang ribao* (Heilongjiang daily), July 8.

Tian Jiyun. (1992) "A Long-Term Arduous Task and Glorious Historical Mission," Xinhua, December 13; FBIS-CHI-92-243, December 17: 21-25.

Tian Yuan and Qiao Gang (eds). (1991) *Zhongguo jiage gaige yanjiu (1984-1990)* (Studies in Chinese price reform, 1984-1990), Beijing: Dianzi gongye chubanshe.

Toffler, Alvin and Heidi Toffler. (1993) *War and Anti-War: Survival at the Dawn of the 21st Century*, New York: Little Brown.

Tsui, Kai Yuen. (1991) "China's Regional Inequality, 1952-1985," *Journal of Comparative Economics*, vol. 15, no. 1, March: 1-21.

Tyler, Christian. (1996) "The Red Flag in China's Wild West," *FT Weekend*, January 6: I-II.

Tyler, Patrick. (1995) "Deng's Economic Drive Leaves Vast Regions of China Behind," *New York Times*, December 27: 1, 4.

UPI. (1993) "Local Governments Ordered to Close Unauthorized Development Zones," United Press International, August 12.

Veeck, Gregory (ed.). (1991) *The Uneven Landscape: Geographic Studies of Post-Reform China*. Geoscience and Man, vol. 30, Baton Rouge, LA: Geoscience Publications.

Vogel, Ezra. (1989) *One Step Ahead in China: Guangdong under Reform*, Cambridge, Mass.: Harvard University Press.

Waiwen Chubanshe Zhongguo Qingkuang Bianjishi. (1987) *Zhongguo gailan* (China Survey), Beijing: Renmin chubanshe.

Walker, Kenneth R. (1989) "40 Years On: Provincial Contrasts in China's Rural Economic Development," *China Quarterly*, no. 119, September: 448-80.

Wang Chu. (1995) "Shenzhen: 15 Extraordinary Years," *RMRB*, September 22: 1, 3; FBIS-CHI-95-203, October 20: 51-53.

Wang Dingchang, Long Liqing, and Wei Fengxian. (1989) "Tidu xiaoying zhong de Yunnan" (Yunnan under the ladder-step effect), *JJWTTS*, no. 3: 25–29.

Wang Fang. (1995) "Dalu zhongyang, difang guanxi riqu jinzhang" (Central–local relations become increasingly tense on the mainland), *ZGSBZK*, December 12: 43–45.

Wang Guoxing. (1991) "Chuangjian gannan lüse chanye tequ de mengxiang" (Initial thoughts on establishing a special green industry zone in southern Jiangxi), *JXSHKX*, no. 2: 29–31.

Wang Haibo and Li Shijin. (1991) "Dui xingcheng woguo jingji xiaoyi biandong tezheng ruogan yuanyin de fenxi" (An analysis of the various reasons for the changing characteristics of China's economic efficiency), *JXSHKX*, no. 2: 1–8.

Wang Hongmo et al. (1989) *Gaige kaifang de licheng* (The course of reform and opening up), Henan: Henan renmin chubanshe.

Wang Qingyun. (1993) "Lun dongnan yanhai qu nengyuan, yuan cailiao de jiejue tujing" (On the provision of energy and raw materials in southeastern coastal areas), *JJWTTS*, no. 5: 59–62.

Wang Sanmin, Xu Fan, and Huang Deli (eds). (1993) *Da kaifang* (The great opening), Dalian, Liaoning: Dongbei caijing daxue chubanshe.

Wang Shaoguang and Hu Angang. (1993a) "Strengthening Central Government's Leading Role amid the Shift to a Market Economy," AFP, September 20, FBIS-CHI-93–180, September 20: 19.

—— and ——. (1993b) *Zhongguo guojia nengli baogao* (Report on the capacity of the Chinese state), Shenyang: Liaoning renmin chubanshe.

—— and ——. (1994) "Zhongguo zhengfu jiqu nengli de xiajiang jiqi houguo" (The decline of the Chinese government's extractive capacity and its consequences), *Ershiyi shiji* (Twenty-first century), no. 21, February: 5–14.

Wang Wenchang and Meng Yanyan. (1988) "Xibu bianjiang diqu jingji shuangxiang fazhan de gouxiang" (Thoughts on the bi-directional economic development in western border areas), *JJYJ*, no. 1: 75–80.

Wang Xingyi. (1993) "Caishui gaige shi zai bixing" (Reforms of finance and taxation are imperative), *Jingji ribao* (Economic daily), September 4: 1–2.

Wang Yong. (1993) "A Freer Market for Real Estate," *CD* (Business Weekly), May 10: 8.

Wang Zenong. (1994) "Ben shiji mo xiangzhen qiye nengfou zai chuang qiji?" (Can rural enterprises repeat their miracle before the end of the century?), *Nongmin ribao* (Farmers' daily), May 12.

Wang Zhenzhi and Qiao Rongzhang. (1988) *Zhongguo jiage gaige de huigu yu zhanwang* (China's price reforms in retrospect and prospect), Beijing: Zhongguo wuzi chubanshe.

Wang Zhenzhi and Wang Chien. (1995) "Create New Advantages and Scale New Heights – Interview with Li Youwei on Central Authorities Attaching Importance to Building Shenzhen Special Zone," *Wen Wei Po*, December 27: A11; FBIS-CHI-96–003, 4 January 1996: 27–29.

Wang Zhigang. (1993) *Zouxiang shichang jingji de Zhongguo* (China makes transition to a market economy), Guangzhou: Guangdong lüyou chubanshe: 135.

Wang Zhiyong and Wang Xiaochun. (1987) "Yunnan jinqi guotu kaifa de zhongdian ying fang zai dong bu diqu" (The focus of Yunan's spatial development should be on the eastern areas in the near term), *JJWTTS*, no. 4: 15–16.

Wang Zhiyuan and Zeng Xinqun. (1988) "Lun zhongguo gongye buju de quwei kaifa zhanlue" (On the locational development strategy of China's industrial distribution), *JJYJ*, no. 1: 66–74.

Watson, Andrew, Christopher Findlay, and Du Yintang. (1989) "Who Won the 'Wool War'?: A Case Study of Rural Product Marketing in China," *China Quarterly*, no. 118, June: 213–41.

Wedeman, Andrew H. (1995) *Bamboo Walls and Brick Ramparts: Rent Seeking, Interregional Economic Conflict, and Local Protectionism in China, 1984–1991*, Ph.D. dissertation, University of California, Los Angeles.

Wei Houkai. (1992) "Lun woguo quji shouru chayi de biandong geju" (The pattern of change in regional income differences in China), *JJYJ*, no. 4: 61–65.

——. (1993) "Woguo quyu jingji zengzhang fenxi" (An analysis of regional economic growth in China), *Jingji yanjiu ziliao* (Economic research materials), no. 7: 16–28.

Wei Houkai and Liu Kai. (1994) "Woguo diqu chayi biandong qushi fenxi yu yuce" (A trend analysis and forecast of regional difference change in China), *Zhongguo gongye jingji yanjiu* (China industrial economics research), no. 3: 28–36.

Wei Houkai and Yang Dali. (1997) "Difang fenquan yu Zhongguo diqu jiaoyu chayi" (Decentralization and regional educational disparities in China), *Zhongguo shehui kexue* (Chinese social sciences), no. 1: 98–113.

Wei Jinkui. (1995) "Fahui tequ youshi, tuozhan guonei shichang" (Give play to the superiority of the special economic zones and open up the domestic market), *Shangye jingji wenhui* (Commerce and economy gazette), February 18: 22.

Wei Shi'en and Guo Zhiyi (eds). (1992) *Zhongguo yanhai yu neidi jingji fazhan guanxi* (Coast–interior economic development relations in China), Lanzhou: Gansu daxue chubanshe.

Wei Wei, Wang Jian, and Guo Wanqing. (1992) *Zhongguo diqu bijiao youshi fenxi* (An analysis of regional comparative advantages in China), Beijing: Zhongguo jihua chubanshe.

Wen Qiangzhou. (1994) "Shanghai Pudong kaifang kaifa de zhanlue jiazhi yu yanjiang jianshe de yiyi" (The strategic value of Shanghai Pudong's opening and development and their implications for development along the [Yangtze] river), *Changjiang luntan* (Yangtze river forum), no. 1: 19–22.

Wen Wei Pao. (1989) "Guidelines Proposed for New 5-Year Plan," *Wen Wei Pao*, October 31: 4; FBIS, October 31: 30.

White, Lynn, III. (1989) *Shanghai Shanghaied? Uneven Taxes in Reform China*, Hong Kong: University of Hong Kong Center for Asian Studies.

Williamson, J.G. (1965) "Regional Inequality and the Process of National Development: A Description of the Patterns," *Economic Development and Cultural Change* 13: 3–45.

Williamson, John (ed.). (1994) *The Political Economy of Policy Reform*, Washington, D.C.: Institute for International Economics.

Wilson, Dick. (1996) "Taking Stock of Mainland Regional Rivalry," *SCMPIW,* May 11: 6.

Wong, Christine. (1991) "Central–Local Relations in an Era of Fiscal Decline: The Paradox of Fiscal Decentralization in Post-Mao China," *China Quarterly*, no. 128, December: 691–715.

World Bank. (1988) *China: Growth and Development in Gansu Province*, Washington, D.C.: The World Bank.

——. (1990a) *China: Between Plan and Market*, Washington, D.C.: The World Bank.

——. (1990b) *China: Revenue Mobilization and Tax Policy*, Washington, D.C.: The World Bank.

——. (1990c) *China: Macroeconomic Stability and Industrial Growth under Decentralized Socialism*, Washington, D.C.: The World Bank.

——. (1992) *China: Reform and the Role of the Plan in the 1990s*, Washington, D.C.: The World Bank: 239.

Wu Guoqing. (1995) "Zhongguo dongbu qiye xiang xibu tingjin" (Eastern enterprises march toward the western region in China), *Jingji shijie* (Business world), no. 12: 4–6.

Wu Jixue and Yang Linjun. (1985) "Chuangjian baokuo fudi tequ zainei de jingji tequ qun de zhanlue yiyi" (The strategic implications of establishing a cluster of special economic zones, including zones in the interior), *JJWTTS*, no. 4: 1–6.

Wu Keqiang. (1993) "It is Necessary to Take the Overall Situation into Account, an Interview with Li Zemin," Xinhua, September 24, FBIS-CHI-93-200, October 19: 31–32.

Wu Ren. (1990) "Quyu jingji fazhan" (Regional economic development), *JXSHKX*, no. 1: 14–17.

Wu Zhe. (1994) "Lun Zhongguo yanhai diqu jingji fazhan de quyu fenyi" (On the regional divergence in economic development of China's coastal region), *Nankai jingji yanjiu* (Nankai economic studies), no. 6: 15–20.

Wu Zhong. (1996) "Reform in Pricing of Materials," *Hong Kong Standard* via World Wide Web, February 26.

Xia Hanxing, Feng Dengkun, Cao Jianfang, and Sun Guoqi. (1989) "Tantan Yunnan minzu diqu de caizheng wenti" (On the fiscal issues in Yunnan's ethnic minority areas), *JJWTTS*, no. 4: 58–60.

Xia Yang and Wang Zhigang. (1988) "Zhongguo jingji 'geju' xianxiang chutan" (Preliminary investigations into China's economic 'warlordism'), *Liaowang* (Outlook), no. 39, September 26: 3.

Xia Yulong. (1994) "An Examination of Comrade Deng Xiaoping's Thoughts on China's Regional Development Strategy," *JJYJ*, no. 12, December: 15–18; FBIS-CHI-95-039, 28 February 1995: 45–48.

Xia Yulong and Feng Zhijun. (1982) "Tidu lilun he quyu jingji" (The ladder-step theory and regional economies), *Kexue yu jianyi* (Science and suggestions), no. 8.

Xiao Min and Kong Fanmin. (1989) "Sanxian jianshe de juece, buju he jianshe: lishi kaocha" (The decision-making, location, and construction of the Third Front: a historical investigation), *Jingji kexue* (Economic science), no. 2: 63–67, 40.

Xie Liangjun. (1996) "Ethnic Groups Live in Harmony," *CD*, January 3: 1–2.

Xie Minggan and Luo Yuanming (eds). (1990) *Zhongguo jingji fazhan sishi nian* (Forty years of Chinese economic development), Beijing: Renmin chubanshe: 107–108.

Xin Xiangyang. (1995) *Daguo zhuhou: Zhongguo zhongyang yu difang guanxi zhijie* (Lords of the empire: The knot of central–local relations in China), Beijing: Zhongguo shehui chubanshe.

Xin Xiangyang and Ni Jianzhong (eds). (1993) *Nanbei chunqiu: Zhongguo hui bu hui zouxiang fenlie* (North versus south: Will China disintegrate?), Beijing: Renmin Zhongguo chubanshe.

Xinhua. (1988) "Zhao on New Economic Plan for Coastal Areas," Xinhua, January 22; FBIS-China, January 25: 10–15.

Xinhua. (1992a) "East–West Economic Ties to Get Closer," Xinhua in English, April 2; FBIS-CHI-92-068, April 5: 42–43.

——. (1992b) "Guangdong Economic Zones Aim to Help Poor Area," Xinhua in English, March 4; FBIS-CHI-92-044, March 5: 43.

——. (1992c) "Guangdong Sets Up Economic Zone to Help Poor," Xinhua in English, March 29; FBIS-CHI-92-061, March 30: 62.

——. (1992d) "Jiangsu to Accelerate Northern Area Development," Xinhua in English, January 15; FBIS-CHI-92-011, January 16: 36–37.

——. (1992e) "Zhejiang Helps Poor Students Return to School," Xinhua in English, February 12; FBIS-CHI-92-029, February 12: 42.

Xiong Siyuan. (1993) "Yunnan duiwai kaifang de gouxiang" (Conceptualization of Yunnan's opening to the outside), *JJWTTS*, no. 1: 59–61.

Xu Changming. (1989) "Guanyu 'qingxieshi' quyu jingji zhengce de sikao" (Reflections on preferential regional economic policies), *JJWTTS*, no. 1: 21–25.

Xu Jialu. (1994) "Jiancha tuoqian jiaoshi gongzi zhaji" (Reading notes on the investigation of defaulting teachers' salaries), *Renmin jiaoyu* (People's education), no. 6: 6–10.

Xu Jingjun. (1987) "Yi hengxiang jingji lianhe cujin minzu diqu de jingji fazhan" (Use lateral economic linkages to promote economic development in ethnic areas), *JJWTTS*, no. 2: 16–19.

Xue Muqiao. (1982) *Current Economic Problems in China*, trans. K.K. Fung, Boulder, Colorado: Westview Press.

——. (1990) *Lun Zhongguo jingji tizhi gaige* (On reforming China's economic system), Tianjin: Tianjin renmin chubanshe.

——. (1992) *Bashi niandai de zhongguo jingji* (The Chinese economy in the 1980s), Beijing: Jingji guanli chubanshe.

Yan Liankun and Chen Zhi. (1985) "Shixing youhui zhengce, jiakuai Yunnan de yinjin bufa" (Adopt preferential policies and speed up the pace of foreign investment in Yunnan), *JJWTTS*, no. 6: 5–8.

Yan Zhengde. (1993) "Guanyu Qinghai jingji shang xin taijie de jige wenti" (Several issues concerning the Qinghai economy's rise to a new stage), *Qinghai shehui kexue* (Qinghai social sciences), no. 1: 3–9.

Yang, Dali L. (1990) "Patterns of China's Regional Development Strategy," *China Quarterly*, no. 122, June: 230–57.

——. (1991) "China Adjusts to the World Economy: The Political Economy of China's Coastal Development Strategy," *Pacific Affairs*, vol. 64, no. 1, March: 42–64.

——. (1993) "Policy Credibility and Macroeconomic Control in China," paper delivered at the American Political Science Association Annual Meeting, The Washington Hilton, September 2–5.

——. (1994) "Reform and the Restructuring of Central–Local Relations," in Goodman and Segal (eds): 59–98.

——. (1995a) "From Planning to Guidance: China's Turn to New Industrial Policies", *Journal of Asian Business*, vol. 11, no. 2: 33–65.

——. (1995b) "Gaiqe yilai zhonqquo shengnei diqu chayi de bianqian" (Reform and intra-provincial inequality in China), *Zhongguo gongye jingji* (China's industrial economy), no. 1, January: 62–67.

——. (1996a) *Calamity and Reform in China: State, Rural Society, and Institutional Change Since the Great Leap Famine*, Stanford: Stanford University Press.

——. (1996b) "Governing China's Transition to the Market: Institutional Incentives, Politicians' Choices, and Unintended Outcomes," *World Politics*, vol. 48, no. 3, April: 424–52.

Yang, Dali L. and Houkai Wei. (1996a) "Rising Sectionalism in China?," *Journal of International Affairs*, vol. 49, no. 2, Winter: 456–76.

——. and ——. (1996b) "Rural Enterprise Development and Regional Policy in China," *Asian Perspective* vol. 20, no. 1, Spring–Summer: 71–94.

Yang Jianrong and Yao Xiaobo (eds). (1993) *Zhongguo diqu chanye jiegou fenxi* (Analyses of China's regional industrial structure), Shanghai: Fudan daxue chubanshe.

Yang Jisheng. (1989a) "'Qishou' zhengzai gengdie" (The changing 'chess players'), *Liaowang* (Outlook), no. 8, February: 16.

——. (1989b) "Dadi meiyou wanli ping" (There is no level ground for 10,000 *li*), *Liaowang* (Outlook), no. 9, February: 10.

Yang Kaizhong. (1989) *Zhongguo quyu fazhan yanjiu* (A study of China's regional development), Qingdao: Haiyang chubanshe.

——. (1993) *Mai xiang kongjian yitihua: Zhongguo shichang jingji yu quyu fazhan zhanlue* (Toward spatial integration: China's market economy and regional development strategy), Chengdu: Sichuan renmin chubanshe.

Yang Tsu-kun and Lin Ping-hua. (1995) "Train of Thought for Formulating Ninth Five-Year Plan – SPC Vice Minister Ye Qing Expounds Three Major Issues," *Ta Kung Pao*, October 7: A1; FBIS-CHI-95–208, October 27: 30–32.

Yang Yingshi. (1995) "New Rules Aim to Cool Development Zone Fever," *CD*, June 12: 1.

Yang Zhongwei, Chen Kaiguo, and Pei Changhong. (1988) "Quyu juezhan, quanguo wending" (Regional [reform] battles to ensure national stability), *JJYJ*, no. 1: 43–50.

Ye Yonglie. (1995) *Chen Yun quanzhuan* (Biography of Chen Yun), Hong Kong: Ming Bao chubanshe.

Yi Jun. (1984) "Kaifa da xinan wenti taolunhui zongshu" (Summary of the symposium on the development of the great southwest), no. 11: 17–20.

Yi Shuihan. (1993) "Nilu shengfen zhaoshang gechu qizhao" (Interior provinces promote innovative strategies to attract businesses), *ZGSBZK*, July 25–31: 50–51.

Yin Yan. (1996) "Hu Angang lilun tai tianzhen?" (Are Hu Angang's arguments too naive?), *Zhongguo shidai* (China times), no. 6: 36.

Yu Honghui and Yan Xiaohong. (1995) "Xinren shengzhang zui guanzhu shenmo" (What the newly appointed provincial governors are paying most attention to), *RMRBO*, March 9: 4.

Yu Jianxun. (1987) "Woguo neidi de waimao fazhan zhanlue" (The interior area's foreign trade development strategy in our country), in *Zhongguo duiwai jingji maoyi nianjian: 1987* (Yearbook of China's Foreign Economic Relations and Trade: 1987), Hong Kong: Zhongguo guanggao yixian gongsi.

Yu Meng. (1993) "Xiang shichang jingji 'kuaichedao' jishi" (Quickly approach the express lane of market economy), *Zhongguo wuzi jingji* (China materials economy), April 1: 4.

Yu Xianpei and Guo Shiping. (1994) "Guanyu Shenzhen jingji shengge de ruogan sikao" (Various thoughts on upgrading Shenzhen's economy), *STB*, October 19: 10.

Yuan Enzheng. (1994) "Deng Xiaoping de fei junheng fazhan sixiang yu Pudong kaifa dui 90 niandai Zhongguo jingji fazhan de daoxiang zuoyong" (The guiding impact of Deng Xiaoping's unbalanced development thinking and Pudong's development on China's economic development in the 1990s), *Mao Zedong Deng Xiaoping lilun yanjiu* (Studies in Mao Zedong and Deng Xiaoping's thoughts), no. 5: 60–63.

Yuan Mu. (1994) "Several Views on Strengthening Special Economic Zones' Construction", *RMRB*, June 25: 2; FBIS-CHI-94–127, July 1: 30–33.

Yuan Shang and Han Zhu. (1992) *Deng Xiaoping nanxun hou de Zhongguo* (China after Deng Xiaoping's southern tour), Beijing: Gaige chubanshe.

Yue Xikuan. (1991) *Zhongguo xiwang gongcheng* (China's Hope Project), Beijing: Shehui kexue wenxian chubanshe.

Yukawa, Kazuo. (1992) "Economic Cooperation Between Guangdong and Inland Areas," *China Newsletter*, no. 100: 9–16.

Yun Mei and Yi Xing. (1987) "1986 nian Zhongguo shehuizhuyi jingji lilun ruogan wenti yanjiu gaikuang" (Summary of research in 1986 on many problems in China's socialist economic theory), in *Zhongguo jingji nianjian* (Chinese economic yearbook), Hong Kong: Zhongguo jingji nianjian yiuxian gongsi: IX–10.

Zhang Annan. (1996) "Xiangnan de kaifang du" (The openness of southern Hunan), *RMRBO*, February 24: 1.

Zhang Haoruo. (1996) "Zhang Haoruo renwei guonei guoji tiaojian jubei, jiakuai xibu diqu fazhan shiji yi chengshu" (Zhang Haoruo believes both domestic and international conditions exist and the time is ripe for speeding up development of the western region), *QB*, May 9: 4.

Zhang Huaiyu. (1985) "Zongjie sanxian jianshe jingyan, cujin xinan de kaifa" (Sum up the experiences of third front construction, promote the development of the southwest), *JJWTTS*, no. 8: 9–13.

Zhang Jinsheng. (1996) "Growth in Open Border Cities Reported," Xinhua, February 12; FBIS-CHI-96–037, February 23: 25–26.

Zhang Jun. (1990) "Lun woguo xian jieduan de caizheng kunjing" (On the fiscal dilemmas faced by contemporary China), *JJYJ*, no. 12: 46–50.

——. (1994) "Dui Zhongguo jingji tequ de jingji fenxi" (An economic analysis of China's special economic zones), *Zhengquan shichang daobao* (Securities market herald), no. 5: 33–34.

Zhang Nianhai. (1995) "Minzu zizhi difang gaige kaifang shiyanqu de zhengce yanjiu" (A study of policies for experimental zones for local reform and opening up in ethnic autonomy areas), *Guizhou minzu yanjiu* (Guizhou nationalities research), no. 1: 31–33.

Zhang Ping. (1988) "Lun gaige mubiao de fenqu daowei yu guo duqu de gaige" (On the regional realization of reformist goals and the reform of transitional areas), *JJYJ*, no. 9: 46–50.

Zhang Pingli. (1992) "Guangdong's Economy Can Develop Even Faster – Interview with Guangdong Governor Zhu Senlin," *RMRBO*, April 20: 3; FBIS-CHI-92–084, April 30: 27–28.

Zhang Shusheng. (1991) "Population Resettlement in 'Sanxi' Areas Scores Outstanding Results," *RMRB*, June 20: 2; FBIS-CHI–91–127, July 2; 34–35.

Zhang Wenhe. (1989) "Woguo quyu jingji fazhan zhanlue de zhuanbian yu xuanze" (China's regional economic development strategy: transformation and choices), *JJYJ*, no. 10: 71–76.

Zhang Yungang and Zhu Xinkun. (1993) *Zhongguo shichang jingzheng lun* (On market competition in China), Kunming: Yunnan renmin chubanshe.

Zhao Shugui and Wang Shuzi. (1988) "Jindai Jiangxi jingji luohou de lishi fansi" (Historical reflections on Jiangxi's economic backwardness in modern times), *JXSHKX*, no. 6: 105–108.

Zhao, Suisheng. (1993) "Deng Xiaoping's Southern Tour: Elite Politics in Post-Tiananmen China," *Asian Survey* vol. 33, no. 8, August: 739–56.

Zhao Tianzhen and Min Zhimin. (1994) "1993 nian Shaanxi xiangzhen qiye fazhan xingshi pouxi" (An analysis of the development of rural enterprises in Shaanxi in 1993), *Zhongguo xiangzhen qiye* (China rural enterprise), no. 7: 37–38.

Zhao Wei and Sun Yuxia. (1996) "Strategic Alternatives for the Absorption of Foreign Capital in Central and Western Parts of China," *Guoji maoyi* (Intertrade), no. 3: 39–41; FBIS-CHI-96–095, May 15: 42–46.

Zhao Ziyang. (1986a) "Guanyu yanhai diqu jingji fazhan de jige wenti" (On several questions relating to economic development of the coastal region), in Tian Fang and Lin Fatang (eds).

——. (1986b) "Kaifa Xinjiang, kaifa daxibei, shi zhongyang de zhongyao zhanlue shexiang" (Developing Xinjiang and the great north-west is an important, strategic, tentative plan of the centre), in Tian Fang and Lin Fatang (eds).

Zheng Hongliang. (1990) "Tidu tuiyi lilun" (The theory of ladder-step evolution), in Zhang Xinjing (ed.) *Gaige shinian shehui kexue zhongyao lilun guandian zongshu (1978–1988)* (An overview of major theoretical viewpoints in the social sciences during ten years of reform, 1978–1988), Beijing: Xueyuan chubanshe.

Zheng Yan. (1994) "Dui suoxiao dongxi bu diqu jingji fazhan chaju de sikao" (Thoughts on reducing the economic disparities between the eastern and western regions), *Qinghai shehui kexue* (Qinghai social sciences), no. 2: 21–25.

Zheng Yi. (1992) *Zhu Rongji pingzhuan* (A biography of Zhu Rongji), Hong Kong: Mingchuang chubanshe.

Zheng Yongnian. (1995) *Institutional Change, Local Developmentalism, and Economic Growth: The Making of Semi-Federalism in Reform China*, Ph.D. dissertation, Princeton University.

Zheng Youjiong. (1984) "Niding diqu jingji fazhan zhanlue de yuanze" (Principles for formulating regional economic development strategies), *JJWTTS*, no. 3: 17–20.

Zhong Liqiong. (1996) "Should Special Economic Zones Retain Privileges?" *Inside China Mainland*, vol. 18, no. 4, April: 61–63.

Zhong Xingzhi. (1993) "Zhongyang yu Shanghai zhengce xing tuoxie" (The policy compromise between the center and Shanghai), *ZGSBZK*, August 29: 19.

Zhongguo baike nianjian 1994. (China encyclopedic yearbook 1994), Beijing, Zhongguo da baike quanshu chubanshe, 1994.

Zhongguo fangzhi gongye nianjian. (1986–91) (China textile industry yearbook). Beijing: Fangzhi gongye chubanshe.

Zhongguo fenxian nongcun jingji tongji gaiyao (Summary Rural Economic Statistics of China's Counties) (1989-93) Beijing: Zhongguo tongji chubanshe.

Zhongguo gaige yu fazhan baogao zhuanjiazu. (1994) *Zhongguo gaige yu fazhan baogao (1992–1993): xin de tupo yu xin de tiaozhan* (China reform and development report 1992–1993: new breakthroughs and new challenges), Beijing: Zhongguo caizheng jingji chubanshe.

Zhongguo gongye jingji tongji nianjian. (1988–94) (Statistical yearbook of China's industrial economy), Beijing: Zhongguo tongji chubanshe.

Zhongguo hengxiang jingji nianjian. (1992–94) (Yearbook of Chinese horizontal economy), Beijing: Zhongguo shehui kexue chubanshe, 1993.

Zhongguo nongcun tongji nianjian 1993. (Yearbook of rural statistics 1993), Beijing: Zhongguo tongji chubanshe, 1993.

Zhongguo nongye nianjian. (1986–91) (China agriculture yearbook), Beijing: Nongye chubanshe.

Zhongguo renkou tongji nianjian 1990 (China Population Statistical Yearbook 1990), Beijing: Kexue jishu wenxian chubanshe, 1990.

Zhongguo xiangzhen qiye (China rural enterprise). (1994), no. 11: 16.

Zhongguo xiangzhen qiye bao (China rural enterprise bulletin).

Zhonghua. (1987) *Zhonghua Renmin Gongheguo guomin jingji he shehui fazhan jihua dashiji jiyao (1949–1985)* (A summary chronology of major events of PRC national economic and social development planning, 1949–1985), Beijing: Hongqi chubanshe.

Zhonghua gongshang shibao (Chinese industry and commerce times).

Zhou Wenzhang. (1995) "Yingdang xiaochu dui tequ renshi de jige wujie" (Several misperceptions on the special economic zones should be dispelled), *STB*, April 12: 10.

Zhu Ling and Wang Yong. (1993) "Bid to Plug Economic Chasm as Zones Close," *CD*, August 18: 1.

Zhu Xianmin. (1993) "Qinghai jingji buju zhanlue zhongdian de zai sikao" (Reflections on the strategic foci of Qinghai's economic distribution), *Qinghai shehui kexue* (Qinghai social sciences), no. 1: 8–15.

Zhu Xinhong, Zhan Weihong, and Guo Wanda. (1993) "Shenzhen qiye weihe xiangwai qianxi?" (Why are Shenzhen enterprises migrating outward?), *RMRBO*, June 19: 2.

Zhu Yaoping. (1993) "Chedi changkai xizang qu men, jiasu kuoda duiwai kaifang" (Completely open Tibet's doors and speed up opening to the outside), *JJWTTS*, no. 9: 54–56.

Zhu Ze. (1993) "Mingong chao wenti de xianzhuang, chengyin he duice" (Present situation, causes and countermeasures of the migrant worker tide), *Zhongguo nongcun jingji* (China rural economy), no. 12.

Zuo Chuntai and Song Xinzhong (eds). (1988) *Zhongguo shehui zhuyi caizheng jianshi* (An outline history of China's socialist finance), Beijing: Zhongguo caizheng jingji chubanshe.

Zuo Dapei. (1994) "Jin xiandai shichang jingji zhong de yanhai youshi" (The coastal advantages in modern and contemporary market economies), *Jingji daokan* (Economic herald journal), no. 4: 61–64.

Zweig, David. (1995) "'Developmental Communities' on China's Coast: The Impact of Trade, and Transnational Alliances," *Comparative Politics*, vol. 27, no. 3, April: 253–74.

ZZGZ 1991. "Zhonggong zhongyang guanyu zhiding guomin jingji he shehui fazhan shinian guihua he 'bawu' jihua de jianyi" (Suggestions of the CCP Central Committee on formulating the 10-year program and the eighth five-year plan on national economic and social development), *Zhonghua Renmin Gongheguo Guowuyuan gongbao* (Gazette of the State Council of the People's Republic of China), no. 2, March 27: 49–50.

Index

Note: Page numbers in **bold** type refer to figures. Page numbers in *italic* type refer to tables. Page numbers followed by 'N' refer to notes.